Let's Pretend
AND THE GOLDEN AGE OF RADIO

by Arthur Anderson

Love to
Charlie
and
...
Arthur
Anderson

Let's Pretend
AND THE GOLDEN AGE OF RADIO

by Arthur Anderson

Foreword by Norman Corwin

Contains Complete Program Log

BearManor Media
2004

For information, address:

BearManor Media
P. O. Box 750
Boalsburg, PA 16827

bearmanormedia.com

Cover design by John Teehan
Typesetting and layout by John Teehan

Published in the USA by BearManor Media

ISBN—1-59393-019-4

Dedicated to the memory of Nila Mack
whose creation Let's Pretend *brought*
joy to a generation of children and
raised the standards of American Radio

Table of Contents

Front cover photo: Gwen Davies, Arthur Anderson, Rosemary Rice, Sybil Trent.

Foreword
by Norman Corwin

"Please send me free a fairy," wrote a child listener to *Let's Pretend*. In one simple stroke this went beyond suspension of disbelief to total abdication of it, a fond dream of drama from the Greeks on.

The most recent setting for dispensation of drama is the unwalled theater introduced by radio and expanded by video. Television is the undisputed champion of the performing media when it comes to funds, apparatus and size of audience. But though vastly richer than radio in those properties, it is also poorer in elements that exercise the imagination. A measure of this claim is that nobody ever wrote to a television program requesting that a fairy or any other creature, gratis or paid for, be sent through the mail.

TV is too young and active to have generated much in the way of genial recollection, but the theater of radio, having been forced into early retirement, bathes in nostalgia.

In addition there exists in the libraries of America a substantial and growing shelf of reminiscences of this latest of bygone golden ages. Of all these memoirs, Arthur Anderson's partly autobiographical account is in my view the warmest and most affectionate. Arthur was one of a group of children recruited by the resolute Nila Mack, and forged by her into an acting company which quickly established itself as the outstanding children's theater on the air. Thanks to Nila's benign dictatorship the program enjoyed a run of 24 years, during which it scooped up almost half a hundred national awards.

Throughout most of the volume, the presence of Nila Mack (originally Mac, but she thought that sounded too much like a nickname and

i

so added the k) is in every way indomitable. Mr. Anderson alludes to her as a "wisecracking surrogate mother [who] chose 'children who seemed simple, unaffected and eager to pretend along with me.'" Her credo was bold and clear: "You don't need to explain happenings. You simply believe or you don't."

There were millions of believers. To this day, half a century after the death of Nila Mack, veteran believers recall their enchantment with the series, recollections so vivid that Anderson does not exaggerate when he writes, "She could have had no idea now strong would be their childhood memories of it."

The Pretenders, as they were called, successfully pretended to be dragons, talking horses, kings, queens, gnomes, dwarfs, princes, princesses, witches, beauteous maidens, assorted knaves, varlets, cats, dogs, nightingales, and various flora and fauna. Anderson himself filled a good many of those roles, once even playing "a pitiful mewing kitten." When the principals traveled in *Let's Pretend*, it was always first class, in golden coaches, wearing purple robes, and as often as not they traversed enchanted forests or lived in castles with emerald halls, rooms of jade, and groaning boards furbished with golden goblets. Not only the lives of rich and famous characters were told, but of wicked and infamous ones. The villains, we are reminded in this memoir, were completely evil and were invariably punished or eliminated by the time each program ended. Virtue was rewarded, and there would be a moral lesson to be learned, "but it always came out naturally."

The book is handsomely researched, with copious data on the subsequent careers of the actors and actresses who performed Nila's stories (130 of them written or adapted by Nila herself), and enriched by anecdotes of great charm. The reader is also indebted to Mr. Anderson for discovering and memorializing marvelous letters from children, including the imperious demand of a determined young listener: "If you do not play "Snow White and the Seven Dwarfs" again…I will tell everyone not to tune in again. I have a lot of friends, and they do everything I tell them." And a joint message from a caucus of eight little girls: "We like all the stories except the stories we don't like, but you make them so good that we like them."

Since, as the author relates, this foreworder once had an office at CBS just a few doors down the hall from Nila's, I may perhaps be permitted to confirm and endorse what is written in the following pages, and, further, be licensed to propose three old-fashioned cheers for Arthur Anderson in recognition of his services as historian, biographer, archivist and anecdotist.

NORMAN CORWIN was largely responsible for the rise of radio drama in the 1930s and 1940s, with programs such as *26 by Corwin* and *The Columbia Workshop*. His prodigious wartime contributions culminated in the classic "On a Note of Triumph" in 1946. His many screenplays included *Lust for Life*, named one of the ten best pictures of 1956. Since 1980 he has been a visiting professor at the University of Southern California.

Introduction

This second edition of *Let's Pretend* is meant for two generations of readers: the older ones who still remember when they sprawled on the carpet in front of the big Philco on Saturday mornings, entranced by the magic and fantasy of our fairy tales, and a larger audience, who were not born then. Many of them, through listening to tapes and CDs, are discovering that old-time radio is fun. It offers an entirely different kind of entertainment pleasure—using your imagination.

This was the world of LIVE radio, where if you said the wrong word it could be heard by millions, from coast-to-coast. But the creative programming of radio brought entertainment, information and joy to a whole generation of Americans.

Though ours was a children's program, it had a sizeable adult audience. To Nila Mack, its creator, a good story was a good story. She did not condescend or "talk down" to children. *Let's Pretend* in its time was an American institution, just as important on Saturday morning as Jack Benny on Sunday night. The following pages tell what our program and network radio were like in those Olden Days B.T. – Before Television, that is.

Sincere thanks to Charles Summers III and to Martin Grams, Jr. and Derek Tague for helping me bring *Let's Pretend* into the computer age.

– *Arthur Anderson*

Cold Hands

In an essay she entitled "Report from a Notion," Nila Mack wrote that at 12 noon on Saturday, August 18, 1930, with "two cubes of ice in place of hands, I, Nila Mack speaking, started the notion that radio was an ideal medium for dramatized Fairy Tales. It's worked pretty well." With one of those frigid hands, the newest member of the Columbia Broadcasting System directorial staff had given a cue from the control room of Studio 3 at 485 Madison Avenue, the network's New York headquarters. Thus began her first broadcast. But it was not *Let's Pretend*.

Nila Mack had inherited a children's radio program which was already on the air. *The Adventures of Helen and Mary*, a 30-minute weekly show, broadcast since September 7, 1929, was written and directed by Yolanda Langworthy. The format was this: two little girls named Helen and Mary, played by eight-year-olds Patricia Ryan and Estelle Levy, play together and imagine all sorts of tales of romance and adventure, which are then performed by a cast of adult actors, with sound effects, and music provided by a six-piece string ensemble. The scripts were from standard works of fiction, adapted for radio by Langworthy, who was Columbia's director of children's programming. She also directed adult programs for the network, including "Arabesque," which had dramatic segments, poetry readings by David Ross, and music by Emery Deutsch and His Gypsy Violins. These programs were only a small part of the daily output of the expanding Columbia Broadcasting System network—and every program was live.[1]

---

1. A live program is one that is actually taking place at the moment the listener is hearing it. The networks in the 1930's had strict policies forbidding recordings on their airwaves. Anyone who wanted to hear a record could play it on their Victrola. The present-day term "live on tape" is a contradiction.

In 1930 radio was almost the only growth industry in a country which was in the throes of a serious Depression. It was the ideal medium for people who didn't have much money and needed a shot of optimism, and that included a very large segment of the population. If you could afford $10 for a little five-tube Emerson or a Fada, the world was yours, and it was free. William S. Paley, son of a Philadelphia cigar manufacturer (La Palinas—10 cents each) had bought a small group of radio stations, starting with WCAU, Philadelphia, which in 1927 became the Columbia Broadcasting System. In the broadcast industry, where nothing was or is immune from criticism or satire, the second word in the title was sometimes changed to "Broadchasing."

Paley presided over his creation in a paternalistic, hands-on fashion at the network's headquarters in four rooms in the Paramount Building at 1501 Broadway. At that time CBS did not even have a New York outlet, and used to buy time on stations WOR and WABC. (WABC is not to be confused with the present stations WABC-AM, FM and TV, owned by the American Broadcasting Company, which in 1930 did not even exist. The old station WABC is now WCBS, New York — AM, FM and TV.)

In December 1928 the network bought WABC, which became its New York flagship station, and in July 1929 proudly dedicated its new studios and offices in a just-completed 25-story building at 485 Madison Avenue, corner of 52nd Street.

Children's programs were just as important on radio in the early 1930s as they are on television today, and the usual broadcast times were then as now early mornings, late afternoons and Saturday mornings. At that time they were all produced by the networks themselves (and on a less elaborate scale by many local and independent stations throughout the country). *The Adventures of Helen and Mary* was meant to be Columbia's premier children's show. The consensus of CBS executives however, and that pretty much meant Bill Paley in this case, was that the program was rather dull, and that a change had to be made. Yolanda Langworthy was apparently not working out as a writer and director of children's programming. Then someone thought of Nila Mack.

Nila Mack was not new in radio, a point in her favor. She had performed on CBS in New York the previous year in a comedy program called *Nit Wits* and on a dramatic series *Radio Guild of the Air*. She had also written a series for the network called *Night Club Romances*, in which she also narrated each week's story as a slightly cynical Texas Guinan-type nightclub owner. She was short (5 feet 6 inches), blonde, blue-eyed and full of energy, enthusiasm and good humor. Moreover, she had an extensive background in show business.

Helen (left), Patricia Ryan; Memory, Harry Swan; and Mary, Estelle Levy.
©1931 CBS, Inc. Used by permission.

She was born Nila Mac, on October 24, 1891, in Arkansas (pronounced
Ar*kan*sas) City, Kansas, the only child of Don Carlos and Margaret Bowen
Mac. She had been a precocious child performer, singing, playing the piano and
dancing. In fact she had won 208 cakewalk contests before she reached her
teens. (A cakewalk was a promenade or march of African-American origin.
Contestants who devised the most intricate or eccentric steps won cakes as prizes.)

In 1906 her father, a Santa Fe railroad engineer, died a hero by reversing
the throttle when his engine derailed at 60 miles an hour, and kept his hand

on it instead of jumping. Though the engine and four of the train's five cars tumbled down an embankment, the last car stayed on the track. There were some injuries, but Don Carlos Mac was the only one killed, scalded to death by live steam. (Another well-known CBS employee whose father was a railroad engineer was Edward R. Murrow.)

After this tragedy Nila's mother sent her to a girls' finishing school in Lake Forrest, Illinois, where she earned some money acting, probably with passing touring companies, when not in class. The next year her mother took her to Boston for training in dramatics, French and elocution, and it was there that she obtained her first full-time acting job, as an ingénue with the Western Repertory Company, doing split weeks and one-night stands for $25 a week. Her mother went along on the tour as her daughter's chaperone.

After two years of touring, the company finally went broke, leaving the actors stranded in the small town of Metropolis, Illinois. Nila, her mother and the repertory company's leading man Roy Briant, instead of accepting this fate, decided to strike out on their own, and they opened a movie theatre in Metropolis. Roy was the manager (and probably projectionist), her mother manned the box office, and Nila was the pianist for the silent films. This lasted about a year, until another touring company was passing through, and Roy and Nila joined it. They were married in St. Anthony, Idaho, on March 20, 1913. Nila Mac was 21.

Nila and her husband performed extensively in vaudeville in sketches he wrote, and later in song-and-dance numbers they wrote together. Later, based in Chicago, her reputation grew, first as an ingénue, then as a leading lady, in both comedy and dramatic roles. She was seen there in 1915 by the famous Russian actress Alla Nazimova, with whom she later developed a close friendship. She played the second female lead with Nazimova in the highly popular and dramatic antiwar play "War Brides," in which they toured the vaudeville circuit. She later repeated the role when it was made into a highly acclaimed silent film. Now based in New York, she and her husband continued to work as actors both together and separately on Broadway, on tour, and in stock companies. Meanwhile, Roy Briant had several of his plays produced in New York, and earned extra money by writing vaudeville sketches and scenarios for silent films.

Nila toured in this country and in Canada for two years with the well-known comedian Tom Wise, sometimes in plays written for her by Roy. She later played on Broadway in a successful revival of the earlier hit play *Fair and Warmer*. By then she had added a "k" to her name, because she said that

"Mac" sounded like a nickname. Her husband moved to Hollywood to write scenarios for Paramount, and died there in 1927.[2]

It was soon after that that time began to catch up with Nila Mack's career. She was no longer the winsome, blonde ingénue, or the striking young leading lady. Moreover, the American theatre was changing. In 1927, a banner year, 268 productions had opened on Broadway, a number never equaled before or since, but from then on the total declined every year, and Nila's various sources of income began to dry up. The rise of the film industry was causing a serious drop in the number of legitimate theatres. Vaudeville was declining, permanent stock companies were no longer able to survive, and the number of touring shows was greatly reduced. Her husband had died. She was alone, and it was time to do some serious thinking.

There was only spotty acting work available in New York. She subsisted by writing film scenarios, including a short for Fanny Brice. Then there was a vaudeville sketch she wrote for Nydia Westman, but a living in show business, for Nila Mack at least, was no longer easy to come by. That was when radio entered her life twice, and both times unexpectedly.

Late in 1929 Miss Mack had applied for a permanent writing berth at Columbia Broadcasting. While working in a stock company she had met Georgia Backus, an actress who was also a writer, evidently with connections at the network, who recommended her. In the meantime, after a long dry spell she got a part in a Broadway play, and things were evidently beginning to look up. But this suddenly became unimportant when in February she received word that her mother was seriously ill in Arkansas City. She left the cast immediately, and took the first train back home. The problem now was how to support them both, since there was obviously no casting in Arkansas City. Ah, but there was. Almost at the time of her arrival back home, radio came to Arkansas City with the opening of station WEEB, and a major part of the operation became Nila Mack. "Mrs. Nila Mac Briant (still using the old spelling), New York actress, playwright and moving picture star, has accepted the position as announcer for the local studio," reported the *Arkansas City Tribune.* "She will be known on the air as Nila," the paper continued, adding that "she possesses a beautiful contralto voice, [and] has broadcast in many sketches over the national chain out of New York City."

2. Did her husband move because of economic necessity? Was there a rift in their marriage? Or was there a strain because Nila's mother had always lived with them, from their early days together? Whatever the reason, it is fact that when Roy was dying, his wife went out to Hollywood to be with him.

Besides being the station's chief announcer, Nila was also producer and director of almost all of its programming. She wrote scripts, she wrote advertising copy, she manned the telephone to sell advertising time, and persuaded many nervous local musicians and vocalists to face a microphone for the first time. Nila Mack's boundless energy and resourcefulness were proving a godsend, not only to her ailing mother but to the new little radio station as well.

The Arkansas City radio adventure lasted six months. Then Nila received a response to her application of the year before—a telegram from CBS in New York offering her a permanent writing and directing berth. It was an exciting offer—a chance to get back into the mainstream of show business. Now that she had been a theatre professional for over 20 years, it is doubtful that she would have been satisfied for long as a big frog in the smallish puddle of station WEEB.

She was reluctant to leave her mother, and there was also one aspect of the CBS offer which to her must have been a shocker. The network was replacing Yolanda Langworthy, and what they wanted was someone to write and direct children's programs. Nila Mack was experienced in show business. She had trouped over much of the United States and Canada, had endured hardships on the road unknown to actors of today, and had written material ranging from vaudeville sketches, snappy one-liners, and songs to dramatic motion picture scenarios, but had never done anything in any medium specifically aimed at children.

Nevertheless, here was steady employment being offered, in her own line of work, in New York, at a time when the country was in the midst of a major economic Depression. Nila's beloved aunt Mrs. P.B. Hanway, who she called Aunt Potie, was willing to look after her mother. So, despite serious misgivings about the children's aspect of the job, she decided to take it. In August 1930, at slightly less than age 39, Nila Mack made an abrupt change in her career and in her life. She ceased performing and writing for the stage, vaudeville and films, and began what was to be her work for the rest of her life — writing, casting, producing and directing children's radio programs for the Columbia Broadcasting System.

None of the Yolanda Langworthy scripts for *The Adventures of Helen and Mary* survive, but we do know that Miss Mack did not like them, and neither apparently did the CBS executives. Something had to be done with the show, and acting on her previous radio credentials and their faith in her, they were giving her complete freedom to revamp it. It was a gamble on their part, and

Nila Mack as a young leading lady, circa 1918. Billy Rose Theatre Collection: the New York Public Library for the Performing Arts Astor, Lenox, and Tilden Foundations.

surely Nila Mack knew that it might not pay off. No wonder her hands were freezing that hot August morning.

The first thing she had done upon returning to New York was to listen to *The Adventures of Helen and Mary* very carefully. She wrote later, "I hoped I could think of something better. I thought back to my own childhood," she continued. "The thing that had given me the greatest happiness was hearing or reading fairy tales and pretending that I was a beautiful princess. And so I had my idea. While I was working it out, I began interviewing and auditioning children. I chose children who seemed simple, unaffected and eager to pretend along with me." She added years later, in the preface to her book of *Let's Pretend* stories in narrative form, what was probably her basic philosophy in writing and casting the show. "One of the nicest things about happenings in the Land of *Let's Pretend* is that fact that you don't need to explain them. You simply believe or you don't. Personally, I enjoy being with those who do."

Surveying *The Adventures of Helen and Mary*, which CBS wanted changed, and pronto, Nila Mack made two determinations: First, how ideally suited to radio would be the classic fairy stories, with their built-in fantasy, adventure and fun. Second, how much better would be a cast of child actors, who could convey much more than grown-ups the openness, innocence and simplicity she wanted for the show. The cast changes came first; the story adaptations would take a bit more time.

Nila Mack's wise judgement and her resolve to carry through this new approach to children's radio programming was to have an effect on the lives of thousands of children in America. She was about to make a gift to them, and to the network, which was to gather kudos for the next 24 years for the program which evolved as *Let's Pretend*, and became the most popular of its kind on the air.

2

The Earliest Pretenders

There were many radio programs which stayed on the air for years, during which the participants formed close bonds and friendships, but *Let's Pretend* was unique in this respect. Nila Mack remained the show's writer, producer and director for almost 23 years, counting from the time she took over its predecessor *The Adventures of Helen and Mary*. Even though there was some turnover in our repertory company every year, a basic group of us eventually formed, who stayed with the program for almost its entire life, and who Miss Mack called upon week after week until her death.

CBS director Earle McGill had this to say in his excellent book *Radio Directing*:

> "The professional child actor is frequently an amazing, sensitive and pliable artist. Billy Halop, the twin Mauch boys [Billy and Bobby], Walter Tetley, Junior O'Day, Estelle Levy, Vivian Block, the Donnelly boys [Andy, Jimmy and Tommy], Arthur Anderson, Jackie Kelk, Jackie Jordan, Joyce Gates, Kingsley Colton, Sybil Trent, Jackie Grimes and Betty Philson are boys and girls who have received most of their training in radio, and every one of them can carry the burden of an entire broadcast and do it complete justice."

Every one of the children he mentions were Let's Pretenders, and probably the only reason more are not included is that he had not yet had the chance to work with them.

The children Miss Mack selected and built into a solid repertory company were a diverse group. We were from many ethnic and economic backgrounds. Some of us had brothers and sisters, some did not. But there were certain things we had in common: almost all of us were born in New York City, and we all had mothers who ranged from mildly to desperately ambitious for us to get into radio. They were able to help us because mothers in general did not have jobs in those days. *Fathers* had jobs, if they were lucky, the early 1930s still being Depression years. The most important trait we shared, though, was a childish naiveté and openness, combined with acting talent and intelligence. Not that we were all Quiz Kids with high IQ's, any more than was Miss Mack herself. She never claimed to be an intellectual, and was slightly suspicious of those who were.

It is important to relate something of our backgrounds and who we were, because we were the privileged ones, this group of child actors who Nila Mack selected, taught, loved, scolded, cajoled, manipulated, helped and directed, both on and off the air. These biographical notes on long-term Let's Pretenders, and others who were important on the show for shorter periods, should give an idea of what kind of people we were, and what it was like to be a child actor in radio.

To begin with, there were some very good child actors already in the cast of *The Adventures of Helen and Mary* when its new director came on the scene. Besides Estelle Levy and Pat Ryan, they included Don Hughes, Ronald Liss, Walter Tetley, Howard Merrill, Roslyn Silber, Madeline Lee, Jackie Kelk, Julian and Elmer Altman, Phyllis Chalzell, Amy Sydell and Ethel Blume. Estelle (now Gwen Davies) and Don were the only ones still on the show when we went off the air. By 1934, when our title became *Let's Pretend*, the others had all been replaced for one reason or another.

Howard Merrill was the son of Fanny Merrill, long-time associate of Gertrude Berg, who created "The Goldbergs." He later became a radio writer. Ethel Blume continued as a busy radio actress, and stayed in radio into adulthood. She later married singer Felix Knight. Madeline Lee grew up as a radio actress, also doing baby cries and cartoon voices. She later became a casting director, then a Broadway producer, and married actor Jack Gilford. Julian Altman became a violinist and his brother Elmer Altman a cellist, and they both played with the National Symphony in Washington D.C. as adults.

Nila possibly felt these children were losing their childish charm as their voices changed, or she may have replaced them because she found others in her auditions better suited to the program.

Then there were youngsters who left *Let's Pretend* because they had transferred their loyalty to Madge Tucker, who produced *The Lady Next Door* at NBC. Little curly-haired Ronald Liss, who also played the violin and had absolute pitch, was one. He remained busy in radio well into adulthood, and eventually became a producer of television programs. Then there was Walter Tetley, who was a great comedian, and who at the age of eight did imitations of Sir Harry Lauder, with kilts, bagpipe and Scottish burr. Walter's voice never changed, and before he died in 1975 in California at the age of 60, he had gained lasting fame in radio annals as 12-year-old Leroy, wisecracking nephew of "The Great Gildersleeve." Another of Nila's youngsters who later crossed over to Madge Tucker was Jack Kelk (then Jackie), who auditioned for her at age nine, playing his ukulele and singing "Would You Like To Take A Walk?" He became very successful in radio in running parts[3]

The cast of *The Adventures of Helen and Mary*, circa 1933, in the CBS studio at 485 Madison Avenue. Standing, left to right: Amy Sydell, Roslyn Silber, Howard Merrill, Lester Jay, Elmer Altman, Florence Halop, Julian Altman, Nila Mack, Donald Hughes, Betty Philson (with ukulele), Billy Halop, and Ethel Blume. Seated: Patricia Ryan, Harry Swan, Estelle Levy, and unidentified. ©1933 CBS, Inc. Used by permission.

---

3. A running part was one which "ran with" the story of a daytime radio serial or a nighttime weekly program. It was an actor's "consummation devoutly to be wished." Anyone landing a running part could expect a steady income from it for a week, a month or even years, even though there might never be a written contract. There were no running parts on *Let's Pretend*, as we did a different story on each broadcast.

which included Junior on *Dick Tracy* and Junior on *The Gumps*, later becoming well-known as Homer, Henry's best friend, on *The Aldrich Family*. He eventually went into the production end of television as an advertising agency casting director.

Each child chosen by Nila Mack had to have the versatility to play many types of roles in her growing library of radio fairy tale adaptations, although as she got to know each of us better she cast us more often in those in which she saw we were especially good. During our director's first four years at CBS these eight child actors: Estelle Levy, Patricia Ryan, Don Hughes, Vivian Block, Albert Aley, Mickey O'Day, Miriam Wolfe and Daisy Aldan became the basic members of the juvenile *Let's Pretend* repertory company:

GWEN DAVIES

In the beginning, there was Estelle Levy. Gwen Davies was not "born" until 11 years later. Nila found little Estelle, age eight, in 1930 playing Helen on *The Adventures of Helen and Mary*, the show she was to take over. She had great vivacity, and great flexibility as a child actress. She was small, and had black hair in long curls, and a voice which she could change from a tinkly, giggling fairy to an aged grandmother. She and Patricia Ryan were the show's framework, and I am sure Miss Mack never considered replacing either of them.

Estelle's father was Greek, her mother Romanian. She was born in Manhattan, an only child. At the age of five she was taken to dancing school, then to a piano teacher. A year later, she and many other children were being taken by anxious parents to audition for the broadcasting companies. It was Depression time. The parents saw not only fame for their children, but money to feed the family.

Once established on the show Estelle's versatility was tested more and more. She would occasionally have a singing part on *Let's Pretend*, and would play fanfares on her saxophone in scenes where royalty was being announced. "I was so embarrassed to do this," she said, "that I would have Pat Ryan carry the saxophone case when we left the studio." Estelle was always used in the lead-in, but frustrated at not getting to play the beautiful princess parts. "I felt like a garbage pail. If Nila had a strange voice to be done, I was stuck with it." She was later glad of this experience when she started to get calls for character voices in radio and TV commercials. For years she was the cartoon voice of Casper the Friendly Ghost.

Estelle Levy (later Gwen Davies), age 9, circa 1931.

During the Depression Estelle supported her parents by radio acting when her father was out of work, and put herself through school, and later Columbia University. She had running parts on *Hilltop House, Mrs. Wiggs of the Cabbage Patch* and other daytime serials, and did nighttime shows including *The Kate Smith Hour* and *The Aldrich Family*. She was Little Cosette with Orson Welles when he did *Les Miserables* first as a serial on The Mutual Network, and later on *The Mercury Theatre on the Air* on CBS. She also had her own show, singing with an orchestra weekly on station WEVD in New York, and working with Molly Picon in dramatic programs on that station.

In the early part of 1937 Aaron Copland was casting his new opera *Second Hurricane*, and, assisted by Hiram Sherman, was auditioning children at the Professional Children's School. (P.C.S. is a private school for children who are

Circa 1937. Studio 1. Nila Mack instructs her cast: Patricia Ryan, Estelle Levy, Vivian Block, Arthur Anderson, Donald Hughes, Florence Halop, and Nila Mack. Note door sound effect in background. ©1937 CBS, Inc. Used by permission.

performers. It was then in an office building at Broadway and 61st Street. In 1937 the tuition was $100 a year.) The chorus and some small parts were to be done by students of the Henry Street Music School and Seward Park High School, but professionals were needed for the leads. Estelle was dying to audition, but for some reason the principal, Mrs. Ethel Nesbitt, did not want her to. Estelle, making believe she had to go to the lavatory, went down to the tiny auditorium on the fourth floor, and stood in the back. The auditions were over. Finally Copland noticed her and said, "Can you sing?" "Well, I don't know what you call it, but I call it singing," said Gwen, which she admits was sort of cocky. Copland said, "Well, come up and sing," and with no music and no accompanist, she sang what we P.C.S.'ers had learned during our Friday assemblies, the Negro spiritual "Let My People Go." "That's my Gwen," said Copland, and she was cast in the role of Gwen in the opera's world premiere, which took place at the tiny Henry Street Playhouse on Grand Street, on April 27, 1937. I sang the role of Gyp, Vivian Block, another Pretender, was Queenie, and Joseph Cotten played the small role of an aviator. The opera was directed by Orson Welles and conducted by Lehman Engel—quite a thrilling and historic premiere, and *Let's Pretend* was well represented.

In 1941 Estelle, now 19, heard that CBS was to do a summer musical show. Dozens of singers had been auditioned, and she had not been called. She tried to convince Perry Lafferty, who was holding the auditions, by continually dropping into the control room. "Come on, Estelle," Lafferty would say. "We know you're a good actress. Can't you leave it at that?" One day when he had lost count of the control room visits and the door opened on Estelle's smiling face, Lafferty said, "NOW what do you want?", well knowing the answer. "Perry, please let me sing." "Oh, all right," said Lafferty, as much to get rid of her as anything else. Again, there was no music and no accompanist, but she did know some chords on the piano. What Lafferty and the others in the control room heard was a warm, sensuous delivery of "Embraceable You," a little reminiscent of Judy Garland, and a world removed from the twinkly elves and doddering old ladies she did on *Let's Pretend*.

After the song, Lafferty said, "Stay there," and went downstairs and got CBS Music Director Lyn Murray. The result was that Estelle got a year's contract with CBS, starting with a show called *The Class of '41*, with orchestra conducted by Walter Gross, guest stars such as Jim Backus and Arnold Stang, and scripts written by Abe Burrows.

There was only one problem: the network said she would have to have a new name. They asked her to come up with one. The first name was easy, taken from the character of Gwen she had played in *Second Hurricane*. The last she took from her mother's Romanian family name Davidescu, which translated to Davidson in English, and she turned that into Davies. And so Estelle Levy became Gwen Davies, and Nila decided to have an official name-changing during a *Let's Pretend* broadcast. After it, she took the new Gwen aside and said with mock severity, "Now listen, Toots—you may be a famous singer, but here you're still Estelle Levy, and you'd better behave yourself." Nila had already become much more than a radio director to many of us. She was a wisecracking surrogate mother, and to a few, including Gwen, her mother and later her husband, a close friend.

Gwen also had a brief career as a band vocalist, leaving *Let's Pretend* for six months in 1943 while she toured with Bobby Sherwood. One day Gwen's mother got a phone call from Miss Mack telling her that *Let's Pretend* was going commercial, and that she wanted Gwen to sing the theme song. The money, of course, would be many times what we children had been getting on the show all those years. Gwen left Bobby Sherwood. Touring with a band was a rough life, and the salary was only $75 a week, out of which she had to pay her own hotel bills and expenses. Though she later did some recording with other bands, namely Artie Shaw and Jan Garber, Gwen stayed with *Let's Pretend* until its last broadcast.

PATRICIA (PAT) RYAN

Patricia Ryan, whom everyone called Pat, was born in London, England, in 1921. As a small child she was brought to New York by her father John Ryan, who was Irish, and her mother, who was English and spoke with a slight Cockney accent. And it was there at the age of four that Pat got her first taste of audience response. At the Park Lane Hotel, where an afternoon social and entertainment was being held, her mother begged and pleaded with those in charge that her little girl be allowed to perform. She sang, she danced, and did a little recitation, as follows:

> If no one ever marries me I shan't mind very much;
> I'll buy a squirrel in a cage, and a little rabbit hutch.
> And when I'm getting really old, about twenty-eight or nine,
> I'll buy a little orphan girl, and bring her up as mine.

The applause was enthusiastic, and Pat was given vanilla ice cream, a piece of cake, and five dollars. That was the beginning of her career, which at first included photography modeling and one-shot theatrical appearances, some paid and some not. At the age of eight she was cast by Yolanda Langworthy in her role of Mary in *The Adventures of Helen and Mary*, the predecessor of *Let's Pretend*, a radio association which for Pat was to last almost 20 years.

The Ryans lived in an aging six-story apartment house on the upper West Side of Manhattan. Mr. Ryan was a steward at the exclusive Metropolitan Club in midtown New York. Pat had two sisters, Peggy, who was older, and June, younger. She attended Catholic grammar school and later Wadleigh High School, meanwhile being a faithful member of the St. Cecelia Choir at St. Michael's Church; her most prized possession was a pin given her for seven years' perfect attendance, and for general excellence.

In addition to her radio acting Pat became interested in writing, and next to the choir pin she was proudest of having had her original story "The Silver Knight" broadcast on *Let's Pretend* in 1935.

Pat had blonde hair and grey-blue eyes. To judge from childhood photographs she seems to have been rather plain, but in her teens she blossomed in poise and attractiveness, leading one feature writer to gush: "A fact to which she is happily oblivious is that she is by way of becoming Columbia's glamour girl. She is also a figuresome find for radio photographers."

There was some truth in the part about being oblivious. The dream world in which Pat lived was expressed partly in her short stories and the radio script she wrote, but also resulted in a slight reserve which no one could ever completely penetrate—even Gwen Davies, who had known Pat since they were small children. Pat was always friendly, and completely honest in the showbiz world in which we were growing up, which had so much affectedness and false glamour. This honesty and sincerity, in addition to a natural talent, probably made her a better actress too. During all of her career she never had any professional training.

Once Pat began doing radio, and learned the knack (not easy) of combining a professional career with schooling, many other shows followed, including *We the People, American School of the Air* and the running parts of Myra Lee on *Joyce Jordan, Girl Interne*, Elly on *The Parker Family*, and Henry Aldrich's friend Geraldine on *The Aldrich Family*. As she reached maturity she also starred in what sounds like a more-maudlin-than-most daytime serial called *Girl Alone*, on the NBC network. For masochist readers, a synopsis follows: "No matter how huge a fortune a girl may have, money cannot guarantee her future against heartbreak—against the fact that many men will propose marriage just to get possession of her money, while the one man who may really love her will shy away rather than have his friends say he married his wife for her money. Patricia Ryan in *Girl Alone* faces that problem." Evidently Pat did not face it for long, because no record shows that the show was renewed, or that it ever got a sponsor.

Things did get better, though. A wonderful break for Pat, indeed one of the high spots of her career, was landing the lead in *Claudia and David*, the serialized radio version of Rose Franken's hit Broadway play of 1941. Publicity blurbs claimed that over 200 actresses were auditioned for the role, to play opposite Richard Kollmar. The show, sponsored by Grape Nuts Cereal, started as a summer replacement for *The Kate Smith Hour* on Fridays at 8:00 P.M. Pat Ryan's naïve quality, plus a slightly breathless vocal delivery, at once ingenuous and sensuous, and rather reminiscent of Margaret Sullavan, plus the complete honesty and sincerity I have mentioned—all made her ideal for the role of the child bride in a woman's body, whom her husband David, and the audience, found so appealing.

Pat's photo, in color, was on the cover of the October 1941 *Radio and Television Mirror*, and the following excerpt from the feature article, by one Adele Whitely Fletcher, though it will admittedly not shed much light on Pat Ryan's career, does provide a good example of fan magazine writing at the time:

It starts out describing gentlemen playing bridge at New York's fine Metropolitan Club, reading the evening papers and watching the New York panorama through the large plate glass windows. The faithful steward Ryan, who has served there many years, brings a scotch-and-soda to a millionaire shipbuilder, then hurries to switch on the radio, and...

> "Into that room came a girl's voice—young and breathless as dawn. Ryan straightened, and the lamplight shone full upon his silvery hair. 'That's my daughter Pat Ryan, Sir,' he said. 'She's making her debut tonight in a new program called "Claudia and David."' Slowly as these rich and powerful men listened, they realized that there were other things in this world besides Stuka bombers and vassal people and war and hatred..."

Adele Whitely Fletcher—where are you tonight?

Nila had for some years predicted great things for Pat, and she was delighted with her success, as she was when any of us made a splash in some other venture. And Pat Ryan kept on turning in excellent performances every Saturday morning on *Let's Pretend*.

DON HUGHES

Don Hughes was one of the earliest Pretenders. Born in 1917, he was 12 years old and already a cast member of *The Adventures of Helen and Mary* when Nila took over the show. He had an elfin face, expressive blue eyes and a cute grin. He was born of theatrical parents. His mother Beth Stone was an acrobatic toe dancer in vaudeville and also in Broadway musicals. She married her vaudeville partner Frank Hughes (Stone and Hughes). They separated before Don was born and divorced when he was three. As a small child he traveled with his mother on the vaudeville circuit, then was put into Professional Children's School so that he could do his work by correspondence when they were on the road. Being in P.C.S. also meant that he and his mother heard about all sorts of casting calls, which eventually resulted in his doing two Broadway plays—*The Enemy*, an anti-war play presented by Channing Pollock in 1925, and *Mima* done by David Belasco, in which Don was an imp, costumed in green oilcloth.

Don took to radio, and especially to *Let's Pretend*, easily. Acting, after all, was fun, and Don was clever and talented. He also had a prominent role in a radio show called *Daddy and Rollo*, playing opposite Nick Dawson. As in the later "Baby Snooks" series starring Fanny Brice, the kid had all the gags, and Daddy was mostly a straight man. *Daddy and Rollo* was sponsored by La Palina Cigars, owned by William S. Paley's father. It was on 15 minutes, three times a week, in 1931-32. The sponsor liked the show so much that performances were increased to six a week, then to nine. But *Daddy and Rollo* disappeared abruptly when the writer, J.P. McAvoy, asked for a hefty salary increase.

Don's busiest time as an actor was in early childhood. Once into adolescence his work tapered off, and as he matured he developed a strong antipathy to "making the rounds," as it was called, of casting directors. It was not laziness. Over the years he and I became close friends, and from time to time he would express the opinion that promoting one's self, in effect saying, hey I'm good, hire me, was somehow immoral, or at least unprincipled. To be successful, said Don, an actor has to have a combination of overweening ego and abject humility. And, to remain true to his own code of ethics, Don sometimes antagonized people in an effort to avoid at all costs the impression that he was trying to curry favor with an eye to getting work.

"I liked acting," Don once said, long after having retired. "I like it to this day. I liked the companionship." Don was also a much better actor than he would admit, to himself or anyone else. Jack Grimes would observe Don's performances, especially when he was playing a lead, such as Faithful John or Rumpelstiltskin, and claimed that you could see Don begin to do a truly brilliant piece of work, then suddenly seem to say, "Oh, dammit—it's showing," and pull back.

Don went on hiatus from *Let's Pretend* at about age 17, when his mother and a friend decided to open a dancing school in West Palm Beach, Florida. Don taught ballroom dancing there and helped his mother in many other ways, including cleaning the studio, and keeping it free of scorpions and palmetto bugs. The venture failed, and when they returned north and settled in Elizabeth, New Jersey, Don was welcomed back on the show by Nila.

It was after Don's return from Florida that we began to notice his writing talents. A young man named Austin Beardsley, an heir to the then considerable Beardsley Codfish empire, hired a studio at Broadway and 56th Street and formed a group called The Young Professionals. All of us were indeed young. After a production of A.A. Milne's *Mr. Pim Passes By*, we did a revue titled *And Be Merry*, to which Don contributed music, lyrics and several sketches. I was involved, as were Albert Aley (by then also a good friend of Don's) and Jack Kelk, among other Pretenders. He was also good at light verse. In the summer of 1941 he composed a set of Epitaphs for some of the *Let's Pretend* cast. Unfortunately most of them are unprintable, leaving only the following as a slight example of Don Hughes' wit:

A.A.

> Kind friend, A. Anderson lies here
> His life was good, though somewhat queer:
> With just one interest in his heart
> He didn't care for sports or art
> Or business, food or drink or sex,
> But only vocal sound effects.
> A legend says that he was born
> Making a noise like an auto horn;
> And this we know: he met his end
> With a sound like a steamboat 'round the bend.

D.H.

> Here's what's left of poor Don Hughes
> Beneath this cold, cold earth.
> He knew not ballads, babes nor booze;
> Hell, he was dead at birth!

Don was away from *Let's Pretend*, beginning in May 1942, for over three years, serving in the Signal Corps attached to the Army Air Force in England, France and Belgium. As soon as he got home, Nila put him right back to work playing wise counselors, talking animals and evil dwarfs.

Don's was a complex personality. He had a brilliantly creative mind, an unusual acting talent and a warm heart. He was able to use only a fraction of his gifts on *Let's Pretend*, but Don, with his distinctive style and sometimes strident voice, was for over two decades one of the show's most important assets.

VIVIAN BLOCK

Vivian came to Nila Mack's attention in 1931 when she was about nine years old. She had already auditioned at station WOV, and after having been referred by the pianist there to Madge Tucker, at NBC, she started being called for her children's show *Coast To Coast On A Bus*. Meanwhile Nila Mack discovered that Vivian was not only a good actress, but had a beautiful soprano singing voice, which developed as she grew older. This was especially effective when we did "Rapunzel." The Prince hears the girl who is held captive by the witch in the stone tower singing (it was "Solvejg's Song" by Grieg), and is determined to rescue her. Somewhere along the line, Vivian does not remember when, she began doing less and less of the Madge Tucker show, and more and more of *Let's Pretend*, becoming another permanent addition to our juvenile repertory company.

Vivian also became a busy actress on other shows, including Nila's own *Sunday Morning at Aunt Susan's*, *Showboat* with Charles Winninger, one of Henry's girlfriends on *The Aldrich Family*, and an early series with Bobby Jordan called *Peter and Pan in Wheatenaville*. She had a running part on the CBS series *Wilderness Road*, with Ray Collins, Bill Johnstone, Anne Elstner and Jimmy Donnelly, and also found time to do baby cries on *The Life and Loves of Dr. Susan*. She was one of the three Pretenders in the world premiere of Aaron Copland's opera *Second Hurricane*. Meanwhile she graduated from the Professional Children's School, and kept up her musical studies as well.

American family life was different in the '30s. If you were young and had a job, you automatically brought your salary home to your parents. At one time Vivian made over $300 a week—a considerable sum at that time. And so she was surprised, but not at all resentful, when she found that it had all gone into her father's business. Vivian once put her head on her mother's lap and cried during the period when the work wasn't coming, and she could not bring home as much as she had been making. There was a solution, though, and it wasn't in radio. At the age of 17 Vivian came to the attention of a Mrs. Kelly, who was the proprietor of an exclusive gentlemen's private club, in a brownstone on East 65th Street. The membership consisted entirely of wealthy male business executives. Delicious gourmet meals were served in softly-lit, luxurious surroundings. The place was immaculate. For musical entertainment there was a pianist and two singers—Vivian and another girl—on Saturday nights. Their repertoire ranged from jazz and pop to classical and operetta. They would also do requests, and the members would tip generously. Vivian remembers returning home from work one night, making her mother spread out her apron, and filling it with ten-dollar gold pieces, ten-dollar bills, and a few twenties.

There were also at least three other attractive young women always on duty at the club—a blonde, a brunette and a redhead. They would talk, eat and drink with the members, and sometimes would leave with them. Indeed, these gentlemen would often book suites at the Plaza Hotel for mutual entertainment. Vivian describes Mrs. Kelly as "a real pro." The working conditions were pleasant, and nobody ever bothered her for any reason other than to request another song. The club could not be described as anything but high class—but one would have to admit that in certain respects it was far removed from The Land of Let's Pretend.

Vivian Block was the first of the Pretenders to marry. In 1942 she chose Dr. Irving Marsh, a dentist whose practice was in Bridgeport, Connecticut. She continued to commute to New York to do the show as long as possible, until she was six months pregnant, which was by then very obvious.

Jackson Wheeler, our CBS announcer assigned at the time, was rather too smarmy for my taste. During the warm-up for the studio audience he would introduce everyone on the program, finishing up with, "And there in the control room is our director, Nila Mack. She's a schweet-heart!" On the occasion of Vivian's last broadcast before becoming a mother, he apparently felt like indulging in a bit of wit. As the cast entered, including Vivian, who was having some difficulty mounting the steps onto the platform stage, Jackson said delightedly: "And here come the kiddies now!" I am sure Nila could have killed him.

Although family had taken precedence over career for Vivian, she retained a strong sentimental attachment to *Let's Pretend* and its director. When she and her husband built their new house, they had it designed with a round stone tower in classic fairy-tale style, or at least as close to that as you could get on the suburban streets of Bridgeport.

When Vivian Block Marsh returned to *Let's Pretend* on July 8, 1944 for a farewell performance before retiring from the show permanently, she once again did her favorite (singing) role of Rapunzel. Her husband was there, and after the broadcast they introduced the Pretenders to their little one-year-old daughter, Nila.

ALBERT ALEY

Albert, born in 1919, joined *Let's Pretend* at the age of 13, in 1932. His father was Spanish, his mother Swiss. His parents had owned their own photography studio, but they lost it in the Depression, and went to work for another photographer. Their little boy Albert was a handsome child with a sensitive face, and light brown hair which always seemed to end in a cowlick at the top.

Albert's first ambition had been to be an athlete, but rheumatic fever in his childhood caused a heart murmur, so he started doing photographic modeling, first for his father's employer, then for others, and his income helped pay family expenses, plus his tuition at the Professional Children's School. The principal, Mrs. Ethel Nesbitt, helped him write a letter to Miss Mack saying why he would like to be on *Let's Pretend*, which so impressed her that she called him for an audition.

Albert was not a character actor, and did not "do voices." He always sounded like Albert Aley, and on our show he was most often cast as either the handsome Prince, or the youngest son who goes out into the world to seek his fortune. These so-called straight emotional parts in our tales of fantasy and adventure could have been ridiculous, but Albert played them with complete honesty and sincerity. Nila used him as one of the two children (the other was our Vivian Block) on her *Sunday Morning at Aunt Susan's,* and on the Thursday *Tales from Far and Near* segment of *The American School of the Air.* Later he auditioned successfully for Frances Von Bernhardi at Air Features, producers of many of radio's daytime serials, and landed the role of Bob James on the long-running *Stella Dallas.*

As Albert grew into his teens he became rather slim and lanky, and stayed that way until past middle age. He certainly did not have a "leading man" demeanor, but that did not matter on radio, which, as far as acting was concerned, was Albert's medium for his entire career. His voice was sympathetic, with attractive "lows." Nila knew that she could depend on him to carry an entire show. She also noticed that as he matured, many letters in feminine handwriting arrived asking for his picture.

By 1937, before he was 18, he was helping Miss Mack in the office, reading fan mail, and making calls to the other actors for the coming Saturday broadcast. When Albert would give Jack Grimes his "Pretend" call at home, he at first mistook him for his mother and addressed him as "Mrs. Grimes." Jack hated this. He was seven years younger than Albert, and his

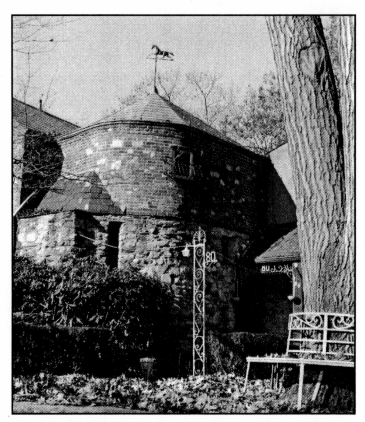

Vivian Block's *Let's Pretend* castle. Photo by the author.

voice hadn't changed yet. He eventually forgave him, and it became a stand-ing joke between them.

Albert was one of the most precocious Pretenders. In 1938 he was billed as "Radio's Youngest Director," when at age 19 he directed our broadcast of "Babes in the Wood" while Nila was on her annual vacation. His writing talents were starting to bud, too. An April 1938 article in *The Jersey Journal* said that he had had scripts produced on radio, and that another would be done soon on New York's station WNEW. His most important early credit was when a script he submitted was broadcast coast-to-coast on *The First Nighter*. When he was 21 he had his only stage experience with The Young Professionals, mentioned earlier, and Albert directed several of their pro-ductions.

Albert's important writing, directing and producing accomplishments were still in the future, but for the time being, though cast sizes varied and Nila could not use all of her "regulars" every week, I cannot remember a

Albert Aley, child model, age 12, circa 1931.

broadcast on which he did not appear. The roles he played, though never spectacular or flashy, were an essential part of the believability of our program.

MICHAEL O'DAY

"Junior" was a popular nickname for little boys in the 1930s, and Michael D'Addario, born in 1920, adopted Junior O'Day as his professional name when he did his first acting at the age of 12 in films in Fort Lee, New Jersey. The D'Addarios lived in Bloomfield. His father was a supervisor with the Prudential Insurance Company. He changed his name to Mickey as he got older, then finally back to Michael as an adult. By whatever name, he was one of the most versatile and talented actors we on *Let's Pretend* had ever encountered.

He may have inherited some of his talent from an aunt who had been in silent pictures, and from a great-uncle who, it was said, had been a Shakespearean actor and a Jesuit priest—an intriguing combination.

Bloomfield was not that far from New York and the radio studios, and Mickey soon became busy in all of them. He joined *Let's Pretend* in 1933. One of the earliest of his other shows was the lead in *Robinson Crusoe, Jr.*, on CBS in 1934. He was soon a regular on Madge Tucker's NBC children's hour known as *The Lady Next Door*, which later became *Coast To Coast On A Bus*. Like *Let's Pretend*, that called for his versatility in character voices. But he was just as clever at playing the mostly stereotyped children's parts on radio we all played: The Mean Kid, The Spunky Kid, The Sensitive Kid, The Crying Kid, not to mention The Foreign or Regional Kid (he was good at dialects, too).

As network radio grew, and Mickey's reputation with it, he began to do important nighttime shows—early comedy programs with Bob Hope, Al Jolson and Fred Allen. When he was 16 he began a long run as Ruth Wayne's little brother Neddie on *Big Sister*, one of the most durable of the daytime serials. It lasted from 1936 through 1952, with Mickey on most of that time. He outlasted five leading ladies (Alice Frost, Nancy Marshall, Marjorie Anderson, Mercedes McCambridge and Grace Matthews) and two sponsors (first Rinso, made by Lever Brothers, then various products made by their competitor, Proctor & Gamble). And for years he was the newsboy who opened *Big Town* with "Get yer Illustrated Press…" To give more of Mickey O'Day's credits would be simply to reel off a list of most of the important dramatic shows on radio.

Nila often cast Mickey and me in the same parts in successive broadcasts of the same story. But one part Mickey retained over all the years we did it was Santa Claus in her original script "The Night Before Christmas." When Mickey played it, you could sense the warmth and love the old man exuded, and you could almost see his fat belly. Nila did experiment with the casting of Santa on one occasion, during our pre-Cream of Wheat days. She had Burl Ives play it. This was before Ives had become a star, so there was no problem with our budget. But it did not work out. Though even in his 30s Ives did look like Santa Claus, this was no help in radio. His voice at that time was rather high, and his acting experience limited. At about the same time—no one knows for sure, but we can assume it was before 1937—Nila was approached by Orson Welles, who also wanted to play Santa Claus. Orson had not yet become a director, and was still a very busy radio actor. Nila told Orson she was sorry, but that *Let's Pretend* only used children in its cast. The mind truly boggles trying to visualize Welles' overpowering presence in our rather low-key, charming Christmas story...not to mention what it would have been like if he had ever become a regular *Let's Pretend* cast member. In any case, as long as we remained on the air after the Burl Ives experiment, Santa Claus belonged to Mickey.

His career had only one drawback, and that was his height. All the D'Addarios were short people, and Mickey never grew to be more than 4 feet 6 inches. He was neither a dwarf nor a midget. His body was perfectly formed. Special shoes partly compensated, and his suits were custom-made. He had good Italian features—black hair, dark eyes and heavy eyebrows. He was always impeccably groomed, and I hardly ever saw him remove his jacket, even on the hottest days. Furthermore, he was always good-natured, though his life surely must have had its frustrations. One positive thing he must have realized, however, as he reached adulthood and the show headed into its long-term sponsorship by Cream of Wheat—there would always be a place for him in radio, and on *Let's Pretend*.

MIRIAM WOLFE

Miriam was born in Brooklyn in 1922. She did her first radio performance at age four, on *The Uncle Gee Bee Kiddie Hour* on station WGBS (the call letters stood for its owner, Gimbel Brothers' Store). Almost from childhood she played older parts on radio. "I never had a child's voice," she says. Before she reached her teens she was playing ingénues and leading women on *Five Star Final* on station WMCA, and doubling as the newsboy signature of the show.

Nila, when Miriam was introduced to her, asked if she could play witches. Miss Mack had decided it was time to replace Ethel Blume and Amy Sydell, who had both reached the advanced age of 16. She was also looking for someone to play The Voice in the Wind in *Beauty and the Beast*, which she herself had always done previously. As for witches, the answer was definitely yes. Miriam had already played Hecate in a Hecksher Foundation production of *Macbeth*, with an otherwise adult cast. And so in 1934 she became a Let's Pretender.

Her best known witch role in radio, besides the many she played on *Let's Pretend* over the years, was Old Nancy on *The Witch's Tale* on the Mutual Network. This show was written, produced and directed by Alonzo

Miriam Wolfe as Old Nancy on The Witch's Tale, age 13, circa 1935.

Dean Cole. The original Nancy, Adelaide Fitz-Allen, had died at age 80, and apparently her replacement was not working out. In 1934 Miriam went to audition for Mr. Cole in the WOR studios at 1440 Broadway at midnight, after one of his broadcasts was over.

Cole thought it was a great joke when he first saw her—a 12-year-old girl with a straw hat and Buster Brown haircut, carrying her school bag. But when he heard the aged, toothless vocal delivery, and the spine-chilling, cackling laugh she produced, his mouth fell open. Miriam was hired. The fee was $10 a broadcast, for which she not only played Old Nancy in the prologue and epilogue, but also doubled other character and leading woman parts in the story.

Meanwhile, Miriam was becoming an attractive teenager, and like many performers on radio, her looks gave no hint of her vocal talents. Besides the Alonzo Dean Cole episode, there were many other instances in later years in which people, especially casting directors, expected her voice to match her appearance. The most embarrassing (not for Miriam but for the director) happened on *Popeye*, a new radio version of the well-known comic strip. The director, Walter Craig, who had never met Miriam, but knew of her reputation for doing older voices, cast her as The Sea Hag. Miriam and the rest of the cast gathered in the studio at the appointed time, but the rehearsal did not begin. The director fidgeted, fumed, lit cigarettes and paced, then finally, exasperated, announced, "I'm sorry, ladies and gentlemen. As soon as that bitch Miriam Wolfe arrives, we'll start." "But I'm here!," said Miriam. Once that misunderstanding was ironed out she became a regular on the show, also doubling as Olive Oyl.

She had a four-year run on *The Witch's Tale* until it went off the air. Her other radio work at that time included weekly stints on *The Bob and Ray Show* and daytime serials such as *Portia Faces Life* and *Aunt Jenny's Real Life Stories*.

Miriam, after Albert Aley, was the next of the Pretenders to branch out into work other than acting, producing and directing dramatic shows for New York City's municipal station WNYC in 1940, when she was 18. Then, recommended by the CBS casting director Marge Morrow, she went to Buffalo to play the lead in a new network serial that would originate there, "I'll Find My Way." Her salary at Station WGR/WKBW was $50 a week. A year later she had become an actress-disc jockey-producer-writer there, all for the same $50. Meanwhile, as she had promised Miss Mack, Miriam returned weekly as needed, to perform on *Let's Pretend*.

Back in New York in 1942, she landed a job on the staff of the Office of War Information, assigning studios and directing overseas multi-lingual broadcasts. Meanwhile Miriam continued as a successful radio actress, and a permanent member of the cast of *Let's Pretend*.

DAISY ALDAN
Theatre was the subject Daisy heard from infancy at home on East 91st Street. Her father was in the costuming business. Her mother Estelle Edel was an actress in silent films, and in the then very active Yiddish theatres in New York. Together with Daisy's two uncles she organized the Yiddishe Folksbiene, which still exists today. So it was only natural that by age ten Daisy was doing imitations of Maurice Chevalier in amateur programs at local movie theatres, and tap dancing on roller skates. She was also writing letters to radio directors asking for auditions. One of them was Nila Mack.

Nila thought Daisy's audition was excellent. There was just one problem. Her voice was too similar to that of Miriam Wolfe, who was already on the show. Miriam and Daisy were good friends, having worked together in a huge pageant done at Madison Square Garden called *The Romance of a People*. And so when a year after the audition Daisy had not been called for a show, Miriam went to Miss Mack and said, "Don't call me for awhile—use Daisy." As a result Nila did call Daisy, and from then on had increased respect for Miriam for her unselfish gesture. Eventually she found that there were enough witches, mothers, stepsisters and enchanted talking animal roles for both of them, and Daisy became a regular on our program in 1934.

The problem of the vocal similarity disappeared as Daisy grew into her teens and developed a drier, more clipped vocal pattern, while Miriam's voice became more resonant, and her speech pattern more legato. Like Miriam, Daisy had an air of maturity beyond her real age, and though she had a secret yen at times to play the beautiful Princess roles on *Let's Pretend*, that ambition was never realized. Nila found Daisy had become much too valuable as quaint old ladies and mysterious voices.

As her mother was too busy in her own acting career to be a stage mother, Daisy did her own promotion. As a small child she appeared at the Heckscher Children's Theatre. She did monologues at union halls for five dollars a performance. She became involved in school dramatics, first at P.S. 151 in Manhattan, later at Herman Ritter Junior High School when the family moved to the Bronx. She would act, for pay or no pay, wherever there was a stage and an audience. Daisy was hopelessly stage struck.

In addition to *Let's Pretend*, her other radio shows included *The Columbia Workshop*, *Big Sister* and *American School of the Air*, but except for our show, radio was not as important to Daisy as it was to the rest of us. Some of her great energy was going in a quite different direction. She had started writing poetry at the age of five, and her first published poem, "In the Dark Hour," appeared in Chicago's magazine *Poetry* when she was twelve. At Hunter College she became poetry editor of *Echo*, the school's literary magazine.

Daisy had always been precocious, graduating from high school before she was fifteen. This caused a brief problem when she began to attend Hunter College in bobby socks, and with her hair in ribbons. The Dean sent for her and said, "You are now a college woman, and you must wear stockings, a hat and gloves."

In 1943, as *Let's Pretend* acquired a sponsor and was about to enter its tenth year under that name, Daisy was already a veteran of nine of them, and long ago had been established as an important member of our now-no-longer-juvenile repertory company.

* * *

In a traditional stage stock or repertory company, which no longer exists in our theatre, the actors were hired according to the guidelines provided by the plays they would be doing: Leading man, leading lady, second leads (male and female), juvenile, ingénue, character man and character woman. *Let's Pretend* was a radio repertory company, but in the sometimes fantastical stories we did, these categories did not always fit.

Who would Nila Mack cast for a talking horse, for instance? Or a messenger bee? Or the West Wind? With the eight child actors just mentioned, plus many more who will be introduced later, she developed a company of players who could handle any of these roles, and many others, as we gained experience and became more and more versatile. Without the instant hit-or-flop pressures which exist today in the theatre, and to a lesser extent in television, Nila Mack was free to experiment with casting, as she expanded, developed and improved the *Let's Pretend* company.

3

The Scripts

Although Nila Mack was convinced that her dramatizations of the classic fairy tales would be an improvement over Yolanda Langworthy's scripts, she could not instantly create a whole new story repertoire out of thin air, and knew that for the time being she had to live with Miss Langworthy's material, which could be repeated, with improvements, she hoped, by herself. Luckily we have Nila's own log of most of the scripts, and their broadcast dates, added to in this edition by Martin Grams and Derek Tague; I am counting those titles which Miss Langworthy wrote as Nila's after she took over *Helen and Mary*, because she did rewrites on every one of them.

For "Sinbad the Sailor," her first broadcast, a laconic margin notation reads "First script, yet." The second story was "Gulnare of the Sea" and was the last one to use an all-adult cast. There is no record of the story on the third show, her first with an all-juvenile cast, but we know that at least into October of 1930 all of the *Helen and Mary* scripts were drawn from *The Arabian Nights*, and many of them were done in two parts.

There was a special Christmas broadcast Nila logged as "Christmas Story—portrait—sick girl," which could have been either an original by herself, or adapted from her predecessor. It was done on the show during the following two Christmas seasons, and afterwards was never heard of again.

It was not until early in 1931 that Nila Mack hit her stride as a writer of radio fairy tale scripts. Her friend Dorothy Stickney had given her the book of *Grimm's Fairy Tales* which she had had as a child, and, before the new year was a month old, Nila had started to phase in her own adaptations from the works of not only Grimm, but among others, Andrew Lang, Charles Perrault and Hans Christian Andersen. She also turned out an original story in time for St.

Patrick's Day, "The Leprechaun," which was charming and touching, and it was repeated every year afterwards for the entire life of the program. Before 1931 was half over, the *Arabian Nights* stories were now only less than a half-dozen among what had become a rich mixture of fairy tales from many sources, and all of them now had Nila Mack's special touch.

The period setting of most of the *Let's Pretend* scripts was from medieval times up to the 18th century, because most of the folk tales upon which they were based had originated then. The language used was present-day, but never slang. People were always courtly and respectful when addressing royalty. When characters spoke roughly or threateningly, you "knew" they were up to no good.

People in our stories traveled on horseback, or in carriages if they were royalty or of the nobility. People who were poor but honest lived in humble cottages. There were noble kings (and an occasional evil one) and gallant knights. There were beautiful ladies who wore fine gowns. There were ancient magicians in long robes, who had grey beards. There were fierce giants. There were scheming dwarfs. And very often there were wicked witches who would point their skinny fingers (obligatory—you never heard of a fat witch, did you?) at beautiful Princesses and cast terrible spells upon them.

The colorfulness of the historical period in which the stories took place, plus the nature of these tales of magic and fantasy—both were ideally suited to what came to be called "The Theatre of the Imagination"—dramatic radio.

One reason parents were pleased that their children enjoyed *Let's Pretend* was its high moral tone. However, the stories were never "throwing goodness at you," as Alfred P. Doolittle put it. It just happened that way. The good people, whether royalty or paupers, were completely and uncompromisingly good. And villains were completely evil, and so had to be, and were, either punished or in some way eliminated by the time each program ended. There was a moral lesson to be learned in each of our stories, even the light comedies, but it always came out naturally, and in the context of the plot, and did not detract from the excitement and adventure.

I do not believe Nila set out primarily to teach and uplift her child audiences. She was savvy enough to know that if you're going to do that, you have to entertain them first. Though we in the cast never heard her express any denominational preference, the religious atmosphere in the Arkansas City of her childhood was strictly Fundamentalist. Her own family were Christian Scientists. Certainly the locomotive engineer's house at 306 South C Street was a place where there was not only order, but love, and Nila, though she once said that she did not "buy" all of the Fundamentalist values, obviously had developed her own set of religious and moral convictions. This could be seen in her scripts.

Why, we even mentioned God on *Let's Pretend*—imagine that. In "Childe Roland to the Dark Tower Came," Roland with his magic sword Excalibur faces the evil King of Elfland:

KING:	Who dares to enter the tower without my permission?
ROLAND:	I do, you monster. Release my sister.
KING:	Oh, no! She belongs to me.
ROLAND:	She belongs only to her God. Release her!!

And, of course, the King does, with Excalibur at his throat. In another story, "The Nuremberg Stove," the little boy August hides inside his beloved Hirschvogel, the beautifully enameled German stove, because he cannot bear to part with it when it is sold by his poverty-stricken father. During a long journey inside the stove, the child falls asleep. When its door is opened, he stumbles out and sees that it is the King of Bavaria who has purchased it. The child kneels before royalty. "Rise, my child," says the kindly King. "Kneel only to your God."

Not that The Deity was dragged into *Let's Pretend* scripts. Nila was not a moralist—she was just a good radio writer. If such mentions were included in a national network program of today, would their headquarters be picketed by atheist organizations demanding equal time?

In dramatizing *Let's Pretend* for radio, Nila Mack had a rich heritage to draw upon. These folk tales from many countries, mostly European, had been handed down for many generations. Most of them, luckily for Nila and for CBS, were in the public domain, meaning of course that no royalties had to be paid.

The earliest, chronologically, were *The Tales from the Arabian Nights*, otherwise known as *The Thousand and One Nights*, authors unknown, but considered classics in world literature. They were thought to have originated in Persia. The first European edition was printed in 1704. The best known, "Ali Baba and the Forty Thieves," "Aladdin and the Wonderful Lamp" and "Bluebeard" were all included in our repertoire.

Charles Perrault, a French poet who lived 1628–1703, adapted and retold eight traditional stories, including "Bluebeard," "Sleeping Beauty," "Cinderella," "Puss in Boots" (originally called "The Master Cat"), "Beauty and the Beast," "Hop O' My Thumb" and "Little Red Riding Hood." According to Nila's notes, this last was done as a vaudeville show—an example of how experimental you could be when so much of radio was sustaining.[4]

Jakob Grimm, a German philologist and folklorist who lived 1785–1863, came next. He and his brother Wilhelm collected and rewrote a great number and variety of folk tales, published between 1812 and 1815, as the celebrated Grimm's Fairy Tales. Jakob also published a German grammar text, and a work on German mythology; the brothers Grimm together produced a 16-volume dictionary, which, though it must have been a monumental work of scholarship, is today all but forgotten, while their fairy tales have become lasting classics.

Hans Christian Andersen (Danish, 1805-1875) was a prolific writer of children's stories. From his works we used "The Emperor's New Clothes," "The Flying Trunk," "The Little Mermaid" and "The Tinderbox."

Richard von Volkmann (1830-1889), born in Leipzig, German, became a surgeon, and wrote scholarly medical treatises on his earliest interest, anesthesia. Forced to wait outside Paris for five months during the siege of that city in the Franco-Prussian War (1870-71), he began to write fairy tales, which he mailed home to his wife a page at a time. They were published later under his pen name of Richard Leander. Those we used on *Let's Pretend* included "The Rusted Knight," "The Invisible Kingdom" and "The Queen Who Couldn't Make Spice Nuts."

Andrew Lang, an English scholar and man of letters (1844-1912), was born in Scotland. He was a poet, interested in myth and folklore, known for his prose translations of Homer's *Iliad* and *The Odyssey*. But he is remembered now mostly for his many translations and adaptations of children's stories, done with his wife Leonora Blanche Lang. *The Blue Fairy Book* was published in 1899, and after that came *The Red Fairy Book*, *The Yellow Fairy Book* and several others. Some of the tales were from the same sources used by the Brothers Grimm and by Perrault, but most were from sources not touched by those authors.

Let's Pretend also broadcast some scripts by living authors, and from unexpected sources.

The first was our own Patricia Ryan, who at the age of 12 authored a radio play called *The Silver Knight*, a well-written adventure story, done on

---

4. A sustaining program was just what the name implies: until a sponsor could be found, the show's production costs would be sustained by the network. In present-day commercial radio and television, of course, there are no sustaining programs. Commercials are only omitted in cases of national emergency.

our program April 27, 1935. A seven-year-old girl named Jean Barhydt, of New Hartford, Connecticut, sent in her story "The Little Black Pot." Its length was only 150 words, and it involved a dispute between a little girl and a witch over the ownership of the pot. It was a charming story, and the CBS publicity department made the most of it. The broadcast, on May 15, 1937, was filmed by Paramount News.

Flora Spiegelberg, an 80-year-old great grandmother, was the author of three stories done on our program, "Princess Goldenhair and the Wonderful Flower," "The Flower Queen's Daughter" and "The Enchanted Toy Store of Fairyland." For the broadcast of the second part of that story, Grandma Spiegelberg, as she called herself, brought along from Connecticut representatives of four generations of her family.

Nila Mack wrote and adapted no less than 130 stories for the program, though several CBS press releases have blown the total up to 200. Some of the most popular and well-known stories we did every year, or oftener, included "Beauty and the Beast," "Cinderella," "Hansel and Gretel," "Jack and the Beanstalk," "Puss in Boots," "Rumpelstiltskin," "Snow Drop and the Seven Dwarfs" (the original title, which Nila insisted upon using), and "Sleeping Beauty."

Certain stories, all originals by Nila, were repeated at the same times every year. These included "The Night Before Christmas," always broadcast on the Saturday nearest to Christmas. In dramatizing the beloved Clement C. Moore poem, she integrated a subplot telling how the Mouse family, which lives inside the wall right next to a beautiful Christmas tree, is getting ready to celebrate the holiday in its own way. The very next week we always did another Nila Mack original, "The House of the World," an allegorical story in which a Little Child meets Good Will, and together they topple the four terrible walls of Selfishness, Greed, Poverty and Intolerance.

Near St. Patrick's Day we would always do another of Nila's original works, "The Leprechaun," the story of Paudeen, the lad who thinks that if only he can catch the wily Leprechaun, the fairies' shoemaker, he will get his wish to have his homely face and twisted back made whole, and win the love of the fair lass Eileen.

Our Halloween observance was always "Fairer Than A Fairy," in which the witch Lagrima, in a jealous rage, lays a curse on the little Princess, because her parents have dared to name her Fairer Than A Fairy. She also has to put up with an annoyingly fun-loving Assistant Fairy (always Gwen Davies), who is constantly fouling up the witch's orders to put curses on mortals.

For a number of years, beginning in 1942, we would always present the classic story "The Little Lame Prince," as a tie-in with the annual March of Dimes President's Birthday Ball polio fund drive. In Nila's dramatization, the little Prince (always played by Kingsley Colton) has ruled wisely as King for 60 years, but now it is time for him to fly to the Beautiful Mountains, leaving his faithful aging Councilor in charge; the Councilor now speaks to the people in the voice of Franklin D. Roosevelt, who himself had been crippled by polio for years. It was done by Bill Adams (first hired for this, before he was Uncle Bill), chosen by Nila Mack because of the faultless imitations of F.D.R. he had done so many times in the dramatized news stories on *The March of Time*. Special permission was granted by Stephen Early, Mr. Roosevelt's Press Secretary, with the proviso that the actor's name be mentioned. It would have been highly unsuitable, and confusing, for people to think that the President of the United States was on *Let's Pretend*. On a later broadcast of "The Little Lame Prince" Bill Adams was unavailable, and the voice was done by Art Carney, which is why he appears in the Appendix as a Let's Pretender.

One of Nila's best original stories, "The Castle of Hatred," was written in 1935 in response to a listener's letter protesting that stepmothers in fairy tales were always mean, and usually turned out to be witches. In Nila's script, a father confesses to his children that he is lonely after the death of his wife, and would like to remarry. The children are very much against this. They've heard what stepmothers can be. Their only friend is a lovely neighbor lady who helps them and their father in many ways. It is only after they have learned to love her that their father reveals that he has married her, and she is indeed their stepmother.

Being limited only by the pattern of doing special stories appropriate to the season, Nila was otherwise completely free to choose whatever script she wished for each broadcast. And if there was a scary tale one week, or one of the few "Let's Pretend" stories which did not have a completely happy ending, such as "The Little Mermaid" or "The Juniper Tree," you might be sure that the following week the story would be light-hearted and gay, or even a wacky comedy such as "The Flying Trunk," or "The Queen Who Couldn't Make Spice Nuts."

As we now have more than one generation which has not been exposed to children's fairy tales (except in their modernized, sometimes overwhelming Disney versions), a little more explanation of what they were like, at least on our radio program, might be appropriate. To illustrate the kind of atmosphere which was created every Saturday morning on the Columbia network, here is a synopsis of one story, "Beauty and the Beast," as it was done on our show.

For the nine years of our Cream of Wheat sponsorship, and until our last broadcast, the story opened with narration by the warm, friendly voice of Bill Adams.

UNCLE BILL: Once upon a time, there was a rich ship owner, who had two daughters...

The spell was cast. Whether Mom was drying the dishes, or the kids were playing in their rooms or outside, they would all get closer to the radio.

In the dialogue we learn that the father, who had lost most of his fortune, is off to the seaport, where, he has heard, his one remaining ship has been sighted. If he regains some of his wealth he promises to bring back a gift for each daughter when he returns. Ethelinda, the eldest, rattles off a list of jewels and perfumes, while his youngest daughter Beauty asks only for her father's safe return—and one perfect rose. "Traveling-on-horseback" music, followed by sounds of seagulls, and many voices, telling us that we are now at a busy seaport. An old codger (usually played by me) tells the father that the ship's dishonest crew have already sold the vessel and divided up the cargo.

Shaken with the bad news, the father starts home, but is overtaken by darkness, and a fierce storm. (Rain, thunder, horse's hooves, whinny of the frightened horse). He glimpses lights from the tower of a castle. A mysterious butler conducts him into a beautiful moonlit garden, where the storm has magically disappeared. (Bird sounds.)

After a sumptuous meal and a refreshing sleep, the father asks to thank his host, but is told by the butler, "My master sees no one." As he leaves the castle through the beautiful garden, he remembers Beauty's request, and picks a rose. A fearsome roar is heard, and a horrible Beast appears. (You, the listener, could of course make that Beast look any way you wanted—tusks, matted fur, yellow eyes, whatever.) The Beast will kill the father for picking the rose, unless he goes home and returns with one of his daughters. The father is borne home on the wings of the wind (wind sound, transition music).

Beauty, to spare her father's life, insists on returning with him to the Beast's castle. She agrees to stay, and the Beast promises that no harm will come to her. After a tearful farewell, the Beast turns a ring on his finger, and the father is magically whisked back to his home. "It's almost as if he were really kind, for all his fearsome looks," says Beauty when she is alone. "I'm not as frightened as I thought."

As Beauty sleeps that night, she has a strange dream…: (Mysterioso music. Clock strikes.)

VOICE:	Beauty…Beauty.
BEAUTY:	Who are you? Where are you? I see nothing but the moon.
VOICE:	I am in the moonlight. I am in the mists and the wind. I am in the perfume of all the flowers, but you cannot see me.
BEAUTY:	What would you have of me?
VOICE:	Do not be misled by appearances. Do not judge by what you see on the surface. Be true to your heart. Be gentle. Don't be afraid.

(When Nila Mack first dramatized the story in 1931 she played The Voice in the Wind herself, but was glad to relinquish the part when Miriam Wolfe joined the cast. Miriam, even at age 12, had the maturity to do it, and as long as she was in New York no other actress played it from then on.)

After a year alone, with no one but her maid Clotilde, and occasional visits from the Beast, Beauty is terribly lonely, and asks to go home for a visit. The Beast reluctantly agrees, but warns her that if she does not return by the dark of the moon it will be too late. At home, Beauty is awakened one night by the mysterious Voice, which warns her:

VOICE:	(Mysterioso music behind) The moon is on the wane. The Beast is dying.

Beauty is taken on the wings of the wind to the castle. She now realizes that in spite of his fearsome appearance, she has come to be very fond of the Beast.

She finds him in the garden, half-dead. With a gasping breath, he asks, "Beauty…will you…marry me?" "Yes, dear Beast," replies Beauty. "I will marry you whenever you wish." "Oh, my dear!" And in an instant the horrible Beast is changed into a handsome Prince. (Sound of a small mouth siren, which

Nila called a "whiz bang," used on *Let's Pretend* for all instantaneous magic transformations.) The Voice now appears in human form as a beautiful Fairy Godmother, and explains that the Prince was the Beast, and had been placed under a wicked witch's spell, which could only be broken by a maiden who would truly love him for himself, in spite of his outward form. "Bless you both," says the Godmother, "and may you live happily ever after." (A few notes of triumphal wedding music, which segues into the *Let's Pretend* theme playoff.)

This synopsis might make the story seem terribly amusing and naïve, but on the actual broadcasts, for 23 years…it worked. Children were moved, and excited, as were their parents.

Synopsizing all our stories would probably not serve any useful purpose, but their titles, listed in the Let's Pretend Broadcast Log, will give the reader an idea of the richness and variety of our *Let's Pretend* repertoire.

In a chapter from *Off Mike—Radio by the Nation's Top Writers*, Nila Mack herself tells how she writes for children: "I don't! When I write it's for people of all ages who enjoy fun and fantasy. No picture comes to mind of pigtails, tow-heads and hair ribbons, but rather the whole family listening and each one finding something in the story for his own personal enjoyment."

She goes on to say that clarity is uppermost in her mind. The listener must be informed either in dialogue or in narration where the scene is taking place, the identity of the people in it, and their relationship to each other. And in radio, a medium with no visual aids, she learned the value of simplicity—in the action and in the words.

For fantasy, which had become her specialty, she found out how valuable sound effects could be, to help tell the story in ways that dialogue alone could not, though she resisted the temptation to add sounds just for their own sake. Our director once said, "I am not of the school who feels there is a great drama in 'footsteps are heard.'" (Her CBS colleague, director Earle McGill, once wrote that there were so many unnecessary footstep sounds in radio that you'd think no American home could afford a carpet.) She took care not to let the sounds become overwhelming, and gave extra clues in the dialogue so that there would be no doubt as to what we were hearing. "If the scene demands a crackling fire in the fireplace," she wrote, "the cellophane sequence[5] isn't quite enough for me. I quickly throw another log on with the first line of the scene."

---

5. For a fire sound, cellophane or other stiff plastic wrap or paper being slowly crushed close to the microphone still sounds very convincing.

Good radio writing can form just as clear a picture in the listener's mind as if he were witnessing the event. As Bill Adams once said in an interview, "Your imagination was part of the cast." It brings to mind the little seven-year-old boy who was asked which did he like better—plays on the radio or on television (that was when both were still equally available). "On the radio," he said. When asked why, he replied, "Because I can see the pictures better." On television, of course, everything is supplied, and there is only one way a viewer can look at it. Perhaps that is what Fred Allen was thinking of when he defined that medium as "the chewing gum of the mind."

Miss Mack had two problems in transforming fairy tales into playable radio scripts: First, the original stories were often bare scenarios. There was plenty of action, but the people in them had almost no individual characteristics. Second, they were written in rather stilted, archaic language. The Brothers Grimm, by the way, said that they did not write their stories for children in the first place. They were merely compilations of old folk tales from many sources, and some were full of violence, and highly unsuitable for young people. For instance, in one there appeared a witch who had made a fence around her house from the bones of her former lovers. (No—we didn't do *that* one on *Let's Pretend*.)

A good example of the technique which Nila learned by doing it was the script for "Rumpelstiltskin," barely four pages long in the original Grimm version. The characters are: The miller, who, to make himself look important to the King, tells him that his daughter can spin flax into gold. There is the King, who is avaricious, and jumps at the chance—the royal treasury is rather low. The poor unfortunate girl Winifred, threatened with death if she does not spin the gold before morning, appeals to Rumpelstiltskin, the little man who magically appears, and he agrees to do it in exchange for her necklace. Pleased with the gold the King orders the girl to spin a second time, also on pain of death. This time Rumpelstiltskin demands her ring. The King and the girl are married, and after a year, insolvency rears its head again, and the King makes the request a third time. (It is remarkable how in almost all fairy stories things come in threes—three beautiful daughters, three wishes, three impossible tasks for the hero to perform, etc.)

This time the little imp demands the Queen's first-born child, and tells her that her only chance to keep the baby is that she guess his name in three days' time. The fourth character in the original story is the messenger whom the desperate girl sends for to try to find unusual names. Through a lucky chance the messenger happens upon the little man dancing around a fire in the forest, gleefully cackling that his name is Rumpelstiltskin. Happy ending. Period.

To "open up" the story for radio, Nila invented extra scenes, and gave the characters more human dimensions. First, the miller, with a few snide remarks to his daughter, is established as a less-than-caring father, before he disappears from the story. The King, more importantly, loses his menace and becomes a cheerful, lovable bumbler, impossibly absentminded, who can't even remember the name of his own kingdom (it was Yaltoria). There are the many giggling maidens who assemble for the King to pick a wife (a new scene created by Nila). There is the patient Councilor ("No, Sire, you haven't grown a beard overnight. That's not the mirror you're holding—it's your hairbrush.") There is the girl herself, who is terrified but courageous. Then there is the baby's nurse, who sends out not one, but two messengers to scour the kingdom for names—two, so that they can have dialogue together in the exciting scene in which they discover Rumpelstiltskin's name, then race on horseback to beat the midnight deadline to save the Queen's child. There was now a full cast of characters to interact with each other, and plenty of excitement, adventure and suspense, with a little comedy thrown in. Nila gave her script a short coda at the end, after the evil elf has angrily stamped a hole in the floor and disappeared, no doubt to oblivion. It went thus:

KING:	(FADE ON) What's happened here? What's wrong, Winifred?
WINIFRED:	Oh, my husband, we had a caller, and he was so angry when he found you were not at home that he stamped on the floor until it collapsed and he disappeared into the earth.
KING:	Who was it?
WINIFRED:	His name was Rumpelstiltskin.
KING:	Rumpel…oh, it's just as well. I never could have remembered it anyhow.
	(Music playoff.)

Helen and Mary **Becomes**
Let's Pretend

As Nila Mack began the task of completely reconstructing the program, scriptwise and castwise in 1930, it was still her responsibility to get *The Adventures of Helen and Mary* on the air every Saturday morning, no matter what changes were taking place. This was not easy, conditions at CBS being what today would be called somewhat primitive. In 1930 there were many dramatic programs originating from 485 Madison Avenue every week, but the sound department consisted of only three people (fifteen years later there were 40 on staff). So Nila called on her friends Georgia Backus, her original mentor when she applied for work at CBS, and Don Clark to pinch-hit.

There were other problems, as Nila recounted many years later:

> "As for the music—we had to be a little resourceful there, too. Emery Deutsch and his ensemble were available—but only for the air show, since they were doing programs like crazy all over the place. In order to get them, Emery, in Studio 5, would sign off the ensemble program while Sidney Raphael, the pianist, would tear into Studio 3 and whip up the opening of our show. About the third musical bridge we were a complete unit.
>
> "Of course I never had a dress rehearsal and had to devise some quaint way of timing strictly by ear. It was almost disconcerting, come the day CBS expanded to the extent of assigning production men to programs—men who could add and subtract—an art I have not learned to this day."

Nila Mack had gone out on a limb with an audacious idea—that of a network dramatic program with all of the parts played by child actors. Now she had to make it work. Nila had confided to friends that she didn't really like children, but she was gregarious, outgoing and made friends easily, and despite her original reservations in dealing with what *Variety* referred to as "moppet thesps," it did not take her long to realize that she had been wrong. She found that she not only began to like children, but grew to love them, and the exquisite patience she eventually developed in working with juvenile performers proved to be one of the most important qualities Miss Mack brought to *Let's Pretend* and all the other children's programs she directed.

However, she was a professional, and expected her cast members to be the same. The program was not like the many radio kiddie talent shows of that time, on which you would do a little song or dance for which you had been carefully coached by your mother at home. Our cast members had to be able to sight-read from a script, which, unless they were very young, they had not been given until first rehearsal. They had to take direction and observe discipline, which meant among other things, pick up your cues, read exactly what is in the script without stumbling, and do not hog the microphone.

Any coaching between rehearsals was frowned upon by our director. ("Frowned upon" is too mild a term. She told the mothers: "Don't do it!") Occasionally, of course, she might ask a parent to go over the words with a very young child who was having trouble with them. I once saw a mother smack her small child in the face in a hallway during a *Let's Pretend* rehearsal break; having the script in advance, she had coached the little boy at home. At rehearsal, Nila, being director, worked with the child and got him to do it her way, but he was then punished for disobeying his mother.

Having made her decision to create a company of child actors, it was our director's job to get to know the children she had "inherited" from Yolanda Langworthy, and to quickly recruit others; and so she started auditioning children for the show, a process she would repeat every few months for the next 20 years, as the talent pool was always changing.

When she auditioned a new child she would always have some *Let's Pretend* scripts to be read from, but around 1934 she developed a new one just for audition purposes. It was a monologue we called "The Dog Script." A little newsboy (it worked just as well for a girl) is happily walking along the street with his dog named Tubby. The dog runs in front of a car and is hit. The child holds the limp animal and sobs: "Oh, please, God—don't let Tubby die. He's such a good dog and he's all I got. Oh, please...don't let him die!" If the tears were real, Nila knew she had probably found new material for her cast, and would often hire the child on the spot. But if the sobs sounded faked, Nila would probably say, "Thank you very much, dear—that was lovely. We'll let you know."

Sybil Trent remembered doing this audition scene under particularly trying circumstances. When nine-year-old Sybil walked into the studio it was pitch-dark, and she stumbled over several bodies on the floor. It seemed that Nila had scheduled the audition during a rehearsal break in the show, and the children in the cast were in the middle of a game called "Murder."

The stodginess of *The Adventures of Helen and Mary* as a children's program probably came from the fact that the two little girls of the title were strictly incidental; the rest of the cast were almost all adults. As Nila Mack later wrote, "It had nothing to do with fairy tales…I went to work, changed the format but kept the title." The new format was one with which children could identify.

Helen and Mary are playing in their attic. Their little friends come up and join them, and they start playing a game of make-believe. They want to hear a story, so they call upon a new character Nila had created named Memory, and this was written for the one adult actor allowed on the program—Harry Swan.

Nila remembered the happy tomfoolery of "Eva the Fifth," a backstage comedy in which she had played two and a half years before at the Little Theatre (now the Helen Hayes), and that Harry, besides playing a drum in his character of a railroad flagman, and being able to sing, was also adept at many voices and animal sounds. He would be very useful on the show. There was never any description of what Memory looked like, but he was obviously small, pixie-like, and rather shy.

On one occasion, in one of the last of the *Helen and Mary* scripts, which Gwen Davies found in a musty trunk in her basement, the children coax Memory to come out of his box and take them to the Land of Let's Pretend for the story of "Melilot." He magically changes a bench into a sight-seeing bus, and they all ride off happily. At the end of the broadcast the announcer says, "So ends another adventure in the Land of Let's Pretend. Was "Melilot" your favorite story? If not, write to 'Helen and Mary,' in care of this station, and they will try to have your story come true."

Helen and Mary had been traveling to that magical country for almost five years when, on March 24, 1934, Nila changed the title of the show to *Let's Pretend*. By then we had long been on in the 10:35-11:00 A.M. time period after a five-minute newscast, so it was no longer necessary for the musicians to frantically tiptoe in from their previous show.

Along with the title change, the format was changed as well. Helen and Mary no longer existed. Estelle, Pat and the others were now simply themselves, in the studio. Memory had disappeared too and Harry Swan became a benevolent straight man (no more pixie voice), known as Captain Bob. In the hundreds of children's programs then existing, both network and local, you would find countless Uncles, Aunts, Captains (probably a few Majors) and other titles, all used to denote friendly, non-threatening authority figures.

Harry still appeared in the program's lead-in, and continued to do animal sounds, and an occasional "Make way for the King!" At the program's opening, having been introduced by the CBS staff announcer, he would start by discussing with the children in the cast the fan mail that had come in asking for favorite stories. Occasionally there would be a misunderstanding, such as the letter Nila received which began, "Dear Niles and Max", and another which started "Dear Nylon Max."

Once the story had been decided upon, there began the ritual of deciding how to travel to the Land of Let's Pretend, which became the program's trademark, and never varied for the next 20 years:

CAPT BOB:	How shall we travel to the Land of Let's Pretend?
PAT:	Walter Tetley—why don't you tell us?
WALTER:	Well, the weather's pretty warm—why don't we all go on a cool, breezy ocean liner?
CAPT BOB:	An ocean liner it is. A-one, and a-two, and a-three! (WHIZ BANG SOUND)

A ship's whistle would be heard, and a gong, and someone would call out: "All ashore that's going ashore! This liner now sailing for Let's Pretend, the Topaz Islands and the story of "King Midas and the Golden Touch"! Everybody would ad-lib "Goodbye, goodbye..." (And I would stick in, "Don't forget to feed the goldfish!" Ah, what innocent days....) The ship's bell and the huge whistle would be heard over the ad-libs, then the orchestra would play the bridge music into the first scene of the story.

In those early years, as Nila later wrote, "Listeners would sit up with a snap when the announcer would say, [as the program ended] 'The Queen Mother played by eight-year-old Patricia Ryan. The Wicked King played by

nine-year-old Billy Halop.' " That was part of the program's unique appeal—
all of the parts, from children to adults to doddering geriatrics, being played
by children. Nila's pioneering idea was a success—so much so, in fact, that as
we child actors became better, and more sure of ourselves under her direction,
she did not replace us when we grew into our teens, as she had most of the
original children on *Helen and Mary*. The device of announcing our ages was
dropped in 1937. They were no longer that remarkable.

The casting had now come full circle, and, as we grew, had gradually
changed back into what it was when Nila took over in 1930—basically adult
actors. As before, the only child actors used were those playing children's roles.
However, there was now a vast difference. These adult actors had been hand-
picked, brought along, trained by Nila Mack, and we had a unified acting
style uniquely suited to fairy tales and to fantasy. We had also developed a
great ease and facility in working with her, and with each other, which Daisy
Aldan later referred to as a "group karma." In any case, by 1940, Nila's tenth
anniversary with CBS and with the program, the Let's Pretenders had become
a smoothly-running repertory company of some of the best young actors in
radio.

It is not difficult to work up a pretty good estimate of what it cost to put
on a *Let's Pretend* broadcast in the early days. Nila Mack, as the show's writer,
producer and director, was on salary as a regular staff member, and so were the
musicians and sound effect people. The classic fairy tales the scripts were based
upon were in the public domain, so that the only net fees payable were to the
actors. When she first went to work at CBS Nila had been given a metal cash
box out of which to pay the cast. Harry Swan, being an adult, probably got
ten dollars. Henry Boyd, our bird whistler, was told by Nila one week that she
had eight dollars for him in the box, and for his next engagement she had only
seven. But all of the children got the same fee: $3.50 for two-and-a-half hours
of rehearsal and a half-hour performance on a national network. This fee was
no doubt based on the proposition that *Let's Pretend* was just like any other
kiddie talent show, and since you were a child getting to broadcast on the
radio, and it was so much fun and all, you didn't really expect to get *paid*, did
you? (Our $3.50 checks remained the same until 1938.) And so the net cost
to CBS for a typical *Let's Pretend* broadcast in those early days, with a cast
consisting of Harry Swan and 12 children, was about $52. A bargain.

When the first contracts were negotiated with the American Federation
of Radio Artists in 1938, the regular rate for a half-hour sustaining show
such as ours was $21, but the networks were able to convince the union to

waive this fee when more than 75% of the cast were children. The kiddie talent show syndrome again.

Though the children on *Let's Pretend* were miserably paid, even by 1930's standards, it was for many of us our first professional performing experience, and the training and confidence we gained enabled us to go on to other shows, some of us eventually earning hundreds of dollars weekly. Nila Mack was once heard to remark, I am sure without bitterness, that some of the kids she had trained were currently earning several times her own salary in their busy radio careers.

During those first few hectic, almost desperate weeks of August and September 1930, Miss Mack was also given additional writing and directing chores, not to mention an occasional acting job, such as the continuing role of Mrs. Webb on a program called *The Magic Voice*, all no doubt included in her weekly salary as a CBS staff member. She directed several other children's shows early on, including *You Decide*, a children's discussion program, and *The Junior Bugle: The Child's Newspaper of the Air*. That was replaced by "Sunday Morning at Aunt Susan's," presented on Sundays for an hour at 9:00 A.M. Nila chose Elaine Ivans, another friend she had worked with in *Eva the Fifth*, for the title role.

There were two children, Teddy and Jean, played by Albert Aley and Vivian Block. It was a family-oriented show, with the same string ensemble as on *Let's Pretend*. It would always open with the family singing a hymn, and conversing. Then guests would drop in—a well-known author, the curator of the Aquarium, an arctic explorer, or some of the actors Nila Mack knew, with made-up names, such as Henry Boyd, who would be called Mr. Robin. He would talk about birds, and do some bird calls. The program was folksy and informative. It went on the air in 1931, and lasted until 1937.

Nila directed several performances of *The Columbia Workshop*, which started in 1936. Two of her earliest were "A Letter from Home," written by her friend Charles Jackson, and "The Ghost of Benjamin Sweet," both done in March 1938, and preserved on tape at the Museum of Television and Radio.

In 1940 she both wrote and directed two Dr. Seuss stories: "To Think That I Saw it on Mulberry Street" with Jack Grimes, House Jameson and Ted DeCorsia, and "The 500 Hats of Bartholomew Cubbins" featuring Jack again,[6] with Howard Lindsay as King Derwin. Nila did not have much opportunity to use her friends the Lindsays in radio—they were always busy in the theatre.

6. She later directed it on *Let's Pretend* (9/25/48) with our regular *Let's Pretend* actors.

She did use Dorothy Stickney (Mrs. Lindsay) on *Let's Pretend* once—there is no record of the part she played. Also in 1940 Miss Mack directed the much-anthologized "Inside a Kid's Head," by CBS staff writer Jerome Lawrence. Nine-year-old Pretender Skippy Homeier played the lead.

The American School of the Air, which had been broadcast since 1930, assigned Nila to adapt the stories for, and direct, their Thursday program *Tales from Far and Near*. Many of us Let's Pretenders worked on that. She also directed the children's quiz program *The March of Games*, starring our own Sybil Trent, and another program for young people *So You Want To Be*, aired on Fridays at 5:45 P.M., beginning in July 1938, in which some person outstanding in his or her field was interviewed by a youngster, who would ask questions from the viewpoint of someone just becoming interested in choosing a career.

There were only two continuous programs assigned to Nila Mack which were not for children or did not involve fantasy. They were *Let Freedom Ring*, a 13-week series for the Department of the Interior, and *Mrs. Miniver*, a series based on the Jan Struther novel, and one has to wonder whether, being a woman, she would have gotten either of them if it were not for the wartime manpower shortage.

Nila Mack had a deep sense of patriotism, and doing these programs must have given her a great deal of satisfaction. They were one direct contribution she could make to the war effort. Another was a book she wrote as a result of a suggestion made by one of the secretaries at CBS, *Animal Allies*. It was a short book for children, designed to answer questions they might have about why we were in the war, and why we had to win it.

All the countries involved in World War II were represented by animals. The book showed how Chief Sam Eagle came to the aid of Stoutheart the Lion, Shaggy Sovietsky the Bear, Chang the Dragon and Kid Aussie the Kangaroo, to prevent Greedy Gruber the Vulture from destroying Pleasant Forest, where they all lived. Mussolini was depicted as a big monkey telling the vulture how strong he was. Emperor Hirohito was a snake who attacked Sam the Eagle's nest, while The Mugwump in Sam's country cried "Quick! Somebody should *not* do something about it!"

In addition to all Nila's directing and writing assignments at CBS, it was of course also expected that she would fill in for other directors during vacations or illnesses, just as CBS directors Earle McGill or William N. (Bill) Robson did for her when she was ill or on vacation. However, whatever difficulties she met at the network, Nila Mack was now firmly established at CBS, and well-liked by all those she worked with. She had proved that she was a versatile writer and director, able to capably handle any of the assignments she was given.

But the jewel in her crown—the program she created and which through the years brought so much honor and recognition to CBS—would always be *Let's Pretend.*

5

Sounds, Animals and Music

As Nila Mack became more skilled at writing and directing *Let's Pretend*, she became more and more aware of how effectively sound effects could contribute to her tales of fantasy and magic. As her CBS colleague Earle McGill wrote, "Sound effects are to radio what scenery is to theatre." And sound helped immensely in our now-familiar device of "How shall we travel to the Land of Let's Pretend?" When we had all decided to ride on a fire engine, and you heard those sirens and clanging bells, and the delighted shouts of all the Pretenders, you were already part of the make-believe, and your imagination was open for anything, before the story had even begun. With sound effects, it was easy to believe that you were under the water with Andersen's Little Mermaid, or at the side of a brave Prince who is given the task of climbing a glass mountain on horseback to rescue the beautiful maiden on top. How do you do the sound of a horse climbing a glass mountain[7]? Our sound men did it with those well-known coconut halves, clopping, sliding and squeaking on a thick pane of glass covered with wet sand. In order to show just how difficult it was for the Prince, and the horse, to climb the mountain (they made it, naturally, to the cheers of the crowd of villagers below), the sound men had to be performers. They were not called sound effects *artists* for nothing.

---

7. Though complete sound effects libraries on compact discs can be cued very accurately, horses' hooves are still one sound which is best done manually, so that the horse can react to the situation in the script. Two half coconut shells are used, with small leather straps on each for handles. Rubber drain plungers are also used. A talented sound effects artist can simulate the horse pawing the ground impatiently, walking, trotting, or at a full gallop (also done on the chest with open palms, perhaps with a few snorts added vocally). The hooves can be done in loose dirt or sand (in a shallow wooden box), on wood, gravel, or whatever surface the action calls for.

Nila wrote that she at first asked with some trepidation for such hitherto unimagined sounds as talking wings, angry dragons, shimmering moonbeams, King Midas' flower garden being changed into solid gold. The sound department received the scripts several days in advance, so there was time for them to experiment in their own laboratory if necessary, and sometimes Nila would be there working with them, and making suggestions.

If an effect was too complicated to do live, they would occasionally cut an acetate recording[8] to be used on the broadcast. But one way or another, when Saturday morning came, everything that our director had asked for was ready.

Admitting some prejudice, I will say that the CBS sound people were the best in the business. When I joined the cast in 1936 there were Walter Pierson (head of the sound department), Ora Nichols, Ray Kremer, Jim Rogan, Henry Gautier and George O'Donnell. Walter Pierson looked like a scholarly scientist who worked in a laboratory, which is exactly what he was, when experimenting with a new or difficult effect in the sound workshop on the third floor at 485 Madison, or perhaps building some sound apparatus from scratch. Ora Nichols, known as radio's only woman sound technician, was rather short, had wire-rimmed glasses, and wore her hair gathered in a bun at the back, making her look like the stereotype of a New England schoolmarm. She had once played piano in a Massachusetts movie theatre, while her husband Arthur played drums, and gradually they began to improvise sound effects in the pit for the silent movies being shown. This led to their having their own vaudeville act, and eventually doing sound effects for CBS. Ora took over her husband's job there when he died. Ray Kremer was tall, thin and laid-back. Jim Rogan looked his Irish ancestry. He was stocky and had a black mustache. He had an extensive music education, and played violin and cello. He co-authored, with our conductor Emery Deutsch, the popular songs "When a Gypsy Makes his Violin Cry," and also "Stardust on the Moon," which was for six weeks on *Your Hit Parade*. Henry Gautier was small, capable and very good-natured. George O'Donnell was humorless, but very conscientious and competent. All of them were unflappable, and at times could be very creative.

---

8. Unlike phonograph records, which were pressed from a mold, acetates were made by grooves being cut in an acetate-coated aluminum disc, and that same disc could be played back immediately, though only a limited number of plays were possible before it started to show wear. Until tape recording was perfected, acetates were widely used to record auditions, special sound effects, and entire programs for later rebroadcast. The use of acetates became a bit chancy during World War II, though. Aluminum was needed for the military. Glass-based records were used for acetates, and woe be to the dolt who dropped one.

Ora Nichols, the industry's only woman sound technician, circa 1938 (from an old newspaper clipping). Note berry box for sound of splintering timbers, branches, telegraph key, pulley and belt, and compressed air tank. Courtesy Anthony Tollin.

Even after having been with the show for some time, I was still fascinated by watching our sound men who, wearing earphones and watching both the script and Nila for cues, might simultaneously be cueing up one or more sound effects records,[9] opening doors, rustling straw, breaking berry boxes to simulate splintering timbers, or maybe running up and down a short flight of prop stairs.

Some of the most important sounds on *Let's Pretend* were those of animals. Though every animal in creation had become available on records, they were far better when done live. The animals, after all, were characters in our stories, and had to react to the situation just as did the humans. Their sounds could never be

---

9. Cueing up sound records was an art. They were all 10-inch 78 r.p.m. records - much easier to find the right groove in a hurry than on a slow-moving LP. The sound man would mark the appropriate groove with a yellow crayon, play the record up to that point silently, heard only on his earphones, then stop the record by holding his thumb on it lightly, while the turntable continued to revolve. When the cue came he would release his thumb and simultaneously turn up the speaker volume, and there was the sound, right on the button - *if* you knew how to do it right.

just "thrown in" at random. However, our sound effects people did not claim to be adept at wolf howls or kitten mews. For those a different kind of specialist was needed, and over the years, *Let's Pretend* had some of the best.

First came Henry Swan, a fixture of *The Adventures of Helen and Mary* and on *Let's Pretend* until his retirement. I remember him in 1936 as being in his mid-50s, with thinning hair, watery blue eyes and a sallow complexion. I found him rather morose. He was not a great actor, but his animal sounds were excellent. It was said that he had been shell-shocked during World War I. We were all occasionally mortified by some of his bitter remarks. Once, when he thought he was underpaid for some animal sounds on a commercial program, he sent the check back to the ad agency with the words "PLEASE DON'T CALL ME AGAIN" written across the front. He left our program and the business before we became sponsored in 1943, and went to live alone in a small house in Hudson, N.Y., which I believe had been his hometown. Every year Gwen Davies would take up a collection to send Harry a Christmas package—we knew he would not take money. In the late 1940s his mental condition had apparently deteriorated, and when officials came to take him to either a V.A. hospital or some other institution, they found that Harry had blown his brains out, and left a note with wording to the effect that "I beat you to it."

Henry Boyd came on the scene not long after Harry Swan. Henry as a boy in East Orange, New Jersey, had always been fascinated by birds, and taught himself to imitate them. In 1923 at the age of 15 he walked into the studios of WOR, (then located above Bamberger's department store in Newark), announced that he could imitate birds, and asked could he be on the radio? Their reply was, of course—you can do a half-hour broadcast. Henry wrote a little narration called "A Walk In The Woods," with all the appropriate bird calls, which he did on the air the following week. There was no audition—but no mention of pay either.

Henry's next radio try was in the early 1930s, at CBS. Luckily Nila Mack was assigned to listen to his audition. By now he had refined his routine into something called "The Bird Opera." Nila not only had him do this on *Sunday Morning at Aunt Susan's*, but also called him for *Let's Pretend* whenever there were stories involving bird songs. These included "The Emperor's Nightingale," "Jorinda and Joringel" and "Thumbelina."

Henry, who was slightly built, prematurely balding, and not really trained as an actor, made his living for 13 years in the '30s and early '40s jerking sodas at Whelan's Drug Store at 8th Street and 6th Avenue in Manhattan, and later at Bigelow's, a few doors up the block. In the early days when Nila still lived on West 10th Street next to her friends the Howard Lindsays, she would come up to the soda fountain on her way home from work and say, "I need you this Saturday, Henry."

Henry Boyd started to get other radio work involving bird songs. He was the whistle of Aunt Jenny's canary, occasionally heard in her kitchen while she told her *Aunt Jenny's Real Life Stories* ("sponsored by Spry, the all-vegetable shortening") to her announcer and straight man Dan Seymour. His biggest success in the business, though, was doing the Rinso White bob white bird whistle. This being before the age of recorded commercials, he was called to the studio to do it live every time the singing duo did the Rinso jingle: "Rinso white, Rinso white, happy little washday song…" Beginning in 1940, he did this every week for 14 years.

Brad Barker came next. He had originally been a good-looking young leading man in silent films made in the East. With the advent of sound, he was on the set one day when a sound effect of frying eggs was needed. The electric frying pan had gone dead, and Brad offered to do the sound vocally. It was a spectacular success. From there it was just a step to doing the sounds of animals, which Brad had always loved. Coincidentally, he was getting on a bit for his young romantic roles, and here was radio—a young, exciting industry. A new career was born.

When he started doing *Let's Pretend*, Brad was already busy on many other shows. His wolf howl was a regular part of the signature of *Renfrew of the Mounted*. He was the original "Arf!" of *Little Orphan Annie's* Sandy. And it is Brad Barker's lion's roar that still introduces literally hundreds of the earlier MGM motion pictures.

The only time I ever saw Brad accept help with any of his sounds was when he first did a horse whinny on our show. As Brad did the lower, guttural part of the sound, Jack Grimes chimed in with the high part, whistled through his teeth. Our first reaction was to laugh, but this combination two-man horse was so real that from then on our director insisted that it be done by both Brad and Jack.

We all knew Brad as a serious-looking, soft-spoken man with a pencil-thin mustache and horn-rimmed glasses, who wore double-breasted suits and a homburg hat. One might think he was a bank executive as he entered the studio with a brown leather portfolio under his arm—until he unzipped it, removed a small wooden box, and used it to make more resonant the frightening snarl of a leopard.

He also had a lively, if corny, sense of humor. I remember his once asking me if I knew the difference between a cocktail lounge and an elephant's fart. Since I didn't, he supplied the answer: "Well, a cocktail lounge is just an ordinary barroom...But an elephant's fart is BARRR-ROOOM!!"

One reason Brad's sounds were so authentic was that he frequented Ringling Brothers' Circus whenever it was in town, and had many friends there, including, I am sure, the animals.

If anyone doubts an animal imitator is also an actor, the following should prove it. Homer Fickett, director of "The March of Time," put in an emergency call to Brad. There was a fast-breaking news story to dramatize on the air that night involving a tiger. Brad got there just before air time, and asked for a script. "You don't need a script —there isn't time," said Fickett. "Just roar when I give you the cue." Brad still insisted that he must have a script. "What for?" said Fickett. "Because," said Brad, "I have to know what the tiger is thinking."

Brad Barker's career in radio lasted almost 20 years, and he was with *Let's Pretend* until he died in 1951.

Brad Barker had an appropriate name, as dogs were his specialty. Harry Swan (and Henry Boyd, if you stretched it a little) both had bird names. All three were gifted and talented artists, and over the years their contributions to radio and to *Let's Pretend* were invaluable.

From the first, music was an essential part of *Let's Pretend*. For the program's entire life, starting with the *Helen and Mary* days, there was always a six-piece string ensemble consisting of first violin, second violin, cello, viola, bass and piano. The only exception was during a short period in 1938 when a 20-piece orchestra, led by Alexander Semmler, provided the music. They were probably all on salary, and assigned by CBS to our show because they had little or nothing else to do at the time. (The orchestra's size was rather overwhelming, though, and it detracted greatly from the program's charm.)

The music chosen for the theme and for bridges between scenes was light classical, or what was termed slightly contemptuously "parlor music" by serious musicians. However, these pieces were ideal for a children's radio program. They were simple and bright, and a definite melodic theme was established within their opening bars, or 15 or 20 seconds, which was all the time there was for each music cue. They included such delightful melodies as "The Flatterer" by Chaminade, "Solvejg's Song" by Grieg, "Dark Eyes," "Song of the Volga Boatman" and Kreisler's "Liebesfreud." Our theme music was "Fairy Tale," originally played in the key of D, written by Karel Komzak (1850-1905) of Czechoslovakia, the second of that name. Like his father he was a musician, a bandmaster and a composer. He wrote no less than 80 polkas, 20 waltzes and 60 marches, and also like his father he introduced Czech folk songs into his arrangements. The first thirteen bars of "Fairy Tale" (never heard on the program) are marked "Andante (with gloomy expression)," but the part used for our "Let's Pretend" theme is marked "Allegretto (very delicately and in march tempo)." If one hums the melody of "Fairy Tale" the "oompah" of a little Czechoslovak band can readily be imagined, with happy couples in a mountain village, stepping and twirling to this bright, lilting tune.

As Nila Mack became more and more confident as *Let's Pretend's* writer and director she also took over the selection of its music. She was well-qualified, having learned much of the kind of music required when as a child she had played piano for her mother's dancing classes in Arkansas City. In the vaudeville and legitimate theatres where she performed later, there was always a small orchestra which played an overture including some of the same kinds of pieces. Thus in her 39 years she had acquired an extensive knowledge of musical repertoire, and all she had to do each week was to send a list of the music wanted to Emery Deutsch, our conductor and first violinist, and it would be rehearsed and ready for Saturday's broadcast.

Emery Deutsch called himself a gypsy violinist. He was indeed Hungarian, by parentage and background, having been born in Budapest. He was a member of the legendary "A & P Gypsies," the first radio musical ensemble to gain a national reputation. He also wrote two hit songs for that genre, "Play, Fiddle, Play" and "When a Gypsy Makes his Violin Cry." When he left, after 12 years with CBS, to lead his own orchestra, Leon Goldman took over as conductor and first violinist, and he stayed with us to the end.

Another long-term *Let's Pretend* musical veteran was Sidney Raphael, who doubled on piano and celeste. His daughter Gerriannne Raphael was a child actress on our show and several others, who later developed a successful adult career, acting and singing in the theatre, and in commercials as well. Our cellist Maurice Brown later became our conductor, and composer of original music for the program, when Cream of Wheat took over as a sponsor. Other long-term members of the ensemble were Isaac Klaas, violin; Howard Kay, cello; and Elias Tenzer, bass. Another of our cellists, Bernard Greenhouse, studied with Pablo Casals and later became well-known in the classical music field.

Though she was experienced in radio, Miss Mack did not truly learn the importance of the engineering department until she began to direct *Let's Pretend*. Anyone who was uninformed might think that the engineer was merely someone who plugged in the microphones, then just sat there in the control room.[10] But she found that the engineer was the master of the sound mechanics of a radio program, and that his skill was just as instrumental in creating a good show as were all the other elements—cast, music and sound effects.

You Are There, first broadcast in 1947, was a program in which CBS news correspondents described famous historical events as if radio had existed then. But all of radio drama could have been subtitled *You Are There*. You were there in "Jack and the Beanstalk" when Jack started climbing that magical plant, and described to his mother the wonders he saw as he rose higher and higher, up into the sky. Jack Grimes always played the title role. One memorable performance of that story took place when we were broadcasting in 1942 before a packed house in one of the Broadway theatres CBS had leased. The dialogue went:

JACK: (GOING OFF MIKE, ON ECHO:) Mother, I can
                   see the top of the church steeple....Now I can see the
                   next village....There's the river...(EVEN FARTHER
                   OFF:) Now I can see the who-o-ole w-o-o-r-l-d!

It was very effective radio, with the help of the echo chamber[11] to give the effect of distance, Jack slowly backing away from the microphone as he spoke. But as Jack said, "Who-o-o-le w-o-o-o-rld!" he fell backwards off the stage of the theatre. Lucky he wasn't badly hurt, and scrambled back on stage in time for his cue in the next scene.

---

10. A control room is a soundproof room where the program's engineer, director and other production personnel sit. There the engineer mixes and regulates sound levels of each microphone as necessary, which are heard on large loudspeakers. Meanwhile, the director can see the performers through a plate glass window, and give them hand signals during the broadcast. Orson Welles, who always performed in the programs he directed, would stand on a podium in the studio, wearing earphones, though most other directors preferred being in the control room, so as to hear the broadcast as it would sound to the radio audience. Photographs of directors standing next to the actors in a radio studio and giving them cues were usually staged publicity shots.

11. Echo chambers were also used on our show for ominous voices, such as that of Aladdin's Genie of the Lamp. Originally an echo chamber was a long concrete room with a loudspeaker at one end and a microphone at the other, with wonderful reverberations in between, the whole effect being mixed with other voices or sound effects in the engineer's console. Some orchestra leaders liked to have a little echo mixed with their music as well. A present-day echo chamber is completely electronic, and the effect is achieved in a gadget no bigger than an attaché case.

Nila Mack learned a lot early on from the engineers with whom she worked, both as a writer and as a director. The first lesson was that the script had to be written so that the listener would always know who the characters were, and where they were. The next, was, you couldn't just put a bunch of people in a studio, turn on the mikes, and expect a believable radio show. The microphones had to be placed correctly for the right sound balance in that particular studio, and each actor, musician and sound effect had to be the right distance from the microphones, to carry out the writer's intent. Anyone in the studio could be faded in or out, either by moving toward or away from their microphone, or by the engineer changing his volume control on that mike, but obviously none of this could happen unless the engineer knew how to achieve these things, and the director knew what to ask for.

Nila Mack once wrote a preface to a published version of her radio adaptation of "Rapunzel," in which she said that this story was a definite challenge to the engineer and to the sound department, as well as to the cast. She added, "Only a fine gradation of sound volume as well as voice will make the action of the scenes quite clear to the listener." What she meant was that as the Witch climbs up the tower on Rapunzel's hair, the director must decide which of them the microphone "goes with." As Rapunzel leans out of the tower to call to the Witch, the echo chamber is used to give the effect of height. Then as the Witch, later the Prince, climbs closer, the echo volume is slowly turned down, then killed. This particular effect was beautiful, and the listener was indeed *there.*

Nila could never be sure which engineer she would be assigned. Those I remember include John Dietz, who later became a CBS radio director, and Fred Hendrickson, who later became the producer of *The Arthur Godfrey Show* on radio. A good audio engineer could be, just as much as the others I have mentioned, essential to the success of any radio show.

Under Nila Mack, with the help of her child actors, and the many other talented experts she learned to rely upon—the sound technicians, the animal imitators, the musicians and the engineering department, a true repertory company was created, in which all of us worked with each other in a spirit of mutual respect, and took pleasure in our work. American radio broadcasting when at its best was a superb combination of artistic creativity and technical expertise, and there was no better example of this than *Let's Pretend.*

6

\Working With Children

It had been Nila Mack's idea to convert the cast of *Helen and Mary* to one entirely made up of children, but now she had to learn to work with them. And so over the months and years, she developed ways of dealing with her youthful cast. Her first instinct, she said, was "to make the children see that I was not their teacher nor yet their mother. I was one of them. We were going to have a grand time—a thrilling time—bringing fairy tales to life."

In a later interview she said that after having been with the show for ten years, "children have taught me that talking down to them is fatal. It gets me in trouble fast. But an eye-to-eye conversation, using words and expressions they can understand, gives the same response that adults give. The same? I mean better."

Another time she wrote:

"There's only one difference between children and adults anyway. Children are more honest. Encouragement is far better than criticism. Confidence draws out better performances. Children accept direction eagerly when given as a means of improving their performances, rather than criticizing their first approach. When a rehearsal begins on *Let's Pretend*, the youngsters sit around a table. The cast is assigned. Then we read the whole script straight through without stopping, so that each gets a clear idea of the story first, along with a clearer picture of his relationship to the other members of the cast. After that is over, and before I

'put it on the mike,' I discuss, in an impersonal and busi-
nesslike way, the characterizations they have given me. I
listen to their ideas, and try to learn just why they read as
they did. If they are wrong, my answer will be something
like, 'I see what you mean. But I believe in this instance,
you can get more out of the part if you tackle it like this.' I
may read one line. But rather than have a group of parrots,
I much prefer to recall a certain movie, or a story, or even
another script wherein there was a character something like
this one being discussed. The response is instantaneous, and
we start to build it along the lines I want. In the meantime,
the child has not been humiliated, and, while he plays it
differently than he originally did, he doesn't feel that his
first reading was unintelligent, or that his ability was ques-
tioned.

"Scolding is no good when there is a broadcast in the
offing....It brings two definite reactions. To single out one
child and scold or punish him creates a 'gang' feeling. The
child mustn't come back with an argument and the others
are embarrassed with and for him, with the result that they
hang together in self-defense. The second reaction is an
unsteady air performance wherein the child will very likely
'fluff' his lines or miss cues because he's thinking of the hurt
he had."

At times when Nila felt direct criticism was necessary, and that could
include our personal conduct, not only our performances, she always had
the consideration to do it in private. None of us was ever humiliated in
front of the others.

Contrary to many newspaper articles and CBS press releases of the '30s
and '40s, our director did not give us acting lessons, or teach theory. That
was not her job. She had a show to put on, and very little rehearsal time in
which to do it. She gave us directions on how to be a better princess, giant,
enchanted frog or wicked witch. We learned by doing, and any child who
proved incapable of learning was eventually not called any more. She would
work patiently with a new child—start the newcomer in small parts (Third
Fairy, Second Goblin, etc.) and gradually nurture the child's talent until he
or she was able to emote as confidently as the rest of us and was, inciden-

tally, often launched on a lucrative career as a juvenile heartthrob on other programs. Nila made real actors out of many of us who would otherwise have been doomed to quick fadeouts after brief careers as "cute kiddies."

In spite of her patience with the youngest children, Nila's sense of humor would occasionally get the better of her. Once, for the sake of a yock, she cautioned a new snippet playing a lady-in-waiting: "No, dear—it's not MADame. It's MaDAME. Just remember—DAME, as in God."

There were also certain technical things to learn, of course. For example, hold your script up and speak directly into the microphone, and don't be a "mike hog"; that is, stand aside a little when someone else on your side of the mike has a speech. Which is the live side of the mike and which is the dead side, and what is the difference between a physical fade (turning or backing away from the microphone while speaking) and a board fade (done by the engineer in the control room). And we all had to learn to be constantly alert for the director's hand signals. Pointing to you means that's your cue to start a speech or a scene. Moving the index finger in a circle means speed up—we're a little behind. Stretching imaginary thread as the two hands slowly separate means slow down, or literally, stretch it out. Cupped hand to ear means I can't hear you—speak up. All of us, no matter how small, had to learn these radio protocols.

Another thing that had to be known, seemingly simple, was ad-libbing.[12] Neither Nila nor any other good radio director was satisfied with a bunch of actors saying, "Walla, walla, walla," the accepted cliché for ad-libs. You were expected to improvise words appropriate to the situation. For instance, if a crowd were in the King's throne room waiting for an announcement, and the script read simply "Crowd murmurs," it might be something like: "Well, I certainly hope they start pretty soon. I'm tired of standing around. Doesn't the Princess look beautiful today. Oh, here comes the King now—maybe we'll find out what's going on..." etc., until directed to fade down (the director's hand held out and slowly lowered) as the King speaks.

If you happened to be eight years old at the time, and had to remember all these things, meanwhile being careful not to fall off the little two-foot-square platform you were standing on to be in range of the mike, it could be rather scary. All of Nila's patience, directorial ability and knowledge of radio were needed for it to come together successfully.

---

12. Ad-lib is short for "ad libitum" which means literally "in accordance with one's wishes." Ad-lib directions in scripts are seldom more specific than (Crowd protests).

There was, even for the most experienced radio actors, always the risk of fluffing a line—saying the wrong word inadvertently. After a broadcast when this had happened to one Pretender, Nila's advise to us all was: "If you make a fluff, don't call attention to it by going back and correcting yourself. Most listeners will not notice, and most of those who do will think they heard wrong."

In live radio, a fluff was always a possibility, no matter how many rehearsals you had gone through. On *Let's Pretend* if a child had trouble with a word or phrase in rehearsal, Nila would change it to something more simple. But the chance always remained. The annals of radio are full of Famous Fluffs, some obscene, some just goofy, but always unplanned. Here are the few that I recall on our show over the years:

Daisy Aldan (intoning mysteriously on the well-known story of the "The Juniper Tree"): I...am the voice...of the Jupiner Tree.

Bill Lipton (on the story of "How Six Traveled Through the World," as the slightly slow-witted Stack the Strong, who discovers that the room in which the Witch has locked them all is an airtight oven with a fire beneath it): Why it's...it's an onion!

Jack Grimes (showing Kingsley Colton through a magical underground garden): And here, Your Majesty, is the Avenue of the Golden Freet Trues.

Our most spectacular fluff also belongs to Jack Grimes. In the original New Year's allegory written by Nila, "The House of the World," the Spirit of Good Will is attempting to break down the walls of Selfishness, Greed, Poverty and Intolerance, and seems to remember this not being their first meeting. Jack (to Good Will): Haven't we wet somewhere before?

Though this might seem to the reader like an insignificant bobble, amidst the tension of a live coast-to-coast broadcast it could well have caused temporary hysteria. In any case both Jack, and Albert Aley, who played Good Will, got through the rest of the broadcast with real difficulty. Rolling on the floor with laughter was not allowed. (The next year when the story was done again, we found that our director had changed both the wording and the rhythm of the line to an innocuous: "I've seen you before, haven't I?")

From *Let's Pretend*'s first broadcast until Cream of Wheat came aboard in 1943, rehearsal and performance took place in one continuous session. When I started with the show our rehearsal began at 8:30 A.M. in Studio 1.

After we'd kissed Miss Mack hello we would sit in a semicircle, boys on one side and girls on the other (our choice, not hers) and study our scripts. All of us would be dressed neatly, the boys in shorts or knickers, with knee-length stockings (no one wore "longies" until they were in their teens), wearing neckties and jackets, even in summer. The girls would always be in dresses, or "middie" blouses and skirts, also with knee-length stockings ("bobby socks" did not appear until 1943) and often with bows in their hair, which might be bobbed (in the early '30s), or worn long, in curls, or in pigtails if they were very young.

Meanwhile Miss Mack sat at a small table in the center with her script, her cigarettes and her stopwatch. She smoked two and a half packs of Kool Menthols a day, and all of us Pretenders have vivid memories of our director coming into the studio with her bustling walk, holding a lighted cigarette, the pack, the matches and the stopwatch in her right hand, and a bundle of scripts and a pencil in her left.

After the first reading of the script there would often be cuts for time purposes, but if a story had been done before there was often no need. Then she would go into the control room, and we would go to the mikes and start working through the story scene by scene, as she gave the actors and sound men directions, speaking patiently and deliberately to the small children who might be newcomers, and in grown-up terms to the more experienced Pretenders. This was a serious work situation, but also a fascinating game. We children were very fortunate, though we did not realize it at the time. We were enjoying the magic of make-believe and the glamour of show business simultaneously—and getting paid for it.

As we grew older, if there was too much clowning during rehearsal, the talk-back[13] would carry the director's admonition: "Now cut that out, or I'll come out there and sock you! And you know I can do it, too!" But all of us knew she wouldn't have.

After this "work-through" and before the dress rehearsal there would be a short break. You could go to the lavatory, or report to your mother in the reception room outside, if you were still young enough that your mother was there. Meanwhile our string ensemble was rehearsing in another studio.

The dress rehearsal was meant to be exactly what the broadcast would be—no stops, no hesitations. After the dress, the tension increased as Miss Mack gave us last-minute notes, and possibly cuts. An audience of about 30 or 40 children and their parents filed in. Then at 10:30, after the opening bars of Komzak's *Fairy Tale*, the announcer said, "The Columbia Broadcasting System presents Nila Mack's *Let's Pretend!*" (Enthusiastic applause.)

---

13. The talk-back is an amplifying system used during rehearsals that enables performers to hear the director's instructions from the control room over a studio loudspeaker.

The longer Nila Mack worked for CBS and directed *Let's Pretend* the more she became devoted to the show and the children on it. Both were in a sense her creations. But because of her insistence on keeping a tight rein on her young performers, many of us were afraid of her at the same time we grew to love her. The proportion of love and fear was different for each of us. As for myself, I distinctly remember feeling a pang in the pit of my stomach when during a rehearsal break in Playhouse 3 (I was then in my mid-20s), Nila pressed the talk-back button and said, "Arthur—will you come into the control room please?" (The memory of whatever minor foible, professional or personal, I had been indulging in is mercifully blotted out by the passage of many years.)

Her concerns also extended to the personal lives of some of us. My mother once received a phone call from Miss Mack, probably about some obstreperous behavior of mine, in which she said, without criticizing Mrs. Anderson directly: "He's been encouraged in these whimsies." Exactly what that meant I never figured out. There were other instances of Nila calling parents about their children's behavior in the studio. Kingsley Colton, a most polite and well-behaved child, was horsing around, as he phrased it, in the corner of the studio one day when our director entered, and he didn't go over and greet her. "Next day," said Kingsley, "she called my father and said, in effect, that I'd better shape up."

We were all in varying degrees precocious, which means in the original Latin "pre-cooked," or "cooked ahead of time." We could and did "act up." We were, after all, children. We could be mischievous, noisy and playful at the wrong times. In general, I suppose, some of us were rather pleased with ourselves. This was evidenced one day during an "American School of the Air" rehearsal when one of my contemporaries (we were both twelve or so) was starting to get obnoxious. Nila Mack was directing, but was out of the room. George O'Donnell the soundman dealt with the child by saying, "Yes, you're a very clever little boy—now shut up!" Nila could have gotten off a much better zinger, I am sure, but the point is, if she had been there the child wouldn't have acted up in the first place. She was pretty good at keeping the lid on our "pre-cooked" behavior.

Though Nila had said early on that she was neither a teacher nor a mother to her cast of children, a mother was what she eventually became— a sometimes strict and even unreasonable mother, but always a loving one. I believe the pattern was formed by her own mother, Margaret Bowen Mac, back in Arkansas City. Her daughter Nila had inherited her humor, and her determination and drive as well. Both of them had carved out new careers for themselves after the death of their husbands. Margaret Mac's at first was managing her daughter's early career. She eventually returned home to Arkansas City to re-establish her former dancing school. As for Nila, her talent, her determination and some good luck had combined to provide her with a new career, and the closeness, leadership and care that she had received from her mother she now bestowed on her own "children."

Her own need to be loved, however, was insistent, and, as will be seen, it sometimes caused a neurotic possessiveness. Another throwback to Nila's relationship with her mother was the loyalty and devotion she expected, and received from us. This increased as we regulars on the show grew to be adults. She was indeed our surrogate mother, and an exacting one.

Nila had said in many an interview that it was her policy not to let any of us get inflated ideas of our own importance. This was unlikely to happen anyway because we were a repertory company—a different play and a different cast every week. If you played the lead one week you would just as likely have a small part with two lines the next—or you might not be called at all. There were no stars on *Let's Pretend*.

This system accomplished several things. It kept egos in check, and it made us a better, more versatile company of actors. It almost meant that there were no jealousies between us. We were a family, and every one of us who survives still has warm memories of that family feeling—and of Nila Mack.

Ever since the advent of the star system in Hollywood, and beyond, there have been news stories of the psychological and sometimes legal problems of former child stars—alumni either of The Golden Age of Films, or The Television Age of Sitcoms. These children had once been highly paid and led quite unnatural lives, and all the rewards and attention of stardom were showered on them, sometimes at a very early age—then suddenly taken away when they reached adolescence. This hardly happened in radio, because child actors were not starred, and especially not on *Let's Pretend*.

In radio during the Depression and post-Depression years, a cute and clever child actor could sometimes earn a lot of money, and since in those days every member of the family was expected to contribute, the child's radio earnings, if Pop was out of work, might be the entire week's bankroll. The child did not feel exploited, and the family did not feel guilty. There were cases in which the parents simply took advantage of their high-earning child, but those were rare. It was just such exploitation, involving the famous child actor Jackie Coogan in Hollywood, which led to California's Child Actors' Bill, better known as The Coogan Law, designed to protect the earnings of future child actors in that state.

What became of a child's radio earnings depended on each family's financial situation, and their code of values. With my first radio money, while I still lived on Staten Island, I was allowed to buy a bicycle, then my own dog—a Boston terrier pup. Later, living in Manhattan, I paid for my own school tuition and clothing. I learned to put almost everything else in the bank. But we were one of the lucky families. My father was always employed.

As Depression financial pressures eased, child actors' families were more likely to put their earnings aside for education. The father of one particularly successful child actor I knew put the boy's earnings into investments, which paid off handsomely when he was grown. Usually children in radio were aware of their families' financial problems, which put unbearable pressures on them. When I was about 13, I once saw another child actor, a boy who was going through adolescent voice change and was not working much, sitting on one of the leather-covered benches on the eighth floor at NBC, looking forlorn and desolate. I asked him what was the matter. "My father told me not to come home until I have a job," he said.

In spite of the casting on *Let's Pretend* being very democratic—what you might call a democracy with a very strong President—Nila did like to boast of her kids who had achieved prominence elsewhere—Patricia Peardon who starred on Broadway in *Junior Miss*, Patricia Ryan who co-starred on radio in *Claudia and David*, the Mauch twins, Billy and Bobby, who went to Hollywood to play in *The Prince and the Pauper*, Billy Halop who went out there to repeat his Broadway role in *Dead End*, and Eddie Ryan, who went the same route to play in the wartime film *The Fighting Sullivans*. All of them had benefited from the acting experience, and the values instilled in them by Nila. She had a right to be proud.

As Bill Lipton said, "She demanded strict loyalty and personal dedication. But she gave a lot to us, too—in attention, and interest in our personal lives, especially when later on some of us married and had children." Jack Grimes remembers, "Most of us were very happy to be on *Let's Pretend*. We had a training ground in radio acting—in voice—in diction—and also in personal behavior."

Though I have sometimes been referring to our director, mentor and surrogate mother as Nila, we Pretenders as children always addressed her as

"Miss Mack." For one thing, said Sybil Trent, "The director was God." And children in the 1930s were taught to respect elders more than nowadays. I do not know when she became "Nila" to each of us, but for me at least it did not happen until after I had returned in early 1946 after three years in uniform, and ten years after I had started as a Let's Pretender.

Nila's insistence on complete loyalty occasionally became unreasonable. She did not take kindly to our accepting other shows which conflicted with "Let's Pretend." She wanted the right to choose which actors to call each week, and did not want to hear that someone was unavailable.

There was also a bit of trouble about Pretenders who worked on Madge Tucker's *Coast To Coast On A Bus* over at NBC, even though it aired on Sunday, and there was no time conflict. The show, which Miss Tucker had started as "The Lady Next Door," was more or less a kiddie variety show, but with a connecting story line of everybody riding a bus on the White Rabbit Line. There was some tension between Nila and Miss Tucker, after that lady had said that anyone who did *Let's Pretend* could not be on her program. Some of those who left *Pretend* for that reason included Billy Halop, his sister Florence Halop, and Jimmy McCallion. Billy and Florence later returned.

Besides total commitment and constant availability, another thing our director expected from all her actors, no matter how young, was good speech. This did not mean cultured pear-shaped tones - just clear and correct pronunciation of the words, and from occasional players to those of us who were on every week, she never let us forget it. To Albert Aley, who usually played romantic leads: "Don't say, 'Lovely Princess, forgimme.' It's two words—forgive—me. And it's not buh-loved—it's BE-loved." She admonished Jack Grimes: "Strength has a 'g' in it—don't say 'strenth'." And to Sybil Trent: "Say, 'I'll wait for you at the castle'- not 'I'll wait FER you at the castle.' This isn't a commercial for the I.J. Fox Fur Company." Sybil learned well these lessons in good speech from Nila, but this once got her into trouble on a daytime serial when the director said, "Don't be so cultured. Why don't you speak like normal people?"

Nila's own speech was exactly what she expected from us—clearly and correctly articulated, but never exaggerated. Her voice was low-pitched, but never weak. (It later became lower and huskier, and punctuated with coughing, because of her constant smoking.) She would look at you directly with her large, hazel-blue eyes, which bulged slightly because of a thyroid condition, and spoke from the front of her mouth, without pushing, except for emphasis. Her speech pattern no doubt came from a strong background of training from her mother, at school, and her years of performing in vaudeville and in the theatre, where your voice had to be audible at the rear of the balcony of any size theatre, without benefit of microphones or amplifiers.

As with any mother, surrogate or not, there was the matter of discipline. Besides the verbal criticism we sometimes got (but always in private) Nila's only disciplinary measure, and it was a powerful one, was simply not calling us. This applied to adult actors as well. Back in the '30s, Nila did not approve of the continuity Henry Boyd had written to go with his bird songs on a *Sunday Morning at Aunt Susan's* broadcast, so she changed it. She was not there for the air show, possibly due to illness, and Henry reinstated his own script. Nila must have heard this on her radio at home, and Henry did not get called for a long time. Finally he went to her office with a large bunch of lilacs, which he knew she loved.

"Are you trying to bribe me, Henry?" asked Nila. "Yes," said Henry. He apologized, and Nila told him that you really couldn't get away with saying whatever you felt like on the radio, and all was forgiven. On another occasion, in the *Helen and Mary* days. Madeline Lee, then a little girl and new on the show, was cast by Nila in a leading role on that week's program. She came down from the Bronx on the subway Saturday morning with her mother, but they took the wrong train, and were five minutes late. When she arrived, Madeline found that her part had been given to another child, and she had just a couple of lines. She burst into tears. But Nila's point had been made—don't be late for my rehearsals.

Our director found that in dealing with the children on *Let's Pretend* and those who aspired to be on it, there were inevitably—*their mothers*. Of course, every small child who performs must have a parent or guardian for the guidance of his or her career, and for an escort to and from performances and rehearsals. But when a mother intrudes in rehearsals and other business sessions, or demands special or star treatment for her child, she becomes—*a stage mother*—a form of life universally detested by all those who have to deal with them.

One of the best-organized and most aggressive stage mothers was Walter Tetley's. For years, until Walter finally moved to the West Coast, any director getting off the elevator on NBC's third floor knew that he would probably have to run into a one-woman road block with flaming red frizzly hair and steel-rimmed glasses consisting of Mrs. Tetley, who could accost him with, "Don't you have anything for Walter today?"

Nila Mack did not suffer stage mothers gladly. First, she did not like them present when she interviewed their children. When the parent did all the talking, or put words in the child's mouth in response to questions, that to her was bad news, and she would usually pass that child up when selecting new cast members.

Eddie Ryan remembered being allowed to sit in when our director was auditioning a very young girl. "Her mother was primping her and giving her last-minute instructions, when Nila asked her to leave the studio," he wrote. "The mother didn't want to go. Nila said, 'I'm auditioning your daughter only. If you prefer, we can just call it off.' Suffice to say, mother left."

The children who came without their mothers, Miss Mack said, had a better chance of pleasing her. It was easier for her to get to know the child's personality and talent. Stage mothers, she found, usually spoiled the children, made them nervous, and, said she, "they get in our hair." (N.B *Stage fathers* are practically unknown.) To quote an early story in *The New York Sun*:

> "Too much temperament on the part of a fond parent
> will result in her offspring's involuntary absence from the
> next program listing, and no more dire punishment can be
> meted out."

Dire punishment indeed. It was not so much the $3.50 that the mothers were interested in, as being able to list *Let's Pretend* in their child's credits, printed on the 3 x 5 cards which all radio actors sent to casting directors for their files.

Most of the mothers of the Pretenders were no problem. They handled their children's calls and business affairs. They brought the youngsters to rehearsals and broadcasts, and were there to pick them up afterwards. Otherwise they were invisible. For the most part Nila got along with them very well. She formed a close friendship with Sandra Levy, Gwen Davies' mother, when Gwen was in her late teens. But this did not change her opinion of stage mothers in general, which she expressed in an article written in 1945: "These grey hairs were never caused by the kids but by some of those horrible, incredibly ambitious STAGE MOTHERS who shall be nameless and, I'm afraid, with us forever."

Beginning with the necessity of keeping her job in 1930, and continuing through her years of experience at CBS, Nila had learned to deal with, work with and love the children on *Let's Pretend*. She possibly had not really articulated her feelings about them until approached by an interviewer in 1947. "Do you think that's why you put fairy stories on the air?" he asked. "Because you are a widow without any children?" "As a matter of fact," she said, "I think it's because I just love fairy stories. I've loved them since childhood."

"And of course you love children, too?" Nila flared at this. "I don't any such thing. I love people—provided they are nice people. If some of those people happen to be children, fine. Children are just as much individuals as grown-ups are, and you can like or dislike them just as much." And in spite of her own insecurities and personal eccentricities, this feeling towards her child actors was apparent to everyone who met her.

Besides Nila Mack's scripts, her genius for choosing and working with her juvenile cast was the main reason the show survived longer than any other dramatic program on the American radio, unless one counts "One Man's Family," which was a continuing serial. In its time *Let's Pretend* won dozens of awards and audience polls as the best children's program on the air. Nila cherished these honors, and the high regard in which she was held on the executive floor at 485 Madison. But more valuable to her was the loyalty and affection of her "kids." Her work was her life, and we were her family.

7

Nila

Nila Mack's personal life as well as her professional life were now very different from the years when she had lived in hotels and rooming houses. Mr. and Mrs. Howard Lindsay (Dorothy Stickney) had become her closest friends. She and her husband Roy had met them while summering at Lakewood, Maine, where the Skowhegan Playhouse was located. Lindsay was director there, and Miss Stickney was the ingénue, and they fell in love and were married in 1927. The Briants, Roy and Nila, had also been part of the happy theatrical community on the shores of Lake Wesserunsett.

When Nila returned to New York from her radio venture in Arkansas City and began her new life working for CBS, she leased an apartment directly down the hall from the Lindsays', in a brownstone row house at 41 West 10th Street in Greenwich Village. From then on she was never without a piano, pianos having been an important part of her childhood. One night when there was a party at the Lindsays' the piano was wheeled down the hall from her apartment into theirs.

In 1934 when Howard Lindsay and Russel Crouse were writing the book for the new musical *Anything Goes*. Mr. Lindsay told Nila that Cole Porter was coming down to let them hear the score for the first time. The ancient upright was wheeled in again, and so the first performance of those now-classic hits "Anything Goes," "You're the Top" and "I Get a Kick Out of You" was on Nila Mack's piano. The instrument did have problems, though. Not only was it somewhat out of tune, but when Porter launched into "You're the Top," the ivory top of one of the keys flew off. (Characteristically, in the version of the story from the CBS publicity department, it was *two* key tops.)

Meanwhile, Nila kept up with other friends she had met during her days in the theatre. Two of them were Georgia Backus, whom she had met in a stock company, and who had helped start her career with CBS, and also Elaine Ivans, whom she had met in the brief road tour of *Eva the Fifth*, and as we have seen she used both of them in radio.

As Nila got into the swing of things at CBS, being gregarious and outgoing, she soon formed friendships with others in the production department on the 18th floor. Jerome Lawrence, later a celebrated American playwright best-remembered as co-author, with Robert Lee, of the Broadway hits *Inherit the Wind, Auntie Mame* and *Dear World* had his office down the hall from Nila. So did Norman Corwin, who became famous for his series *26 by Corwin*, which he wrote, directed and produced, along with many other brilliant radio plays, on the network's pioneering series *The Columbia Workshop*. Edward R. Murrow (no doubt with cigarette in hand) would poke his head into Nila's office to say hello. And of course William S. Paley, who everyone called Bill, and who kept in personal touch with all the network's workings, including program production, was never far away.

Her closest friend at Columbia, though, was Charles Jackson, whose scripts for the network never attained any fame even remotely approaching his best-selling novel *The Lost Weekend*, later made into a film starring Ray Milland.

As I got to know Miss Mack better, I became increasingly impressed by the contrasting sides of her nature. She had the ability to be sentimental—even reverent, when human values were in question, expressed so well in her scripts—then the ability to instantly show her other side in a hearty laugh at someone's ribald joke, or by a quick-on-the-uptake gag of her own. It was especially her humor that endeared her to the many adults she worked with at CBS—actors, production people and executives.

Once when Nila entered a crowded elevator on the 18th floor, she saw at the back one of her dear friends, a CBS vice-president. Between them stood the Deep River Boys, a black vocal quartet under contract to the network, and just leaving rehearsal. Without hesitation she greeted her friend: "Doctor Livingstone, I presume."

Then there was Frank Readick's urine. Frank, whose distinctive, slightly rasping voice was heard regularly on *The March of Time* and many other networks shows, had just come from his yearly physical, and was boasting to his fellow actors at Colbee's Restaurant downstairs that the doctor had said his urine was as clear as a bell. "Nila ought to know about this," one of them said. Frank went over to a pay phone, dropped a nickel in it, and called her office. "Nila, this is Frank. Guess what? I just had my physical, and my urine is as clear as a bell!" "Good," snapped Nila. "I'll take two cases." And hung up.

Of course, none of this is to say that Nila Mack did not have a temper, or wasn't hard to get along with at times. She did have what Jerry Lawrence called a dark side, which could be attributed at least partly to the executive pressure cooker in which she was now sealed. Though Douglas Coulter, her immediate supervisor, was a friend and protector, Nila Mack was nevertheless pretty much a lone woman in a man's world.

The only other women on the staff in the mid-'30s were Nila's close friend Dorothy Gordon, who produced educational and public service programs; Margaret Lewerth, a writer who probably did not have any executive input; Marge Morrow, the casting director; and Lucille Singleton, who auditioned vocalists and staff singers. Otherwise the executive and production floors were all male, except for secretaries and receptionists. Nila was intelligent, resourceful and high-spirited. She could match any of the men, idea for idea, joke for joke and drink for drink. But it could not have been easy. During all of her career at CBS, she was always conscious of being a woman, and thus a member of a very small minority.

In 1936 the Lindsays moved from West 10th Street into a house they had bought on West 11th, and Nila had already moved uptown, to be nearer to her work. CBS was at 52nd Street and Madison Avenue, and she found a floor-through apartment with a large terrace, two flights up, in a brownstone at 55 West 53rd Street, less than four blocks away. This was to be her home for the rest of her life, and it was a place many of us got to know, since we were all invited there for Christmas parties and other special occasions. Besides the apartment itself, one of the most permanent and dependable parts of her existence from then on was her black maid Maud Wilson, who stuck with her loyally for 18 years.

Nila, much too busy to long nostalgically for the good old days in the theatre or vaudeville, was using her talents to the fullest. In a 1937 newspaper "thumbnail biography" she was described thus:

> "She'd like to look like Miriam Hopkins, and have Dorothy Parker's brains."
> "Current hobby: Trying to understand 50,000,000 children."

"Likes very feminine clothes, large 'show' hankies and turkey dinners. Is unusually mechanically inclined." (Nila often wore dark-colored dresses with polka dots and wide collars, and a bow in her hair. As for her being mechanically inclined, I never saw any evidence of that.)

"Favorite star: Charlie Chaplin."

"Attracted to sincere, honest he-men and regular, feet-on-the-ground women." (She was definitely still attracted to the opposite sex. Some surviving Pretenders have vague memories of a romance with a man who worked at CBS, but there is nothing to indicate if it existed, if it was very serious, or of more than brief duration.)

"Has never had enough dancing, congenial companionship or seen enough mountains."

"Weighs 130 lbs., is 5'2" tall, has curly blonde hair and blue eyes." (I would describe her hair as ash-blonde, and as for her weight, she did gain a few pounds in the years following that interview.)

"Programs: *Let's Pretend* and *Sunday Morning At Aunt Susan's*."

Elsa Maxwell, in her newspaper column *Party Line* described Nila in 1943 as "plump and soft. She laughs constantly. She has hair the color of wheat, a pink skin and a tough mind." *Newsweek* the same year saw Nila as "large, plump, hard-boiled and shrewd." All of these writers, on very short acquaintance, were trying to sum up Nila by describing her as the tough New York nightclub proprietor she had once played on radio in 1929, an image no doubt reinforced by her constant smoking. They failed to see, or at least completely left out, her warmth and sincerity, qualities that were also present in abundance in her scripts.

In 1940, *Time* magazine, on the occasion of Nila's tenth anniversary with CBS, also mentioned, only incidentally, one of her chief interests: "Scripteuse for *Let's Pretend*," they wrote, "is blonde, broad-beamed Nila Mack, who used to be an actress, now lives with a cat in Manhattan." The cat referred to was a grey Persian named Cloudy. Nila had several cats over the years in New York. Another was Mr. Pinney, her white Persian who was called that, she said, because no one knew him well enough to call him by his first name.

A newspaper article described Pinney as liking water in a big way. "He drinks directly from the water faucet," it added, "and likes to curl up in the wash bowl to take a siesta. A guest in the Mack ménage knows he is welcome when Pinney leaps up to the broad brim of the bowl and supervises ablutions."

One of Nila's friends, CBS engineer Jack Mason, once went to her apartment to repair her radio. "She used to have at least one cat there," he remembered. "They clawed the devil out of the sofa—the furniture. When I first saw them doing it I got upset. She said, 'Let them alone—they get so much fun out of it.'"

In Nila's later years, at one of the Christmas parties she gave for the Pretenders, Sybil Trent's husband Andrew Nieporent, who had never been in her apartment, was admiring a pair of perfectly-matched life-sized statues of faun-colored Siamese cats, placed on opposite ends of the fireplace mantel in Nila's living room. As he came nearer to examine them, the two statues leaped off the mantel in perfect unison and scampered away, almost giving him a heart attack, as he later described it. The leaping felines were her two Siamese, Sapphire and Tsing-Fooey, who had been posing as cats do, and inspecting the crowd from a safe vantage point.

Nila may have preferred dogs originally. There had always been dogs in the Mac household from her early childhood, but now, living alone and with a busy professional life, cats were just the thing. She later started a collection of cats made of porcelain and crystal.

Like Dorothy Stickney, she also collected music boxes. At the time of her death she had dozens. Other than the cats and music boxes, she liked reading, mostly historical novels, eating well, and going to the theatre. Those of us who survive do not believe she was particularly happy when alone.

Her chief satisfactions in life were her work and the people she worked with—mostly her family of young actors on *Let's Pretend*.

As we regulars on the show formed closer bonds over the years with our director (early newspaper accounts always referred to her as "directress"), we learned more of the things that amused or pleased her, and the things she could not abide. Among other things she had always been strongly patriotic. She once stopped a rehearsal of "The March of Games" during World War II to read from the control room a communiqué that had just come in (she was so excited that she pronounced it "communeek") to the effect that our Navy had just sunk 23 Japanese ships.

Circa 1938. A party at Nila Mack's apartment. Maud Wilson, Arthur Anderson, Kingsley Colton, Jack Kelk, Jack Grimes, Patricia Peardon, Vivian Block, Harry Swan, Estelle Levy, Arthur Ross, Betty Jane Tyler, Nila Mack, Miriam Wolfe, Patricia Ryan, Daisy Aldan, Sybil Trent, Michael O'Day, Albert Aley, Eddie Ryan, and Sidney Lumet. ©1938 CBS, Inc. Used by permission.

From time to time we would catch glimpses of the things she had been exposed to in her years in vaudeville, such as the dialogue (possibly from Weber and Fields) that went like this:

> "Say! Vot's de difference between ah cynic and ah stoic?"
> "I couldn't even emegine."
> "It's simple. Ah stoic is vot brings de babies, and ah cynic is vere you vash dem."

As was often said back then, that's what killed vaudeville.

For several years before our Cream of Wheat sponsorship there were annual *Let's Pretend* Christmas parties at the New Weston Hotel, at Madison Avenue and 50th Street. There would be a long table in the oak-paneled

Circa 1936. A *Let's Pretend* Christmas party at the New Weston. Standing, rear: Elaine Engler, Albert Aley, Arthur Anderson, Jack Jordan, Don Hughes, unidentified, Vivian Block, Milton Kamen, unidentified, Patricia Ryan, Estelle Levy, Patricia Patterson, Patricia Goodwin, Joyce Gates, and Miriam Wolfe. Extreme rear, against wall: Andy Donnelly, and Eddie Ryan. Seated, far side of table: Margaret McKee, Harry Swan, unidentified, and Ronald Liss. Near side of table: Florence Halop, Lester Jay (note cigarette), Lloyd Barry (the boys that year were given Burgess flashlights), Betty Philson, Nila Mack, and unidentified. ©1936 CBS, Inc. Used by permission.

dining room, and a large Christmas tree. The menu was pretty much the same every year: Chicken croquettes with gravy on mashed potatoes and Holland rusk, with green peas, rolls and butter, and ice cream for dessert. Each of the boys would get the same present, and each of the girls another. I still have the binoculars from one year, which have weak lenses but immense sentimental value.

There was always a piano there, and Nila would do one of two acts: The first consisted of some of the thumping revivalist songs she had heard as a girl in Arkansas City, which she would sing in her throaty voice. One of them was titled: "I'm H-A-P-P-Y Cause I Am S-A-V-E-D," and another was: "The Bells of Hell Go Ting-A-Ling-A-Ling For You But Not For Me."

More familiar, because she did it at almost every "Pretend" cast gathering, was Nila's rendition of the silent film music she had played back in 1912 in Metropolis, Illinois. As she played the cues for "Danger," "Romance" or "Chase," you could see reflected in her large expressive eyes exactly what was happening on the imaginary screen.

The Christmas parties at the New Weston are for me a marvelous memory of my childhood, and the Yuletide season. Needless to say, parents were not invited. At one of them, someone (we are pretty sure it was Lester Jay) crawled under the entire length of the long, white-clothed table to give another boy a hotfoot.

And if you, dear reader, do not know what a hotfoot is, you may congratulate yourself on your youth.

8

The Cast Grows

Nila Mack once said that when she found one child during each of her semi-annual talent auditions who showed promise of fitting into the *Let's Pretend* cast, she considered herself fortunate. They were either too self-conscious, too brash, or more usually, just did not have any feeling for how to read lines or relate to a script, or to other actors. But the need was there, for children were constantly either dropping out, or were being eliminated by Nila as it became obvious to her that they were no longer integrating well into the Land of Let's Pretend.

Gradually Miss Mack did find more child actors who were versatile and talented. There were eight more long-term Let's Pretenders, who, starting in 1935, stayed with the show and became part of its identity. They were, in the order of joining the cast, Sybil Trent, Arthur Anderson, Jack Grimes, Kingsley Colton, Betty Jane Tyler, Bill Lipton, Bob Readick and Rita Lloyd, the last to join us, in 1948, whose career will be outlined in a later chapter.

SYBIL TRENT

Sybil Trent, together with Gwen Davies, is still more closely identified with *Let's Pretend* than any of us, first because during our sponsored years she and Gwen Davies would open every show with the Cream of Wheat theme song, and also because very often she would have the female lead in the story.

Sybil was an only child. During the Depression her father was a salesman for The Swee-Touch-Nee Tea Company. The family originally lived in Brooklyn, moving to midtown Manhattan when Sybil got a part in a Broadway show. For many years they lived at The Whitby, an apartment hotel on

West 45th Street just down the block from what was then the Martin Beck Theatre (now the Al Hirschfeld), where most of the tenants were show people.

Sybil was three-and-one-half years old when her mother took her to Warner Brothers studios in Brooklyn to audition for the "Our Gang" comedies. Though nothing came of that audition, she was called within a week to do a short subject with Fatty Arbuckle. She then became a member of the Warner Brothers stock company, doing singing, dancing or dramatic roles in more than 25 shorts, as well as features, for RKO. These included *The People's Enemy* with Lila Lee and Melvyn Douglas, *Keep 'em Rolling* with Walter Huston, and short subjects with Ruth Etting and Sammy Davis, Jr. (New York in the 1920s and early '30s was still a major studio production center.) By the time *Let's Pretend* entered her life, Sybil was at the age of nine already a show business veteran.

When Sybil did her first *Let's Pretend* broadcast in late 1935 she was fresh from a more spectacular triumph, having opened November 16th in Billy Rose's extravaganza "Jumbo" at the huge Hippodrome, which occupied the entire block of 6th Avenue between 43rd and 44th Streets.

The Hippodrome probably hit its high point during the run of *Jumbo* which played 233 performances, closing in June 1936. The huge house was only 30 years old at the time, but had been closed five years previously, no doubt due to the Depression, and the high costs of producing any show big enough to fill its 5200 seats. It later had a few desultory bookings of lesser known opera companies, then wrestling matches, then nothing—until 1952, and now only the name remains at that location: The Hippodrome Parking Garage.

The score of *Jumbo* was by Rodgers and Hart, conducted by Paul Whiteman and directed by George Abbott (book) and John Murray Anderson (musical numbers), and starred Jimmy Durante, Donald Novis and Gloria Grafton. Miss Grafton dreams of being in the circus, whereupon little Sybil Elaine, as she was then known, enters in a silver and crystal coach with grey satin seats, drawn by two white ponies. She tells Miss Grafton the circus isn't under canvas, but in your heart. This was known as The Spangled Dream Scene. The classic song "Little Girl Blue" was later sung to Sybil, after which she made her exit riding on an elephant.

Another major part of Sybil's early background, shared by many other child performers of the early 1930s, was the influence of Mabel Horsey, a large black lady who, assisted by her husband Leonard, ran a performing school on West 46th Street. Children sang, danced, did monologues and imitations, and under Miss Horsey's tutelage performed in benefits at Town Hall and many other places in the New York area. Her pianist was Hazel Scott.

By the age of six Sybil was emceeing her own radio show on station WHN, "Baby Sybil Elaine and her Kiddie Revue," sponsored by a Brooklyn furniture store. She would imitate Joe Penner (with cigar) and the Block and Sully comedy team, finishing her act with a tap dance, and closing each show by singing "Thank You for a Lovely Evening." Another of her numbers was the sure-fire crowd-pleaser "I Wish There Were a Radio Up in Heaven So Mother Dear Could Listen In to Me." The culmination of her musical career was later, when she sang "I Love You from Coast to Coast" on *The Kate Smith Hour* on the CBS network.

In 1935 Sybil was attending P.S. 17 on West 47th Street when Nila Mack and Dorothy Gordon went there to interview children for *The Children's Forum of the Air*. Sybil was not chosen for this, but Miss Mack said, "Why don't you come and audition for *Let's Pretend?*

Nila found she liked everything about Sybil but her name. "No one can go through life with two first names," she said, and after a conference with Sybil's mother, Sybil Elaine became Sybil Trent. Not only was it short and easy to remember, said Miss Mack, but the initials were the same as those of Shirley Temple, who hadn't done so badly herself.

Sybil had black hair, lively brown eyes, a ready smile and was very good-natured, but most important for radio was the fact that she had great emotional range, could read lines and follow directions easily, and also had a remarkably warm and sympathetic vocal quality. In one interview, Nila called Sybil her future Claudette Colbert.

The radio production industry in New York in the mid-'30s was a comparatively small group, and word about Sybil Trent got around quickly. Once she had been auditioned by Air Features, that most prolific producer of daytime serials, she started being busy on shows for them and for many others. She remembered playing a little blind girl on *David Harum* early on, and doing a running part on "Front Page Farrell." She was also on two of the five-a-week segments on the CBS-produced *American School of the Air*.

For two years Sybil was The Drum Major on a children's quiz program, *The March of Games*, which was on two weekday afternoons a week in 1939, later shifted to a half-hour on Sundays. There were questions to test

Sybil Trent emcees her own kiddie show at age 6, circa 1932.

vocabulary and general knowledge. There were tongue twisters and musical questions as well. Master of Ceremonies was another Pretender, Arthur Ross, who billed himself as The Youngest M.C. In Radio. Sybil appeared in full costume, with visored hat, white satin and red dress and cape, carrying a baton. How she was able to also hold her script I do not remember.

As Sybil grew into her teens her two occupations were acting on radio, and completing her schooling. Her mature vocal quality won her emotional adult roles on several daytime serials, including Thelma, the lead, on *We Love and Learn*, as well as on night-time shows including *Gangbusters*, *The March of Time* and *Famous Jury Trials*.

Though Sybil became one of the mainstays of *Let's Pretend* she was not called steadily until 1943 when we were sponsored, and she and Gwen Davies became the show's musical signature, as well as usually appearing in the story and in the commercials as well. However, neither of the girls, or for that matter any of us, ever had written contracts in advance. None of us could assume we would be on that week's show until called the previous Tuesday. Nila had said many times she did not want any of us to get swelled heads. It is most unlikely that Sybil ever would have anyway, but a rule was a rule, with no exceptions. Our director was taking no chances.

ARTHUR ANDERSON

I came on the *Let's Pretend* scene May 9, 1936, and from then on until our last broadcast, except for military service, I was on consistently almost every week. My father was Danish. He was an engineer with the Mack Truck Company. My mother was English, born as Violet Brookfield. My great-uncle Charles Brookfield, born in 1857, was a British actor in plays and in vaudeville, a well-known wit, and later a playwright.

I was born on Staten Island, N.Y. in 1922, and had two elder brothers, Edward and George. I came to radio indirectly through my first drama teacher Cecyl Grimes, who ran The Children's Playhouse in Dongan Hills in a little barn in her front yard. My first role there, at age eight, was Rip Van Winkle in a Christmas pageant, and it included a song to my dog Schneider. A character man already. I started appearing regularly in 1934 on a kiddie hour on station WMCA, emceed by the *New York Mirror* columnist Nick Kenny, who with his brother Charles, Miss Cecyl's friend, formed one of the foremost songwriting teams of the '30s ("Love Letters in the Sand," "There's a Gold Mine in the Sky," "While a Cigarette Was Burning," etc.) Charlie Kenny also wrote songs independently of his brother, of a more fanciful nature. Some of his titles were: "I Wear My Glasses to Bed Ev'ry Night So I Can See You in my Dreams," "Ev'ry Street is Canal Street in Venice" and "I'm Planting Little Onions So I Can Cry Over You."

On Uncle Nick's program, I did little two-minute sketches written by my mother and myself, doing all the voices, plus dog barks.

It was through a friend of my mother's that I got my first paying radio job in August 1935, as an orphan boy named Buddy who cried a lot, on a show called *Tony and Gus* on the NBC Red Network, sponsored by Post Toasties. Once I had done a general audition and had been put in NBC's talent file, I was cast in many of their programs, including the lead in a series

Arthur Anderson, age 12, on NBC's *Tony and Gus*, 1935.

called *Peter Absolute*,[14] the adventures of an orphan boy in the Erie Canal days of the 19th century. And it was the writer of *Peter Absolute*, David Belasco Howard, later to become my good friend and mentor, who introduced me to Nila Mack.

From the first, at age 13, I was an all-round character man on *Let's Pretend*. I was good at "doing voices." If there was a mysterious old man sitting by the side of the road who warned the Prince of danger ahead and gave him a magic charm to protect himself, that was me. I was always one of the three talking crows in "Faithful John." I was a crooked innkeeper who stole the magic gifts that had been given to the innocent young hero in "The Donkey, The Table and the Stick"—and innumerable others over the years.

All of us juvenile actors on the show could "get into," or assume the characters we were playing, but I was one of the few who could do a com-

---

14. In 1998 I revived *Peter Absolute*, adapting and directing it in recordings which are now sold by Radio Spirits, starring Dick Beals, originally the voice of Speedy Alka-Seltzer, as Peter.

plete voice change, using different inflections, rhythms or age characteristics—sometimes a dialect—whatever I though was called for when I saw the script. It was great fun. Miss Mack saw at once where my talents lay, and thanks to her I used them to the fullest. I do not believe that what I or any of us did on *Let's Pretend* was hokey or exaggerated—she would not have allowed it. We were dealing in fantasy, but our director insisted that it be played legitimately.

Because of the great variety of roles I played on the show, people were sometimes confused when I told them I was a Let's Pretender. They could never identify me with any particular part, or even any kind of part. I did not mind. Not only did I get what I thought were the juiciest roles, but I was on almost every week. It is often said that some people become actors to escape reality, and if this was/is true of me, nowhere did I have the chance to do that more completely in my career than on *Let's Pretend*.

My mother and I spent an abortive two months in Hollywood in September-October 1936. David O. Selznick had optioned me to star in a planned spectacular production of *Tom Sawyer*. My life might have been very different but for the fact that bad weather in Hannibal, Missouri, where the film was to be shot, meant postponement, and it became obvious to the film people that by next spring I'd have grown too much to any longer be a cute kid. So it was back to radio and back to *Let's Pretend*. I did not feel any failure in that. I was glad to be home again.

My parents and I had long since moved from Staten Island into Manhattan, where we lived over the years in various parts of West Greenwich Village. Many other radio shows followed on both CBS and NBC, including *Bambi* with Helen Hayes, and *The Phillip Morris Playhouse*. After I had worked for Orson Welles in Aaron Copland's opera "Second Hurricane," I was cast by him as Lucius in his historic Mercury Theatre modern dress production of *Julius Caesar*, which we played on Broadway (1937-38), in repertory with the bawdy Elizabethan farce "Shoemakers' Holiday." In that I was listed as "Boy," and spoke the prologue. Orson also used me in radio on *The Mercury Theatre on the Air* as Jim Hawkins in Robert Louis Stevenson's "Treasure Island," and later in the Mercury's *Campbell Playhouse*.

Shortly after joining *Let's Pretend* I went into my awkward years, not knowing whether I was a child or a grown-up, and not feeling I fitted into either category. My voice started changing - too serious for a child radio actor. When I was called for an afternoon or evening show I knew I could carry off the 12-year-old and younger parts I was cast in, but a morning show was a problem. (I knew nothing about voice warm-up techniques, of course.) That was another reason I felt secure and happy on *Let's Pretend*. When doing a giant or an enchanted frog, adolescent voice change was not a problem. I was gangling and bony, with a sensitive face, wavy brown hair and slightly protruding ears.

In those days I masked my shyness and insecurity by clowning—by doing vocal sound effects and acting silly at parties, where I felt particularly vulnerable. Meanwhile I had become quite good at singing and playing the ukulele. I constructed my own Two-Man Band ("Who's the other man?" "I'm both men"). It consisted of kazoo and train whistle mounted on a coat hanger around my neck; the uke, and various electric and mechanical bells and horns, I operated with my feet.

There was occasional mischief, but it was mostly harmless. Whenever *Let's Pretend* publicity photos were taken at 485 Madison Avenue, I would collect the flashbulbs (they were made of glass, and almost as large as regular light bulbs), and drop them one by one down an unoccupied air shaft from the 21st floor. Each one made a satisfying pop as it exploded far below. Another escapade, which could have been more serious, took place at the National Theatre, where the Mercury was now playing *Julius Caesar*, in March of 1938. (John Houseman in his book *Run-Through* said that I was supporting my widowed mother at the time. Actually, my father was very much alive and proud of what I was doing, with the possible exception of what I am about to relate.)

I had a long, boring wait in my fourth floor dressing room during every performance, and during one Wednesday matinee I applied a match to a sprinkler head on the ceiling, expecting the metal in it to slowly ooze down. Instead the head popped off instantly. The water inundated the dressing room, then cascaded through a fire door and down onto the main switch-board, and eventually the stage. This resulted in the only intermission there had been in any Orson Welles production up to that time. Miraculously, no one was electrocuted, and the story, which was run in every New York daily, was no doubt a help at the box office.

Nila Mack used me on some of her other CBS shows, including the Thursday "Tales from Far and Near" segment of *The American School of the Air*, as well as on *The March of Games*, but I was not as aggressive in looking for work as were some of the other Pretenders (and their mothers). By January 1943 this didn't matter anyway, for right after doing a commercial on *Big Sister* ("My wife washes my shirts white as snow with Rinso") and the following Saturday doing my favorite *Let's Pretend* role, King Feodor in "The Queen Who Couldn't Make Spice Nuts," I was drafted.

I played a distinctly non-starring role in the U.S. Army Air Force for over three years, but whenever I was home on furlough, Nila would always find a part for me, such as a mysterious voice which could be done in an isolation booth or behind a screen. She felt, and rightly, that a soldier in uniform shouldn't be seen on a children's radio program.

JACK GRIMES

Of all the Pretenders, Jack Grimes was the most successful in his radio career. Rather than trying to catalogue his credits, it would be easier to mention those shows he did not do. The list would be much shorter. In fact, during the years 1937 to 1943, Jack and Kingsley Colton, another Pretender, between them probably played close to 90 per cent of the male child parts in New York radio.

As a child Jack was small for his age. He had blue eyes, sandy brown hair, freckles, a button nose and an impish grin—a cheerful, altogether likeable typical-American-boy type. He also had a great facility for understanding the script and reading lines intelligently, and was a quick study.

In April 1937 Nila Mack went to see a new Broadway play, *Excursion* with Shirley Booth and Whitford Kane, at the Vanderbilt Theatre. Jack was in the cast. She went backstage and asked him to come and audition for *Let's Pretend*. Jack, incidentally, had not long before celebrated his tenth birthday in Tulsa, Oklahoma, while on the road with Helen Menken and Judith Anderson in *The Old Maid*.

When Jack did "The Dog Script," one of great pathos, as part of his audition, he cried real tears—sobbed, in fact. Nila told him he would be used on the show. "Okay," said Jack, "but I don't want to do any of that sissy stuff—any of those princes." And she never did cast him in any romantic parts—he was much better at other things anyway. For instance, he always played the long-suffering Fisherman in "The Fisherman and his Wife," who has to go back time after time, more and more embarrassed, to the Magic Flounder (always Albert Aley) each time his wife (usually Gwen Davies) demands a bigger house, then a castle, ad nauseum. He was Terry in the Hans Christian Andersen story "The Flying Trunk"—a charming con artist who uses his wits and his good luck to gain great riches, and the hand of a Princess.

Another of his favorite roles was the brave Jack in "Jack and the Beanstalk." In fact, his specialty on *Let's Pretend* became feisty parts that

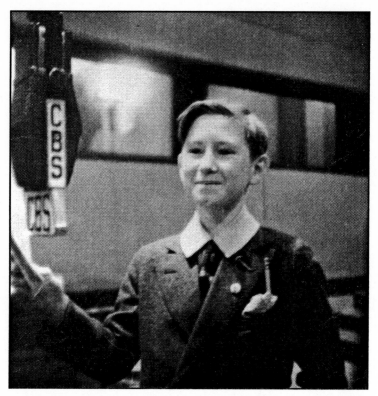

Jack Grimes, age 11, in Studio 1, circa 1937. Photo by the author.

called for great energy, and which usually made use of his great talent for comedy. Jack found these much more fun than the child parts he played on other shows—the conventional cliché roles that all of us were called upon to do—orphans who cried, kids who were constantly physically or emotionally abused, etc. Sadly, it cannot be said that all dramatic fare in those dear old Golden Days of Radio was necessarily great.

The contradiction in the Jack Grimes story is that, to hear him tell it, he didn't enjoy this at all. Jack came from a close-knit Irish Catholic family, in which family ties and family support were all-important. In the early 1930s the present network of government assistance as we know it did not exist. Families took care of their own. Once it became apparent to Jack that his talents could bring in money, he became a juvenile workaholic.

There was need enough in the Grimes family. Jack's two female first cousins had been orphaned in their teens, and had joined the household. Then there was Jack's older brother Pat, his younger sister May, and his father and mother. Mr. Grimes' carpet business was a casualty of the Depression. He was laid off by the carpet departments of Namm's, then Gimbel's, and suffered a complete nervous breakdown while still in middle age. And so Jack, starting at the age of ten, was eventually supporting seven people, including himself. There was no turning back. He had to keep working. And so, as Jack tells it, he withdrew from parochial school and simply stopped being a child.

In the post-Depression years, with unemployment widespread but radio work expanding, there were many households partly or even completely supported by the child actor in the family. The Grimes family was one of them.

(A devastating comment on this was made at the time by Parker Fennelly, best known as Titus Moody on "Allen's Alley," but a fine actor in many other roles. One day Parker was sitting reading a newspaper on the third floor at NBC when the entire juvenile cast of Madge Tucker's *Coast To Coast On A Bus* came trooping by, towed by their proud mothers. Without looking up, Parker took his pipe out of his mouth only long enough to say quietly, paraphrasing the well-known Biblical quotation, "And a little child shall feed them.")

In spite of his full-time radio acting, Jack achieved an education. He transferred to the Professional Children's School, but since he was only in class about two hours a week, he did his work by correspondence, usually using a piano top in a radio studio for a desk. Later, after graduating from high school, he somehow found time to complete four years at Columbia University.

A typical week for Jack meant working seven days and doing at least 15 shows—at times more than 40. A child actor in radio was a miniature grown-up, generally paid the same money as adult actors, but always subject to the same responsibilities. That was one reason why his weekly hours with *Let's Pretend* came to mean so much to Jack. Nila Mack and the other kids were a second family, with a family's friendship and support, but without the sibling rivalry that often goes with it. The only radio association that even approached this closeness for Jack was what he felt for the cast of *Second Husband*, which starred Helen Menken. Jack was on that show from 1938 until the mid-1940s, when it went off the air, as a member of the Cummings family, which included Miss Menken (Brenda), Joe Curtin (Grant), Jack (Dick) and Charita Bauer, another Pretender, as Jack's sister Fran.

Meanwhile William S. Paley, the president of CBS, who ran the company very much as a personal operation from his office on the 20th floor, had taken an interest in Jack. He had a few actors under personal management contract, and Jack was one of them, but Paley never collected any commission from him. When Jack was 12 years old and beginning to grow, Bill Paley had a sign posted in the lobby at 485 Madison:

CONGRATULATE JACK GRIMES TODAY –
HE'S WEARING HIS FIRST LONG PANTS

When Jack began on *Let's Pretend* he wore a matching tweed jacket and shorts, like other schoolboys his age, and a small tweed cap with a little visor in front. He showed up one Saturday morning in a pork pie hat with a brim, which he was so pleased with that he refused to take it off, even for the broadcast.

As Jack grew into his teen years, people thought he was becoming more and more cocky. Besides the built-in securities any actor has, working or not, Jack explains that he was always introverted and shy, especially because of his height. The cockiness was a cover, and a very successful one, and it certainly helped get him a lot of work he might not otherwise have had. During his teen years his idol was Mickey Rooney. "If he can do it, so can I," thought Jack. Rooney after all was only five feet tall, and Jack was not much taller.

The early 1940s brought important transitions to the lives of all the Pretenders. The child actors inhabiting Nila Mack's world of make-believe had turned into adolescents. Many of them disappeared from the show and from radio, as their voices and their interests changed. But there was no aging-out for Jack. His phone continued to ring.

Jack Grimes had great energy, and, as we have seen, ever greater motivation. The feisty little Irish kid was a survivor. He successfully made the transition from cute kid parts to mature adult roles, and could now reasonably expect to remain active and successful in radio for many years to come.

KINGSLEY COTTON

Kingsley, having a methodical turn of mind, knows for a fact that his first *Let's Pretend* appearance was on July 31, 1937. He was already busy as a commercial model, signed with the John Robert Powers Agency. That came about when Kingsley was in a school play in Flushing, New York, and the father of a fellow cast member told his father that Johnson & Johnson was looking for a kid to pose for an ad—a little boy crying, with a dog. More childhood pathos, but it kept many of us working, and sometimes quite lucratively.

Kingsley was what in those days was called a beautiful child, with hazel eyes, and brown curly hair. He once did a screen test for the lead in the motion picture "The Yearling." When Claude Jarman, Jr. was chosen, Kingsley was not heartbroken. Though he did enjoy being a child actor ("It was okay—it was pleasant enough," he says), he was never emotionally involved with it, either positively or negatively, as were some of the other Pretenders. Kingsley was rather shy and low-key, though not painfully so.

He had an appealing quality—was energetic, intelligent and dependable. If a radio director in the late '30s wanted a feisty kid who could talk fast and project excitement, he would very likely call Jack Grimes. But if a more laid back, earnest, even cultured quality was wanted, he would use Kingsley.

In 1938, acting on a personal referral from a friend, Kinglsey's father contacted the casting director of the B.B.D.&O. advertising agency, and as a result Kingsley started having a very busy full-time career on network radio, starting with their shows, which included *The March of Time* and *Cavalcade of America*. Mr. Colton had diligently followed up the lead. And this recalls the fact that Kingsley Colton was the only one of the Pretenders to have a father, not a mother, promoting his career.

Due to word-of-mouth referrals from directors and casting directors, Kingsley soon had a running part on the daytime serial *Valiant Lady* and another, *John's Other Wife*. For over a year he was Betty Garde's little boy on *My Son and I*. This was the poignant story of a vaudeville trouper who is widowed, and struggles to keep her self-respect while raising her child. The suspense was once prolonged for several weeks on that show when both mother and son were held captive in a cave by Mexican banditos.[15] On *Let's Pretend* Kingsley always played straight parts—not comedy, and not character voices. His sincerity and earnestness made any magical situation believable. He and Sybil Trent played the husband and wife Yeng-Ki and Hatsu in "Princess Moonbeam." It is the beautiful story of a poor Japanese couple whose prayers for a child are finally answered by the Moon Goddess. She sends a tiny baby whom they find in the bell of a flower. In the classic story of "The Little Lame Prince," which we did every year, Kingsley always played the title role.

After returning in 1946 after three years in U.S. Army Signal Corps Intelligence, Kingsley determined that the insecurity of an actor's life was not for him. That decision, he said, may have been made when one day he

---

15. *My Son and I* and *The Aldrich Family* were both radio programs first heard as weekly segments on *The Kate Smith Hour*. The same device was used on *The Rudy Vallee Hour*. They were the equivalent of out-of-town tryouts of Broadway plays.

saw several grey-haired actors on the third floor at NBC, waiting to audition, and visualized himself at their age, still knocking on casting directors' doors. Though his life after V-J Day went in a very different direction, Nila Mack continued to call him as long as he was available.

BETTY JANE TYLER

Betty Jane Tyler, born in 1928, probably first appeared on *Let's Pretend* in 1937, when she was nine years old. She, her father, mother and brother lived in Washington Heights in upper Manhattan, and it appears that Betty Jane broke into radio through the connections provided by a local dancing and dramatic school, and the periodic showcases of its students for whatever casting people could be persuaded to attend. These tenuous connections were always augmented by a strong network of ambitious mothers, who would exchange tips on whom to see and who was casting in the magic world of radio.

Her first running part was little Midgie, Marge's daughter on *Myrt and Marge* when it moved to New York from Chicago and became a daytime serial. She was also the North's niece Susan on *Mr. and Mrs. North*, and had long before made her professional debut in movie shorts starring the fast-talking news commentator Floyd Gibbons. *Let's Pretend* was an important part of Betty Jane's career. She was particularly valuable to Nila Mack because even in adulthood she could still do a little-girl voice. When she was a small child I remember her doing the title role in "Thumbelina," and standing on a platform to raise her to microphone height, as so many of us did in our early years.

There was a long period during which Betty Jane was not available for our show, beginning in 1943 when she won the part of Isabel, one of the leads, on *Land of the Lost*, another Saturday morning children's program, on the ABC network. One of Betty Jane's fellow cast members on that was Art Carney, who played Red Lantern, a magical talking fish.

The world of live radio was as glamorous for child actors as it was for grown-up performers. There you were, acting your heart out in a tall skyscraper on Madison Avenue, or the RCA building in Radio City, for an unseen audience of possibly millions. You were being complimented and flattered and well paid. None of us realized at the time, though, that the pressures we were under could be traumatic and damaging. A child radio actor had to be a miniature adult—a little business man or woman. Betty Jane was dealing with directors and casting people at a very early age. She had to be charming, and sometimes ask them to grant conflicts.[16] Even a simple "just thought I'd check and see if there's anything I'm right for today" phone call involved aggressive salesmanship, and the possibility of rejection that is part of any actor's career. But for a ten-year-old child it could be traumatic. (Gwen Davies' mother used to give her a dollar's worth of nickels, and send her to Whelan's Drug Store to make calls to casting directors.)

In addition to this, you were expected to be no less than perfect on the broadcast. There were no recordings or retakes in radio in the '30s and '40s, and directors would no longer call anyone, child or adult, who fluffed their lines too often, or did not observe promptness and studio discipline. Added to this pressure was Betty Jane's constant awareness that her mother, besides being proud of her, was tremendously anxious for her to succeed. With all these things going on, something was left out. There was no time for Betty Jane to simply be a child.

Though the glamour of radio carried with it the pressures we have seen, especially for child performers, *Let's Pretend* was somehow different. It was, after all, Fairyland. And when Betty Jane, as tiny Thumbelina, threatened with an unwanted marriage with a mole, was rescued, and flew through the air on the back of a friendly swallow, musically whistled by Henry Boyd to the tune of "Birds and the Brooks," the stresses and strains of being a miniature grown-up simply vanished in a fairy dust.

BILL LIPTON

Bill Lipton was yet another Pretender from Brooklyn—born there in 1926. His start in radio came from the fact that his mother knew Floyd Neal, an announcer at station WOR, and Neal introduced Bill to Bob Emery, the producer of *Rainbow House*, another kiddie talent show. When Emery heard Bill sing and then read some lines, he told him, "You're not a singer—you're an actor." So at age 11 Bill did his first radio work appearing in sketches on the show, and getting up at 4:30 A.M. every Sunday to make rehearsal.

After passing his audition for Nila Mack in 1938, he got his first call for *Let's Pretend.* It was relayed by a neighbor, as the Liptons did not have a telephone. The message was "be at CBS between 2:00 and 5:00 on Thursday" (we were then broadcasting midweek, with a 5:30 P.M. air time). So Bill got there between 2:00 and 5:00, choosing 4:00 P.M. for his arrival.

---

16. A conflict meant that an actor's broadcast conflicted with the rehearsal for his next show. The director of that show might grant the conflict on condition that he hire another actor to be his stand-in at the rehearsal he would miss. The other actor would not only get paid for the rehearsal time, but it might serve as an entree to the director's list of favored actors.

Naturally, the rehearsal had started at 2:00, so Bill's introduction to "Let's Pretend" was not a pleasant one. He remembered two other things about his first show: that it was "The Princess on the Glass Mountain" with Lester Jay doing the handsome Prince, and also (Bill could not have been feeling very good about the rehearsal call mix-up) that one of the girls flashed a lovely smile his way. It was Sybil Trent. Bill was instantly smitten, and ever since had a heartfelt affection for her.

Though there were sometimes other feelings of affection between us Pretenders, from the surviving members I have talked to, they were always secret. Sybil, for instance, early on had a crush on Albert Aley, who usually played Princes. "To me, he personified what a Prince was," she said. Her affections later shifted to Kingsley Colton—she pinned his picture over her bed—then to Jack Grimes. I had amorous thoughts about Pat Ryan for some time. We even went out on a date once. But there were no serious romances between *Let's Pretend* cast members. By the time we were adults and our respective teenage crushes had subsided, we had formed such long-standing brother-and-sister relationships that anything closer would have seemed unnatural.

Bill, with his mother's help and guidance, became a busy child radio actor, and the family moved to Manhattan on West 56th Street. His father meanwhile had his own problems. Mr. Lipton was not able to support the family as a singer, for which he had been trained, and so went instead into the scrap metal business. When that enterprise was no longer successful, there were several years when his son's radio earnings were the family's entire income. This was possible because Bill was now on the Air Features casting roster, and by 1938 was doing dozens of network shows.

As a child he played Skeezix on *Gasoline Alley*, later progressing to the lead in *Chick Carter, Boy Detective* on the Mutual network (a spin-off from *Nick Carter*), and eventually going on to older parts such as Dr. Malone's son David on *Young Doctor Malone* and another doctor's son, John Brent, on *Road of Life*. Remembering those last two shows, incidentally, brings to mind the old French proverb which translates: "The more things change, the more they are the same." After 70 years, and the transition from radio to television, daytime serials are still preoccupied with doctors, hospitals and serious illnesses. (The only difference is that now you can *see* the suffering.)

Bill, in addition to his flourishing career on daytime serials and night-time programs such as *The March of Time*, continued on *Let's Pretend* playing not only romantic leads but character parts as well, and, like Jack Grimes and Kingsley Colton, interspersing his radio work with studies at Columbia University.

Looking back on his career, Bill was particularly proud of some of the sustaining programs he did for the networks. The reason, he said, was that they were not bound by sponsors' strictures or ad agencies' fears, but could afford to be experimental. The ones he remembers best were *The Columbia Workshop*, on which he worked several times, and *Mrs. Miniver*, the CBS wartime serial on which Judith Evelyn played the lead, and Bill was her son.

Some of Bill's busiest radio years were just after Pearl Harbor. By then he was playing 18- and 19-year-olds, and young GI's. Soon his own military service would be inevitable, so Bill decided to join the Navy while he still had a choice. Ironically, this came just at the time when his blue eyes, blond hair and square-jawed good looks were becoming more and more of an asset. In 1943, the day after he was sworn in, 20th Century-Fox called from Hollywood and offered him a contract. But for the time being, show business and Bill's happy memories of *Let's Pretend* would have to be put on hold.

BOB READICK

Bob Readick (called Bobby when he was a child) was the last one to be added to Nila Mack's permanent roster before we became sponsored. He joined *Let's Pretend* in 1939. Little Bobby did not break into show business via the proud mother route. He did it completely on his own, by bluffing.

Bob was the fourth generation of a theatrical family. His great-grandfather, George Randall, was an actor. Before that he had been a cavalry private in the Civil War, assigned as the groom to the horse which had been the only survivor of the Battle of the Little Big Horn. Bob's grandmother was the original female lead in the 1922 Broadway long-running classic *Abie's Irish Rose*. He lived for years with his mother Dorothy Randall Readick, who was separated from his father Frank Readick, one of the busiest and best-known radio actors of the 1930s and '40s.

The child was rather thin and gangly. He had grey eyes, a longish nose and a pale complexion. It apparently never occurred to either his mother, or his father, whom he saw occasionally, to "put him into show business." One day in 1939 his mother, who had a radio show to do at CBS, left her little 11-year-old boy in Colbee's Restaurant, downstairs at 485 Madison. In Colbee's he saw many little boys his own age who were obviously radio actors. He followed them upstairs to the studios, where each went in to audition, came out with a script, and threw it in a wastebasket in the reception room. Bobby fished out one of the scripts, and when the last child emerged, went in and announced that he was there to audition, too. P.S.:

He got the job. It was a running part on a daytime serial. The pay was $24 a show, and, with no help from his mother, he was launched.

Having now become a professional actor, Bob appeared in two Broadway plays, first as the pesky little kid Raymond in *George Washington Slept Here* (1940), and later, at age 16, in *All in Favor* (1942).

Bob was a clever and versatile actor, and Nila cast him in a wide range of parts, from the addlepated King in "Rumpelstiltskin" who couldn't remember why he had asked the maiden to spin the flax into gold, to the wicked Bluebeard in the scary classic of that name from "The Arabian Nights." After Pearl Harbor, too young for the draft but with quite a mature and resonant voice, he was able to fill the roles on *Let's Pretend* and on many other radio shows usually done by those who were away in uniform. It was then that Bob came into his own as a steadily working actor in adult parts, and seemed destined for a long and successful career.

* * *

There were other Pretenders during the pre-Cream of Wheat years, each of whom was for a time as important to the show as any of the long-termers just described, but who left for various reasons....The first and most prominent was not one but two—the Mauch twins—Billy and Bobby—born in Peoria, Illinois in 1922.

Their mother brought them to New York when they were ten. Modeling and radio jobs followed, including *Let's Pretend* and *The March of Time*. In 1936 Billy was hired to play Frederic March as a child in the Hollywood film "Anthony Adverse," and Bobby was his stand-in. The twins did not tell the director until the picture had finished shooting that they had taken turns playing the boy Anthony. Billy and Bobby both made a big success in 1937 with Errol Flynn in *The Prince and the Pauper*.

The twins were then in the picturization of Booth Tarkington's "Penrod and Sam" in 1937, and in two forgettable sequels in which Penrod and his twin brother were juvenile detectives. When the twins would return to New York for a visit they would be welcomed back to *Let's Pretend* and given maximum CBS publicity coverage. Their film acting careers eventually faded, but they remained in southern California, and both found new employment in and near Hollywood, as film editors.

Billy Halop, born in 1920 to a lawyer and a professional dancer, made his first radio success as the lead in *Bobby Benson and the H Bar H Ranch*.

Let's Pretend was only one of his many radio shows. In 1935, already in his teens, he originated the role of Tommy, leader of the gang, in the Sidney Kingsley Broadway hit play *Dead End*, then on to Hollywood in 1937 to repeat it in the film version, starring Sylvia Sidney. From then on he was known, and typed, as a "Dead End Kid," and he and some of the other boys from the original cast made a series of highly lucrative but assembly line formula films based on the same type of characters. In the early days he made a few trips back East, and was always welcomed back on our show by Miss Mack and the rest of us.

After a stint in the Coast Guard in World War II, he returned to Hollywood and the bitter disappointment of being unable to get out of the Dead End Kid type of role. After a bout with alcohol, threats of suicide and a nervous breakdown, he gave up drinking and went into training as a registered nurse, to better care for his wife, who had contracted multiple sclerosis. He did bit parts toward the end of his career, including Mr. Munson, owner of the taxi service which employed Archie Bunker, in *All in the Family*. He died in 1976.

Nancy Kelly, born in Lowell, Massachusetts in 1921, had, like Sybil Trent, already done several films as a small child when she came to *Let's Pretend*, and had played Dorothy in a serialization of *The Wizard of Oz* on the NBC network. She played in *Susan and God* with Gertrude Lawrence at age 16, interspersing her Broadway plays (a total of 13) during her teens and early adulthood with a great variety of radio shows, including *The March of Time*. She also specialized in screams for adventure programs such as *Gangbusters*.

She eventually became an important actress in Hollywood, repeating there in 1956 her performance as the mother in *The Bad Seed*, for which she had won a Tony Award on Broadway. By then, her childhood acting on *Let's Pretend* had become just a memory.

Patricia Peardon was another Pretender who grew up in radio. She had a round face, blue eyes and curly, flaxen-colored hair. She started on *Let's Pretend* at the age of ten, appearing on such other shows as *Orphans of Divorce*, *Second Husband*, *The March of Time* and *Cavalcade of America*. She had a soft and most sympathetic-sounding voice. Nila Mack always cast her in romantic leading roles. Meanwhile, after appearing in an undistinguished Broadway play called *The Hook-Up* at age 11 in 1935, she created the part of Judy Graves in *Junior Miss*, one of the biggest hits of the 1941 season. She became a star at the age of 17.

Patty's long run in *Junior Miss*, (two and a half years on Broadway and a coast-to-coast tour) was followed by 14 months in the same role overseas for the USO, and by the time she came back she had decided there would be no more radio in her life. She temporarily retired from acting, married, and bore two daughters, Christine and Anne. She returned to the theatre in 1955 as Cindy, the spitfire daughter, in the Tony Award-winning Broadway production *The Desperate Hours*. Among her many other distinguished acting credits were several seasons at the Stratford, Connecticut Shakespeare Festival, and yearly Shakespearean roles with Arnold Moss at the Library of Congress in Washington.

Patricia Peardon made a surprising career switch about 1961. She became quite a successful sculptor, with several prominent exhibitions and many private commissions to her credit. At the time of her death in 1993 she had for some time been specializing in small cast bronzes of dancing and flying sprites—lovely groups of magical beings. It is easy to imagine that they were inspired by the fantasies of *Let's Pretend*.

Little Lorna Lynn's first *Let's Pretend* appearance in 1941 was an abortive one. Only six and a half years old, she was fired by Miss Mack after one performance, she said, because she could not read the script. Six months later she had learned to read, and worked on the program many times after, as well as on Ed Wynn's program *Happy Island*. She landed a running part on *The Brighter Day* and did many other radio shows.

Lorna also appeared in twelve Broadway plays. In 1961 she married, and in her later years was quite content managing some of the business affairs of her husband, who owned gas wells in Texas.

Eddie Ryan was a regular on our show in his childhood and early teens, but left for Hollywood in 1943, under contract to 20th Century-Fox to play opposite Anne Baxter in the wartime epic *The Fighting Sullivans*, the true story of those five heroic brothers who went down with their ship. Co-starred with Thomas Mitchell in *Within These Walls*, he later played important roles in five other films, did *The Charlotte Greenwood Show* on radio for two years, and formed a vaudeville act, which toured the country for two seasons.

It was in the early 1950s that Eddie decided on a career switch, which worked out very successfully. He went into sales and marketing, and was successful at it for 40 years. "I found," he later said, "that acting and selling are the same business."

Unfortunately Roddy McDowall must be listed not as a Let's Pretender but as an almost-Pretender. A child refugee from the London Blitz in 1940, he had already appeared in films in England. After he had auditioned for her, Nila Mack cast him in several of her radio programs, and would have used him on *Let's Pretend*, but his English accent was too distinctive.

While I was away in uniform Arnold Stang, known in radio and later in television and in three Broadway plays as a comedian, played some of the same character roles I had done in numerous pre-war *Let's Pretend* broadcasts.

Sidney Lumet, born in 1924, was a Let's Pretender during his teens, until he entered the Navy in 1942. A child of the distinguished actor Baruch Lumet, he had done several Broadway plays during his childhood, one of the earliest being *Dead End* in 1935, followed by the religious epic *The Eternal Road*, and William Saroyan's hit *My Heart's in the Highlands*, but did not do much radio except for our program. In 1955 when I worked for him in the Phoenix Theatre production of Shaw's *The Doctor's Dilemma*, Sidney was already a successful CBS television director (*You Are There, Omnibus, Alcoa Theatre*, etc.) It was thanks to his experience directing live television that he was able to complete *12 Angry Men*, the first of his brilliant screen successes, in just 20 days. It is certain that none of us on *Let's Pretend*, including Sidney, could have guessed that his radio acting days would be little more than a hint of things to come.

Jimmy Lydon, a freckle-faced, cute, redheaded kid born in 1924, was on *Let's Pretend* for three years—1937 to 1939, before a motion picture he made in New York, *Back Door To Heaven*, propelled him to Hollywood, under contract. He started there by playing teenage roles, including the lead in a series of nine Henry Aldrich films, which lasted from 1941 to 1944. Jimmy acted in over 100 Hollywood motion pictures, but found that he enjoyed life behind the camera much more than in front of it. He now produces, writes and directs for his own company, Spectrum Productions.

* * *

It would be oversimplifying to say that Nila Mack had built a repertory company of child actors. It simply would not stay built. There was constant turnover from the day she directed her first broadcast until the last show she cast before her death. First, not all of those whose careers I have outlined were always available. Then there was the group who had defected to Madge Tucker's camp over at NBC, after that lady's ultimatum that they could not play both sides of the street, or, in this case, the dial. And last, there were those whom Nila would phase out as she decided they were no longer suitable as Let's Pretenders.

Besides those I have profiled or will mention elsewhere, there are certainly others who are left out because they were on *Let's Pretend* only occasionally, or perhaps once, and so are not included in any surviving records. Those actors I have been able to document, though, who were on the show at some time during its 24 years (25 including its predecessor *The Adventures of Helen and Mary* before Nila Mack took over), add up to a total of 181 (see Appendix B). This does not include CBS staff announcers, who were assigned by the network and not cast by Nila.

The motivations of the Let's Pretenders' parents included dreams of glory for their children, economic necessity, or a combination of both. The children's motivations probably ranged from obedience to what Mommy wanted, to the desire to experience the fun of acting out fairy tales, with many gradations in between. Nila Mack, I am sure, had no idea when she started out how successful she would be in molding this extremely varied group into a good radio acting company. That it became that was a tribute not so much to our individual talents as to the lady who brought them all together every Saturday morning, and who built *Let's Pretend* into the institution it became.

9

Please Send Me Free a Fairy

Let's Pretend was now attracting fan mail, press notices and awards. Nila Mack was also much in demand to give interviews, and make speeches before women's clubs. In May 1934 someone cooked up the idea of having her write a weekly column called "The Child's Hour," which appeared in *Radio Guide Magazine* (five cents a copy).

Our director was highly touted in the introduction to the first column: "Nila Mack, director of all children's programs at CBS [is a] friend to children...one of the outstanding students of child temperament and an authority on juvenile behaviorism." Nila herself wrote this disclaimer: "Let me begin by putting my readers at ease. I am not a child psychologist. Children have taught me everything I know about them."

The subject of the first article was how to cure thumb-sucking, and contained the advice to use a metal thumb guard, or for older children a rough adhesive bandage. It concluded, "Take from thumb-sucking the comfort, solace, contentment and cheer it gives, and you have broken the habit." Later articles discussed such things as Shy and Imaginative Children, The High Strung, Tense Child, The "Lazy" Child, and The Spoiled Child. By implication, some of these were personality problems supposedly afflicting the Let's Pretenders. Though God knows some of us were rather complicated, high-strung children, no one reading these articles who knew Nila could believe that this bat guano was anything but ghost-written, though it is possible that the actual writer consulted with her from time to time.

Radio Guide (later *Radio and TV Guide*) was a pulp-paper magazine which every week featured complete program listings, gee-whiz feature articles, photographs of star personalities, and a fictionalized murder. *The Child's Hour,* which lasted 8 months, gave it a touch of class it otherwise sorely lacked, and also of course helped publicize CBS and *Let's Pretend.*

From the first, the ending of each of our broadcasts had always included an invitation to the children listening to "Write to *Let's Pretend* in care of your local station, and ask for your favorite story." Miss Mack said, "It's not only good for the children to get used to writing letters, but it's also good for me. They never leave me in doubt as to what story they want to hear." It also reminded the local affiliates of how popular the program was.

As our show developed into an institution, the mail volume grew. By 1940 we were receiving over 1,000 letters weekly. They were in three categories: Requests for stories, requests for photographs of the Pretenders, and requests for auditions. From their early teens onward, Albert Aley, Gwen Davies, Miriam Wolfe and Daisy Aldan would help in the office by opening and handling the fan mail. When Nila was interviewed she would usually mention some of the more interesting letters received recently, and that way a few of them have survived.

From eight little girls: "We like all the stories except the stories we don't like, but you make them so good that we like them."

"Dear Let's Pretenders: I've had almost every germ you can get, and now I have the mumps, but I think I would feel better if you played 'Snow White and Rose Red.' I like all the stories you have played. Thank you."

In August 1938, the office was literally deluged with mail, 5,334 letters, in response to a single announcement of a prize for the best letter on "Why I Listen To *Let's Pretend.*" The prize was 10 dollars.

Not all of the letters were necessarily charming. One little boy wrote: "Dear *Let's Pretend*: If you do not play 'Snow White and the Seven Dwarfs' I will never tune in again. If it takes too long, you can have it continued. I am 10 years old, but I still like 'Snow White.' If you do not have it I will tell everyone not to tune in again. I have a lot of friends, and they do everything I tell them."

Many other letter writers had very definite ideas of their own: "Dear Actors: If you get a letter from James please don't play that story because I think you played it. Therefore I got a better story, and here it is—'Aladdin and his Magic Lamp.' I like it because my teacher read it to me. So long, actors."

Nila answered a fan who requested "Snow White" telling her we would play it later, but evidently a friend of the writer became impatient: "Dear Let's Pretenders: You told a listener friend of mine that you would play 'Snow White' later. Well, now it is later. I have to eat my supper now, so goodbye."

Our letters ranged from poignant to grasping. One of the most unsettling ones came from the mother of a girl, age undetermined, who hoped we would interrupt the broadcast to send a personal message. The letter read: "She has always listened to your program. Please tell her, wherever she is, to come home to her heartbroken mother."

Nila would often take the time to dictate personal notes to the writers of the letters. One letter she took particular trouble with came from a little girl named Phyllis Knapp, age 11, in Utica, New York:

> Dear Let's Pretenders, I do think your fairy tales are grand.
> I love the music that is played while we're in Fairy Land.
> And Nila Mack, I want to say how much I love your plays.
> (The ones you write yourself, I mean, for special holidays.)
> I have one wish I'd like fulfilled, and it is simply this:
> If you could act "The Snow Queen" I'd be such a grateful miss.
> And then if you are tired of our wishes never ending,
> Just act a play to suit yourselves, despite the notes we're sending.

And here was Nila's reply:

> Dear Phyllis Knapp, just past eleven, your poem put me
>   right in heaven.
> How very nice to take the time to put your story wish in rhyme.
> But oh my dear, I'm in a spot (but tell me nowadays, who's not?)
> I have the "Snow Queen" in my files, but it's too long by
>   miles and miles.
> To try to shorten it to present it, I'll leave out parts, and fans
>   resent it.
> But maybe on some magic day, I'll try again to find the way.
> And when I do, I hope you'll hear, and write some other
>   poems, dear.
>   I really think you have the knack. My love to you, Miss
>   Nila Mack.

Among other letters were these:

Please send me a baby sister.

I love your hour.

I like it, but it made me have bumps on the neck.

Dear *Let's Pretend*: I wish for $80.

The all-time favorite, though, of Nila and indeed all of us, was this letter from a little girl in Chicago, which showed not only childish innocence and trust, but also incidentally, the power of radio to completely involve its listeners:

Dear Lespertend: Please send me Free a Fairy.

* * *

As the CBS publicity department ground out each new press release about *Let's Pretend* it would never fail to mention the many awards and popularity polls we had won. There were such a large number of them that the network had reason to be proud. One of our first was the *Motion Picture Daily* Award for best children's program on the air. "Pretend" won this award five times in the six years from 1938 to 1944. *Radio Daily* gave us its award for the years 1939, 1940, 1944, 1945 and 1946. In 1939 we won a grand slam of three awards as top children's radio program from *Motion Picture Daily*, The Women's National Radio Committee and the 600 radio editors polled by Scripps-Howard Publishing. Winners in various categories in the Scripps-Howard poll, announced in February, 1939, were:

Favorite Program and	
Best Comedian	Jack Benny
Quiz Program	Information, Please
Light orchestra	Guy Lombardo's
Male popular singer	Bing Crosby
Female popular singer	Frances Langford

Classical singer	Nelson Eddy
Symphonic conductor	Arturo Toscanini
Dramatic program	WABC Radio Theatre
Announcer	Don Wilson
Sport Announcer	Ted Husing
News Commentator	H.V. Kaltenborn
Favorite quarter hour	Amos n' Andy
Outstanding new star	Orson Welles
Children's program	Let's Pretend

Each new award was always acknowledged by a letter from Nila, and mentioned during the opening of the following week's broadcast. Sometimes she would make a brief speech of thanks on the air (her only radio performances in the last years of her life), then hurry back into the control room to direct the rest of the show.

The count of awards and polls won by our program varies with each CBS press agent's telling, and has gone as high as 60. Undoubtedly the most prestigious was the Peabody Award, known as the "Pulitzer Prize of Broadcasting." The awards, established by the University of Georgia School of Journalism in 1940, were named for George Foster Peabody, a Columbus, Georgia native who was a successful New York banker and philanthropist, and was one of the University's trustees. *Let's Pretend* was the first winner in the new category of "Outstanding Children's Programs," established in 1943. The citation reads:

> The award for outstanding children's program goes to *Let's Pretend*. Directed by Miss Nila Mack, this dramatization of great fairy tales has contributed both to entertainment and education, both to the passive and active development of children. The dramas are played chiefly by children, themselves.
>
> In addition to the merit of this program's direct contribution to the imagination of American children, it has become one of the most unusual child-acting schools of the air—numerous veterans of its "troupe" have gone on to play remarkable juvenile parts on Broadway.

As each new plaque, figure or citation came in, Nila would put it on a shelf or on the wall in her office, no doubt with satisfaction—and would then get on with the day's business of preparing for next Saturday's broadcast.

Every newspaper or magazine feature about *Let's Pretend* would mention these awards, and usually add its own tribute to the quality of the program, its appeal to youngsters, and the moral values it taught them. The closest thing to a straight critique I found was in the trade paper *Billboard*, in 1938, and that was not entirely a rave. It concerned our dramatization of "Dick Whittington" who by pluck, ambition and good luck becomes Lord Mayor of London:

> "Script was good, clear and well-balanced. Dialogue and clean continuity made it an easy one to follow. Nevertheless it was not suited for the juvenile cast of fifteen-year-olds who played it. Youngsters were not capable of handling the Irish and English brogues and dialects to make the script sound authentic. Script contained enough action to prevent youngsters from terming it a sissy show. An undercurrent of sympathy which shied away from anything approaching pathos made it simple to follow and a natural to be approved by parent-teacher groups."

My favorite follow-up comment was, naturally, more complimentary. It appeared in New York's newspaper *PM* in September 1940. After mentioning the latest awards won on this, the program's tenth anniversary since Nila Mack took it over, the tabloid called us "the blue-ribbon children's show on the air" continuing:

> Most radio programs for children face a particularly thorny dilemma. What the children like, the parents usually don't like, and vice versa. One kid program, however, on which both children and parents, as well as child psychologists, PTAs and all sorts of air-minded busybodies see eye to eye is CBS' *Let's Pretend*.
>
> *Let's Pretend* is a program by children, for children, which goes on WABC at 12:30 P.M. on Saturdays. It

hollers no hotcha, and sells no cereal or Dunko-Malt. It just acts out fairy stories, a shade professionally, but extremely well.

It was in 1940 that Nila was approached by two songwriters who wanted her to hear a new pop tune they had written called *Let's Pretend*, with the thought that perhaps it would become our new theme song. Our director invited them to let us all hear it. And so one Saturday morning during a rehearsal break in Studio 1, the composer, Abner Silver played it, while Gerald Griffin sang the lyrics. (Abner Silver was the composer of "Farewell to Arms" and "My Love For You," among many other hits, while his collaborator Gerald Griffin's solo efforts included "It's Only a Step from Killarney to Heaven.") All of us Pretenders listened politely and attentively, and Nila told them she'd let them know. Though hers was of course the ultimate decision, we all agreed that the song was very nice, but that our instrumental "Fairy Tale" was still the best. Although Nila Mack's mind was not closed to experimenting, her formula for a successful children's radio program had now become firmly established, and even when we acquired a sponsor in 1943, the basic format of *Let's Pretend* never changed.

10

CBS and WABC

The world of which *Let's Pretend* was a part was that of network radio. This huge new industry was the product of technical advances which made two things possible: First, clear radio broadcasting over long distances, and second, the transmission of broadcasts nationwide by many stations simultaneously, due to their being joined into networks by long-distance telephone lines. The United States, now in the midst of a major Depression, was ripe for an entertainment medium which was cheap, and radio provided it. You didn't have to go to a theatre and buy tickets for radio. The entertainment and information, in great variety, came to you for free.

The economics of radio were originally based on stations being owned either by manufacturers of radio sets, or department stores that sold them. The more and better programming available, the more sets people would buy. Eventually that proved inadequate in paying the costs involved, and stations then began offering time for sale to sponsors. Sponsors would pay the costs of putting on the programs, and thus be identified with them, and this increased their sales, and their importance. It worked marvelously— and still does, of course.

The sponsors got results, the stations and networks reaped income from time sales, and the listeners got free entertainment. Part of the system was that those time slots that were not sold were filled with sustaining programs such as *Let's Pretend*, which helped the network to keep the loyalty of its affiliated stations and its listeners, by providing presumably high-quality programming. Our children's show fitted ideally in that category. It was the best of its kind in radio, and generated enormous good will, both for the network and the affiliates.

Better still, because our production costs were so low, the Columbia network was under no great pressure to find us a sponsor—nor did it want to, once the program started winning national radio editors' awards and became so closely identified with the network by its loyal audience. Like the CBS *American School of the Air*, which was broadcast into classrooms five days a week, and like the NBC Symphony, *Let's Pretend* was not for sale.

There were many other sustaining programs on CBS and the other networks in the 1930s and well into the '40s, especially dramatic shows, which did fine work precisely because they were not sponsored. CBS had on its payroll such highly creative people as Norman Corwin, Max Wylie, Jerome Lawrence, Irving Reis and Charles Jackson, and it encouraged them to try new ideas in radio drama. Such programs as *The Columbia Workshop* could never have been produced by advertising agencies, whose main goals were not excellence, but simply large numbers of listeners, to move large quantities of merchandise off dealers' shelves.

The wholesale shift of radio program control from the networks to the advertisers had not yet taken place. It was lucky for Miss Mack and for *Let's Pretend* that it had not—she was given complete freedom by CBS to do her own experimenting.

Columbia Broadcasting was named "The Tiffany Network," no doubt by its own publicity department. Bill Paley was proud of providing quality programming for all of America. He had already boasted in the early '30s of having this country's largest radio network. NBC had more stations than CBS's 116 at the time, but they were divided between the Red and the Blue networks, so the CBS claim was in a way true.

WABC (860 on your dial) was the New York flagship station of the Columbia network, and the originator of much of its programming, which was fed to member stations by A.T.&T. long lines (today long since replaced by satellite transmission).

These telephone networks were a marvel of American technology, though very rarely lines might go down due to extreme weather conditions, or someone could switch a program to the wrong circuit.

A human error of a different sort occurred once in the 1940s when a telephone lineman, who had climbed a pole somewhere west of Denver to check some circuits, found that he had connected his headset to the line carrying *The Romance of Helen Trent*. He listened for a minute, then made an obscene suggestion to Helen Trent as to what she could go and do. Little did he wot, as Shakespeare would have put it, that he was broadcasting on the entire Western section of the CBS network.

In the mid-1930s CBS began leasing Broadway theatres to broadcast shows with large studio audiences, but 485 Madison remained its New York headquarters. There were (and still are) two sets of elevators in the building. The three on your left as you entered went to the lower floors, and served non-CBS tenants in the building. The three on the right went from the 14th to the 23rd floors, and served only CBS. (Note: "The 14th floor" at 485 was actually the 13th floor, but no one called it that. To this day, in many of the newest glitziest New York office buildings, you will find no 13th floor. Even in this time of enlightened thinking, triskaidekaphobia is not dead.)

The 18th floor contained the offices of Nila Mack and the other directors, as well as the staff writers and the casting director, Marge Morrow.

Nila Mack's office was no larger than 10 by 12 feet. Just like all the other production department offices, its walls and door were frosted glass, framed in dark-stained oak. It was high over Madison Avenue, and sunny, with a western view. From its one large window Miss Mack could see the back wall of Best's department store and St. Patrick's Cathedral on Fifth Avenue, and beyond them the towers of Radio City, which contained the NBC studios, and her rival, Madge Tucker.

Other floors up to the 19th contained CBS business offices, and on the 20th were William S. Paley and his top executives.

CBS had seven studios at 485 Madison Avenue ranging in size from Studio 6, which had been converted from a coat room, to Studio 1, the largest, which could, and sometimes did accommodate a full symphony orchestra. It was up a flight of ten steps from a cheerful, north-lit reception room on the 22nd floor, raised in this way to provide extra ceiling height for Studios 3 and 5, on the 21st floor below. All the CBS radio studios were on these two floors, with two exceptions: the News Room on the 17th floor (later expanded when the Columbia news division began to make a name for itself with its pioneering overseas broadcasts before and during World War II), and Studio 7, about the size of someone's not-too-large living room, and isolated from the others on the third floor. Master Control was near the top of the building, on the 23rd floor.

CBS had created a broadcasting center in a medium-sized office building (120 feet frontage on Madison Avenue, and 100 feet on East 52nd Street) very unsuited to such a use—but it worked surprisingly well. The only real problem was those ten steps that led to Studio 1, especially when a grand piano, or a heavy sound effects console, had to be lugged up or down.

When I started working on *Let's Pretend* in 1936, the studios at 485 had recently been redecorated. Their walls originally had art-deco murals of skyscrapers, bridges and ocean liners. The microphones had mostly hung from the ceilings—very impractical, as this meant they could not be moved around to suit the needs of each program. Part of the studio redecorating scheme was that large areas of the walls now had walnut paneling extending from wainscot to ceiling, and full-length beige curtains.

The paneling and the curtains, besides being handsome, had an important acoustical use. The studios, or any part of them, could now be made "live" or "dead," depending on whether the curtains, which were soft and sound-absorbent, were pulled back, exposing the hard and sound-reflecting panels, or were pulled over them. Other parts of the studio walls, and the doors, which had large semi-circular stainless steel push panels, were painted in not-unpleasant warm grays and blues. There was modern, recessed ceiling lighting. Reception rooms were done in art-deco style, with mirrors, light walnut paneling, receptionists' desks with rounded corners, and large, handsome built-in brown leather sofas.

This new and modern layout was no doubt in response to NBC, which had recently (November 11, 1932) moved into its spectacular new studios in the RCA building of Rockefeller Center, than called Radio City. The old NBC headquarters had been on the top floors of 711 Fifth Avenue, at 55th Street.

During my first two years on *Let's Pretend* we always broadcast from Studio 1. This was the studio where Orson Welles originated his weekly *Mercury Theatre on the Air* broadcasts, including the famous, or infamous, "War of the Worlds," and where Fletcher Markle later originated his *Studio One* radio drama series in 1947. (The name was kept for the later very successful live TV show.)

The large, single door at the top of those 10 steps was on the left side as you entered. On the left-hand (north) wall was the raised control room, three steps up, which one entered by first going through a glass-windowed sound isolation booth. This could be used for clients to view the broadcast, or a mini-studio, for actors whose voices were on echo, or on filter.[17]

17. Filters, like echo chambers very effective in radio, are still used in television drama and all sorts of audio productions. A filter usually eliminates the low frequencies from a designated microphone circuit, making a rough and high-pitched effect, such as a voice on the telephone. Since there were no telephones in the Land of Let's Pretend, filters were used for people's inner voices, or characters who were enchanted and could not speak normally.
If you were an actor "on filter" on "on echo," you would stand behind a sound-deadening screen or in an isolation booth so that your microphone would not pick up other actors' voices, and you would have earphones so that you could hear your cues.

Two-thirds of the distance from the control room to the opposite wall, slightly to the director's right, was a large round supporting column, which was sheathed in stainless steel. It didn't interfere very much with the director's view, but it was yet another reminder that 485 Madison Avenue had not been designed with radio in mind. Bill Paley and associates had signed a ten-year lease on the space just in time to have the studio floors redesigned (high ceilings, no windows, mechanical ventilation) before the building was completed in 1929.

High on the studio's east wall was a large art-deco clock which had metal bars in place of numbers. Beside the clock was a semi-circular scale, half green, half red, with a movable pointer which could be regulated from the control room. When it was moved all the way to the right (3 o'clock, on the red side) that meant that the broadcast was one minute ahead, and to slow down. All the way to the left (9 o'clock, on the green side) meant a minute behind, and to speed up, and there were many gradations in between. But in all the years I worked in Studio 1, I never saw the device used. It was completely impractical. Everybody in radio had learned to depend on hand signals from the control room, and no electric gadget could replace eye contact between the director and the performers.

Restaurant, watering hole and the center of a good deal of the off-mike social life of people who worked at CBS was Colbee's (originally called Lebus, but hardly a soul is now alive who remembers that). Though the main entrance to Colbee's was on the building's 52nd Street side, you could enter directly from the lobby, through double-doors and down a narrow flight of stairs (485 Madison was built on a hillside). I remember going down them many times, and finding myself in a noisy, friendly place which smelled of food, liquor and cigarette smoke.

While there I could telephone casting directors about jobs, use the lavatory, or call my message service[18] free of charge, on a direct line (beepers were of course unknown). Then I would often have lunch at the large oval bar in the center. My favorite was a chicken salad sandwich, with lettuce, on white toast, with a pickle on the side, and a chocolate milkshake.

Though the food at Colbee's would not have won gourmet prizes, it was good, and hearty. Jack Grimes remembers that you could get a great

---

18. Telephone message services were the radio performers' lifeline. Anyone at all active in the business was seldom home in the daytime, being out either performing, or at auditions or other appointments. There was Reg, the actors' nickname for Radio Registry, Lex, which stood for LExington 2-1100, and later Artists' Service and Billie's Registry, both started by operators from the other two.

bowl of black bean soup there for 25 cents. You could eat, or drink if you were of age, either at the bar, or in one of the booths which lined the walls. Nila Mack would regularly hold court in one of them—she did not plan it that way—it was just that her many friends would naturally gravitate to her booth to say hello or exchange the latest jokes when they saw her there. And for those of her friends who were actors, these meetings were also a subtle way of asking for jobs. Between Nila's popularity as a person and the fact that she was a director, it is surprising that she had time to get any nourishment at all in Colbee's. In fact, a reporter who once tried to interview her there almost gave up, there were so many interruptions.

A more sedate establishment was Louis & Armand's, just one door east on 52nd Street, on the ground floor of a brownstone. I never set foot in there in my childhood days—it was strictly for grown-ups. The food, the atmosphere (wood paneling, dim, shaded lights) and the prices were all more upscale than Colbee's. CBS executives were among its best customers, as were some of the more successful actors.

Both Colbee's and Louis & Armand's had one thing in common; if you came in at all regularly, the staff knew you, and would greet you like family. In the exciting but insecure world of radio, both restaurants were important contact points for many actors—places to make themselves visible, and perhaps pick up casting tips, or wave to a director. They knew that whether they were working or not, they would always find a welcome within these little enclaves, or at least someone to share a cup of coffee or a drink, and agree that the business was going to hell.

Child actors too were welcome at Colbee's. Smaller children would come there for lunch with their mothers, and the older ones alone. As miniature grown-ups, we too were on the lookout for possible passing directors, as well as for a good lunch, and Colbee's was a way station for the Pretenders as much as for everyone else who worked at CBS.

485 Madison Avenue and 30 Rock, as the RCA building at 30 Rockefeller Plaza was called, were the foremost creative headquarters of network radio in the United States for at least twenty years. The main difference between them was that at CBS the activity was all concentrated in a smaller space. In the CBS building you could almost feel the excitement, the energy, and the creativity moving and pulsating—in the studios, the elevators, the offices, the reception rooms, the hallways—and certainly in the restaurants. If you were a child actor growing up in radio, it was an exciting time to be there, and even more so if you were on *Let's Pretend.*

New Times, New Studios

With the almost explosive development of radio programming, beginning about 1930 when Nila Mack joined CBS, came great variety. There was a wide range of programs affording listeners experiences completely outside those available in the theatre or motion pictures.

First, there was music—both classical (NBC and CBS both maintained symphony orchestras) and popular ("And now, from the Grill Room of the Hotel Taft, here is Vincent Lopez…"). There were top comedians, incisive news commentators, quiz programs, church services, exciting play-by-play sports, and round table discussions of social issues, not forgetting the amateur hour craze of the mid-'30s. But what we are most concerned with is the great variety of dramatic programs—especially those for children.

Some of the earliest children's radio programs had been those that told stories; Ireene Wicker, "The Singing Lady" on NBC (who started on station WGN, Chicago in 1931) and *Let's Pretend* on CBS. Also on the networks and locally, there were numerous "Uncles" and "Aunts" who spun yarns for small children.

Beginning in 1932 broadcasting companies and especially advertising agencies started to develop a new breed of children's programming: dramatized adventure serials, most of which were broadcast in the late afternoons or early evenings, Monday through Friday. Though there was a great variety of subjects, and heroes and heroines, all of these shows had this in common—danger, adventure, sometimes physical combat or gunshots—and all were continued stories. This meant that the hero or heroine was always in some kind of peril or danger, and the situation was never resolved at the end of a 15-minute episode. In the infrequent instances in which one particular villain or villains had finally been brought to justice, there was always a new danger introduced, either in the wrap-up of the current adventure, or in the announcer's teaser for the next episode.

These were true cliffhangers, as were the old movie serials our parents had watched at the Bijou on Saturday afternoons, in which Pearl White would literally be left hanging from a cliff at the end of an episode. Back then the children had to beg a dime from their parents to see the next one, meanwhile being kept in suspense for a whole week. What the next generation's children had to beg was permission to tune in the next day's program.

Eventually, educators and parents' organizations began to protest about the effect the adventure shows were having on children. Though it may not have been typical of Heartland America, a study was made in 1936 by Azriel Eisenberg of more than 3,000 children in the New York metropolitan area. The study found that children listened an average of more than six hours a week (piddling compared to surveys of television watching by young people today), and that among their favorites were *Buck Rogers, Bobby Benson, Little Orphan Annie, Jack Armstrong, Skippy, The Lone Ranger* and *Let's Pretend.* Of these, our program was the only one not of the law-and-order/violence/cliffhanger type.

More important, though, were the children's reactions to the programs reported by Eisenberg. Twenty-seven percent of them had told of lying awake at night thinking about the shows they had heard, 43 percent said they had dreamed about them, and 72 percent of these dreams were unpleasant. All of the programs except ours was broadcast in the late afternoon, or, in the case of *The Lone Ranger*, early evening (7:00 o'clock Eastern Time).

Marilyn Boemer, in her excellent book *The Children's Hour* about children's radio programs from 1929 to 1956, tells us that a survey by *The Ladies' Home Journal* found 63 percent of the women of America thought some of the programs were too exciting for children. However, they did sell a lot of Wheatena, Cocomalt and Ovaltine, and for years broadcasting companies and ad agencies preferred to ignore the criticism.

However, to quote another readable radio history, *Don't Touch That Dial* by J. Fred McDonald:

> By 1938 the pressure against mayhem on the air became overwhelming. The adults assailed adventure series aimed directly at youngsters—programs like *Jack Armstrong*

which featured an athletic teenager fighting pirates, hostile natives, and diabolical gangsters; "Jungle Jim," an adult character who struggled against enemies similar to Armstrong's rivals; *The Green Hornet*, an urban vigilante whose programs included beatings, shootings and murder; and "Howie Wing," an aviator and do-gooder who usually encountered crime and brutality. These programs often relied on fistfights, loud action and death to add spice to the plot. They also featured cliff-hanger endings guaranteed to draw kids back to the radio the following day.

Groups like the Parent-Teachers Association argued that this programming left children on edge, upset their normal upbringing by placing destructive ideas in their young heads, and generally made them violence-prone.

Children, as might be expected, did not share these feelings. One early survey (1933) of children in Scarsdale, New York, reported that almost half (47%) preferred thriller-type programs, and one child specifically requested "a blood-curtle murder." [sic]

The networks finally became nervous about all the protests. They did not want to offend listeners, sponsors, and particularly the Federal Communications Commission, which had the power to refuse to renew stations' licenses, and they responded by dusting off their standards for children's programming. CBS's credo, adopted in 1935, had apparently gathered a lot of dust. Children's programming was not, it said, supposed to exalt as modern heroes gangsters, criminals and racketeers. Disrespect for parental authority was not to be encouraged, nor were cruelty, greed and selfishness. Conceit, smugness or an unwarranted sense of superiority over others less fortunate were not to be presented as laudable. Recklessness and abandon should not be falsely identified with a healthy spirit of adventure. It also stated that programs that caused nervous reactions in the child (a bit hard to define?) were not to be presented.

William S. Paley went further. CBS had an advisory board on children's programming, and it advised him to simply cancel what he called the "blood-and-thunder" children's programs. The order went out, and this was done. However, as he later related in his autobiography *As It Happened*, "Our sponsors deserted us on the replacements. The children deserted us too, turning to the same type shows on other networks." One of the replacements of the "blood-and-thunder" shows was *Let's Pretend*, and in January 1938 we were shifted to two broadcasts a week, late afternoons on weekdays, and from a great variety of studios.

First it was Tuesdays and Thursdays from 6:00 to 6:30 P.M. (New York time). In April we started doing the show half an hour earlier. In October our days were changed to Mondays and Thursdays, and in January 1939 the time period was again changed, this time to 5:15-5:45 P.M. These midweek broadcasts meant that all the Pretenders had to leave school early on broadcast days to make early afternoon rehearsals—something positive or negative depending on one's attitude towards school. We were all pleased, however, that the fee had been raised from our former $3.50 per show to $5, and those of us who did both broadcasts in a given week were making out fabulously...at least percentage-wise.

During July and August of 1938 and 1939 we would do our broadcasts from one of the several Broadway theatres that CBS had under lease. It was vacation time for school children all over the United States, and just a couple of announcements about sending in for free tickets brought thousands of requests. For the first time we in the cast had the experience of playing to audiences of hundreds of enthusiastic youngsters who filled every seat, cheering and clapping when Hugh Conover or Jackson Wheeler would make the opening announcement.

The shortage of studio space being what it was, there were also times in the winter months when we did the show from a sunlit studio on the top floor of the Steinway building on West 57th Street. This had been the original home of the Columbia Phonograph Broadcasting System before it was bought by Bill Paley & Co.

I enjoyed the afternoon *Let's Pretend* broadcasts most when we were in Liederkranz Hall. This large old four-story red brick and sandstone building at 115 East 58th Street had been built around the turn-of-the-century by Deutscher Liederkranz, a German-American music society organized in New York in 1847. By 1938, the average age of their membership now being on the high end, the Society was no doubt very pleased to get a steady rental from Columbia Broadcasting for their spacious ballroom on the third floor.

(A good-sized photograph of the old building appears in *Orson Welles on the Air*, once published by the Museum of Television and Radio. *The Mercury Theatre on the Air* moved there from Studio 1 because Liederkranz had become Columbia's largest single studio space.)

I am sure the rococo, Old-World style of the building appealed to Orson's sense of the dramatic. I had also imagined his being able to finagle sumptuous meals from the German kitchen downstairs, but diligent inquiry proved I was wrong. It turns out that Orson always had his rehearsal break Mercury meals sent over from Toots Shor's.

The ballroom must have been magnificent at one time. It had at least a 30-foot ceiling. The lower parts of the walls were covered with red figured brocade, interspersed with long, narrow, vertical mirrors. The upper walls were decorated with now-dingy murals of classic scenes such as zaftig maidens sporting with flute-playing centaurs.

The network made some changes. First, movable black curtains, to control acoustics, were attached at a point about two-thirds up the walls, and huge basketball court lights with wire guards were hung from the ceiling, which no doubt had once been graced by crystal chandeliers. Also, a soundproof control room was built within the ballroom. From a decorator's standpoint, the place was ruined, but it was just what CBS needed—a large studio in a midtown location. Furthermore it had excellent acoustics, especially for music. Many records were cut there for the Columbia label.

It was an adventure doing *Let's Pretend* in Liederkranz Hall, climbing the two flights of wide, gently curving stairs with their oak banisters. There were also temptations. Though CBS had the upper floor, the Club still maintained its business, including full dining room, on the floors below. As I peered over the railing outside the ballroom, I could see two floors below an old, bald German waiter tending his stacks of clean dinner plates, ready to fill them with Wiener schnitzel from the fragrant kitchen. One day during the rehearsal break, Mickey O'Day and I could not resist pouring little droplets of water from paper Dixie cups down onto the plates, then pouring more as the old waiter, perplexed, took each plate away to wipe it with a clean napkin. Shortly after an announcement was made by Miss Mack from the control room that whoever was doing this had better cut it out. So, back to business.

Bill Paley's experiment in good citizenship had ended when on April 22, 1939, we returned to broadcasting on Saturdays from our old home in Studio 1 on the 22nd floor at 485 Madison Avenue, this time in the 12:30-1:00 P.M. time period. July 13, 1940, we made another studio move—this time to the new, seven-story studio building at 49 East 52nd Street, which was now ready for occupancy.

Forty-nine East had originally been constructed in 1908 by the Vanderbilt family as a guest house. It was designed in English Renaissance style, with brick front and handsome (though by 1940, old-fashioned) carved stone window lintels. In 1924 it had been sold to the Juilliard Music Foundation as auxiliary space for its school. The former guest rooms, now classrooms, were oval in space, and in each Juilliard had installed two Steinway grand pianos.

CBS was lucky to get the building, located as it was directly across the street from 485 Madison. Still expanding, the network badly needed more studio space. Besides leasing the Liederkranz Hall ballroom, by then it was even using studios of a New York local station, WMCA, which was then on Broadway between 51st and 52nd Streets. Its size and location made the new building ideal for radio studios, more so than the original space ever was. CBS bought it from Juilliard in 1939, and completely transformed it into what *Architectural Forum* described as "the last word in broadcasting design."

For better soundproofing, the windows on the building's front were completely eliminated except for those on the top floor. The front was otherwise completely plain, and covered with white stucco. The only variation was that the building's ground floor was covered with one-foot square blue and grey terra cotta tiles. There was a simple, modern marquee over the entrance on the right side, with "CBS" in small bluish neon letters above it. The whole effect was starkly modern, and quite striking.

Inside the architects created eight studios, two of them quite large, meant to be used for audience shows. They were Studio 21, one flight down from the softly-lit lobby and reception room, and Studio 22, one flight up. Each of these could seat an audience of over 300. Upstairs, reached by two elevators, were six smaller and also ultra-modern studios, as well as plenty of space for the sound effects department, for acoustical research, and for equipment storage.

Let's Pretend broadcast from Studio 21. The double-doors for the audience were at the front, at the foot of the wide stairs from the lobby. At the back end of the studio was another door, to the control room and the playing area, for which a portable stage was built in sections so that it could be easily dismantled.

To prevent sound waves from bouncing around randomly, the ceiling was made in a shallow zigzag pattern. And on the rear and left-hand walls of the studio were what CBS called Acoustivanes—handsome, three-foot-wide vertical walnut panels which reached from floor to ceiling and were pivoted, so that when they were closed, sound was reflected from their hard surfaces, and when open, it was absorbed by a soft cloth backing.

The control room was three or four steps above the studio floor level so that everyone could see the director better. Painted surfaces in these studios were those same cool CBS blues and soft grays, the whole effect being perhaps a little less friendly than the old studios, but the new building was a vastly more efficient place to work. It was to be the home of *Let's Pretend* for the next three years.

* * *

It was on Tuesday December 24, 1940, that all of us, busy with our radio careers and happy in our *Let's Pretend* security, got a rude shock. Gwen Davies (still Estelle Levy in those days) telephoned all of us to say that Miss Mack was in the hospital.

Gwen, who lived only two blocks away, had been passing that evening, and saw fire engines in front of 55 West 53rd Street, where Nila's third floor terrace apartment was located. Miss Mack had been there, about 8:00 P.M., opening Christmas presents, in front of a cheerful fire in the fireplace. As she opened each package she threw the wrappings in the fireplace. But one box was apparently filled with shredded paper padding, called excelsior, and this instantly flared out into the living room, setting fire to Nila's chair. She attempted to throw the flaming chair out the window, which set fire to the curtains, and then to her dress.

Apparently Maud Wilson was not much help. Nila later did an imitation of her frightened maid standing by the door, wringing her hands and saying, "Oh, whatever are we going to do? Why doesn't somebody help us?" Eventually neighbors did come and help, and the New York Fire Department put the flames out. Our director was taken to Roosevelt Hospital with second-degree burns about the face, hands and arms. She was not back in the studio for two weeks.

* * *

It was also in 1940 that CBS had started making noises about *Let's Pretend* acquiring a sponsor. Radio was becoming bigger and bigger financially. The actors, singers and announcers had become unionized

(American Federation of Radio Artists, known as AFRA), and for this and many other reasons, programming was becoming more expensive. The idea of having so many sustaining programs, for prestige and to keep local affiliates' loyalty, was now less attractive to the networks. However Nila, being in charge of all children's programming originating in New York, and having the loyalty and respect of the CBS top brass, had for all practical purposes the right of refusal of any potential sponsor, though it was surely not spelled out in her employment contract.

Miriam Wolfe, Gwen Davies and Sybil Trent, to whom I am indebted for so many facts about Nila Mack and *Let's Pretend*, remembered that once CBS had let it be known that the program was available for sponsorship, there were many suitors for the honor, but that for at least three years she had turned them all down as not being suitable. Though the program being under sponsorship would mean more income for her personally, she felt a responsibility to the children in her audience, and to their parents, refusing to allow our program to be identified with any product that would cheapen it, or cast it in a bad light. She preferred to wait.

Meanwhile, I had been thinking for some time that it was really unfair for a national network program, a prize-winning, top dramatic show, to be paying its actors a fee of $5, while other sustaining programs exactly comparable to ours, with the same number of rehearsal hours, were paying their actors $21. The reason was the "Children's Program Waiver" in the network's contract with AFRA, which stated that if more than 75% of the cast were children, regular union minimums did not apply. The "kiddie show" syndrome again. But we long-term Pretenders mentioned earlier had by this time reached an average age of 16½, and more than half of us were 20 or older. Bona fide children were not now, by any stretch of the imagination, more than a small minority in our cast.

I called George Heller, Executive Secretary of AFRA. (Heller, formerly a dancer and an actor, had done many Broadway shows, the last of which was *You Can't Take It With You*, in the role of Ed Carmichael.) When I explained the fee situation, his reply was an unprintable epithet, then, "They can't do that to you! I'll see about this, Arthur." The result was a compromise: a month later our fee had been raised to $10. This did not take place without some anxiety on Nila's part, however. The network management had apparently told her they were not at all sure they were willing to pay what turned out to be an average of $60 in additional talent fees per broadcast. I never told her or anyone else that I had "blown the whistle" to AFRA. There is no way of knowing whether my complaint to the union, and the resulting higher fees, played a part in her decision, but when Cream of Wheat came along in 1943 Miss Mack, like Goldilocks and the three bowls of porridge, decided that this one was just right. The nine years of their sponsorship (1943-1952) made some changes in the program, mostly for the better, great changes in our lives (and pay checks), and marked one of the strongest product identifications in the minds of listeners ever known in radio.

12

Cream of Wheat
Is So Good To Eat

On August 18, 1943, the following item appeared in Variety:

13-YR-OLD SUSTAINER LANDS A SPONSOR

After 13 years on the air as a sustainer, *Let's Pretend*,
Nila Mack's kid dramatic series Saturday mornings on CBS,
has been sold commercially. Cream of Wheat will bank roll
the show...Sept. 25 in the same 11:05-11:30 time slot.

Deal calls for the show to air over the full CBS network on a 52-week basis, with 13-week cancellation periods. Miss Mack, currently on vacation, will continue to
write and direct the series. B.B.D.&O. (Batten, Barton,
Durstine & Osborn) is the agency.

The marriage between Cream of Wheat and *Let's Pretend* was an ideal
one. Cream of Wheat touted itself as *The Great American Family Cereal*,
and, like the product, ours was a family program, suitable for all ages, not
just for children. The company itself was an old American institution,
started in Minneapolis, Minnesota, in 1896. It only made one product, a
smooth white farina which came from the heart of the wheat berry, called
choice middlings. Enriched Five-Minute Cream of Wheat, a quick-cook-
ing variety, did not come along until 1938. The company was operated
along very conservative lines. For years two of the principal stockholders
would take turns being President. Every summer the entire plant would
be closed down for two weeks for employees' vacations.

131

Cream of Wheat's only previous experience with network radio had been when it sponsored Alexander Woollcott, the writer and commentator known as *The Town Crier*, on the CBS network for one season in 1933. The association with *Let's Pretend* was destined to last a lot longer.

Though our program had since 1934 been important because of the prestige and good will it created for CBS, it was now bringing in revenue as well. The show was sold to the sponsor as a package. The network figured its costs, including transmission charges to the member stations, and added a lump sum which was its profit. Because of this, CBS could also afford to budget more money for publicity. The institution that was *Let's Pretend* was never better known or better promoted than during those sponsored years.

As we have seen, Nila Mack was not disposed to allow any sponsorship to change the character of her show, or cheapen it. We may be sure that conferences were held between her and the BBD&O people in New York to determine the new format, and how the commercials would be integrated into the program. First of all, the familiar Komzak theme music *Fairy Tale* was now given lyrics, written by Nila Mack, to be sung by our Sybil Trent (melody) and Gwen Davies (harmony), and here they are:

> Cream of Wheat is so good to eat
> Yes, we have it every day,
> We sing this song, "It will make us strong
> And it makes us shout HURRAY!"
> It's good for growing babies,
> And grown-ups, too, to eat,
> For all the fam'ly's breakfast
> You can't beat Cream of Wheat!

The music, which had always been played rather lethargically, was now given a more sprightly tempo, and reset in a higher key, so as to be in comfortable range for the singers.

The music was much improved by our sponsorship because the budget now allowed for original music, composed especially for each broadcast. It was written, arranged and conducted by Maurice Brown, who for years had been the cellist in our orchestra. Leon Goldman, our former conductor, stayed on as first violinist. No longer did we use standard works from the music library. Brownie, after reading the script, would write bridge music for each scene break. He had a genius for creating a musical "button" for the scene just ended, then a segue to set the mood for the next scene, all in an average time of about 15 seconds. The old standards "Dark Eyes," "Estrellita," etc. were now used only if they fitted in with the mood which needed to be created.

Just how valuable the new format was to the program became evident once when Brownie's contract came up for renewal. He asked for a raise, and the sponsor was not willing to give it to him—until he reminded them that in the contract the original music remained his property, and could not be used if the contract was not renewed. Brownie got his raise.

I remember a lovely waltz he wrote for the scene in which Cinderella dances with the Prince. In the last scene, as the Prince discovers that the poorly-dressed girl by the doorstep who was forbidden by her stepmother to try on the glass slipper is indeed the maiden he had fallen in love with, the waltz sneaks in again under the dialogue. The glass slipper fits perfectly. As the scene ends the music swells, segues into the triumphant notes of Mendelssohn's wedding music, and that in turn into the *Let's Pretend* playoff music denoting the end of the story. It was a superb example of how effective music could be in radio drama.

Another improvement in the show which came with sponsorship, and more money in the budget, was the addition of a narrator for our stories. What we had had in the sustaining days were various CBS staff announcers, who would merely introduce the program in the beginning, then read the cast and other credits at the end. Once we had decided how we would travel to the Land of Let's Pretend there would be music, and the story would start cold: that is, with no further introduction or explanation. This could be confusing, especially for some of our younger listeners. Now Nila was able to hire Bill Adams, to be known on the show as Uncle Bill, a choice she would surely have made years before if she had had the budget for it.

William P. (for Perry) Adams was born in Tiffin, Ohio in 1887. He attended Heidelberg College in his hometown for pre-law courses, then decided upon a singing career, for which he began studying at the College of Music in Cincinnati. While there he was hired by the celebrated Shakespearean actors Edward Sothern and his wife Julia Marlowe, who needed a young actor for their Cincinnati engagement. In 1912, right after graduating from the College of Music, he joined their company with a long-term contract.

From then on Bill was a busy actor, stage manager and later a director. He was with John Barrymore in a production of *Peter Ibbetson*, which also starred Constance Collier, played with Barrymore in 101 performances of *Hamlet* on Broadway for Arthur Hopkins, and then directed Barrymore's own production of *Hamlet* in London. A list of his other stage credits would fill a page.

When he became our narrator/spokesman for Cream of Wheat, Bill, now 56 years old and the father of a grown daughter, had long since ceased to depend on the theatre for his income. He had for fifteen years been occupying a comfortable niche in radio.

Bill Adams was the epitome of a working actor—never starred and seldom featured, and in radio usually not even identified by name—but always working. He gave solid, believable performances in whatever show he was cast. His running parts went back to Uncle Henry on *The Collier Hour*, first broadcast in 1927, and included *Pepper Young's Family* (Sam Young), *The Story of Mary Marlin* (Franklin Adams), and *Big Town* (Fletcher). He was often called for one-shots on important shows such as *The Light of the World* and *Cavalcade of America*, but until he became Uncle Bill, he was best known in the business for his many roles in the dramatized news events of *The March of Time*, and especially for his fault-less impersonation of Franklin Delano Roosevelt.

"Show us how he spoke," asked an interviewer. "He didn't speak," said Bill. "He sang." And indeed, if you listen to a recording of one of FDR's speeches before a large crowd (not his Fireside Chats), you will recognize that Roosevelt's was indeed a singing voice. Bill said the President had a two-octave speaking range, compared to a less than normal one, which held this entire nation (or at least the Democrats) spellbound for almost four terms. Bill, being a lifelong Republican, personally had no use for the man.

When not performing, Bill Adams was active in the New York local of AFRA as a Board member, later as President. He enjoyed smoking cigarettes, having a drink with his friends at the Lambs Club, and shooting pool, at which he was an expert.

If you were inventing an Uncle Bill you could not have found a better type than Bill Adams. Rather tall, he had a long nose, a kindly creased face, naturally wavy gray hair, and most important for radio, a beautifully resonant voice. Besides his warmth and believability when he narrated our stories, Bill was also the delight of the ad agency and the Cream of

On the air: Gwen and Sybil sing "Cream of Wheat is so good to eat" while Miriam Wolfe, right, awaits her cue. In background: Violinist Leon Goldman, actress Betty Jane Tyler (hidden), conductor Maurice Brown, and pianist Sidney Raphael. ©1944 CBS, Inc. Used by permission.

Wheat people. You could not help but trust that what he told you about Cream of Wheat ("Yes, Pretenders, it's full of phosphorus, to build strong bones…") was the absolute truth.

Because the stories were what *Let's Pretend* was all about, we now had a time problem—a double one. First, the nation was on a war footing, and since April 1943, CBS had been broadcasting five minutes of news at 11:00 A.M., on Saturdays, which took five minutes out of our broadcast time. And our commercials cut further into the time available for the actual story.[19] That had been over 27 minutes in our sustaining days, and was now pared down to 18.

Did the stories suffer because of our new time limit? To some of us who remembered Nila's original radio versions they did, but this may have been our own prejudice because we knew the scripts so well from

---

19. During all broadcasts there was a production man at the director's elbow, who had made timing notations at 15-second intervals on the margin of each page at dress rehearsal, and would tell the director whether the show was "on the nose," or whether to give the cast a "stretch" or "speedup" signal.

having performed some of them so many times. (Indeed, there are some lines which the few surviving Pretenders still remember, and repeat to each other for a sort of word game when we get together.) But compromises obviously had to be made.

In "Rapunzel," for instance, the first two scenes were cut entirely. In the first a husband, John, and his wife, Marian, who is ill, are looking out of their window at the garden of a witch, who lives next door. She is growing beautiful lettuce, which Marian is sure will make her well. The Witch refuses to sell them any, threatening to put a curse upon them if they bother her again. The husband climbs over the garden wall that night to take some of the lettuce. As he does so he is caught by the wicked Witch. As the price of saving them both from a terrible curse, she forces him to agree that if the couple should ever have a daughter, she will belong to the Witch. "Now take the lettuce," says the Witch grimly, "and go back to your wife and tell her the good news!" (Ominous music, segues into "Rock-a-bye, Baby"). The (cut) commercial script begins with the third scene, which Uncle Bill introduces only by saying that a happy couple are trying to decide on a name for their new baby girl. After this is established the Witch suddenly bursts in to claim the child. Nila inserted new dialogue which explained why in just 30 seconds. Establishing the menace of the Witch next door, and how it came to be that the husband and wife are in her power—the scary scene of the husband pounced upon in the dark while taking lettuce—all were lost. The cut material in this case equaled almost exactly five minutes—enough to accommodate all the Cream of Wheat commercials. Though it was a shame to lose the two scenes, it was a good cut. It meant that the remaining scenes could be done intact, and the listeners did not miss what they never knew had once existed.

In "The Donkey, The Table and the Stick" the innocent, good-hearted hero Jack is given magical gifts by the three artisans to whom he is apprenticed in successive years. The first two, a donkey whose ears drop gold coins at the world "Bricklebrit," and a table which is covered with a sumptuous meal at the words "Little table be covered with food of my choice," are stolen by a dishonest innkeeper. The scene in which Jack receives the third gift, a magic stick which beats unmercifully whomever he tells it to, was cut. We never find out how he got it. All we know is that in the last scene he uses it to punish the rotten innkeeper and force him to return his loot. By then the story had gained its momentum, and this omission prob-

Circa 1949: "Uncle" Bill Adams and Jimsey Somers (note platform). Billy Rose Theatre Collection: the New York Public Library for the Performing Arts Astor, Lenox, and Tilden foundations.

ably mattered very little to the radio audience. Meanwhile, a much-needed three minutes had been cut from the script.

(There was another problem with this story which had nothing to do with timing, but with Nila's rapidly-maturing actors. The magic words to make the stick fly into action were originally, "Up, stick, and whang the life out of him!" But there was much giggling during rehearsals, because we adolescent sophisticates were always reversing the words "stick" and "whang" when not on mike. It eventually became such an in-joke among the boys of the cast that Nila, much as she probably enjoyed it herself, changed the line to "Up, stick and *beat* the life out of him!" and it stayed that way forever after.)

Each script that had to be cut to accommodate the shortened commercial format presented a new challenge, but our director, who by now had 13 years of radio writing experience behind her, surmounted each one successfully, preserved the show's charm and character, and if anything made it better.

Once the new format had been set for *Let's Pretend* under Cream of Wheat sponsorship, it hardly varied for the nine years they were with us. The opening was Gwen Davies and Sybil Trent singing the Cream of Wheat jingle, and enthusiastic applause and yelling from a theatre filled with 1,000 children and parents. Then Gwen or Sybil would tell Uncle Bill what today's story would be, and we would do our decades-old ritual of deciding how we'd go to the Land of Let's Pretend.

Once we were on our magical way, Uncle Bill, or more accurately the copywriters at the ad agency, would find a way of connecting that with Cream of Wheat. To give a sample:

UNCLE BILL:	And now, Sybil—what's the story for today?
SYBIL:	The Six Swans, Uncle Bill.
UNCLE BILL:	The Six Swans it is. And who'll say how we travel to the Land of Let's Pretend?
SYBIL:	It's Bill Lipton's turn today.
BILL:	Well, what do you say we travel by giant rockets?
GWEN:	Bill, that's terrific. Rockets it is. One for each of you, and a great big one for Uncle Bill and me. Everybody ready?
CAST:	(Ad-libs sure, etc.)
GWEN:	One—two—three!
SOUND:	(WHIZ BANG. ROCKETS)
GWEN:	Gosh, Uncle Bill—did you ever in all your life see anything so fast as these rockets? And so smooth, too.
UNCLE BILL:	Almost sounds as if you're talking about our favorite breakfast treat, Gwen. Yep, Enriched Five-Minute Cream of Wheat is mighty fast, and smooth, too. You

see, it cooks to full digestibility, even for babies, in just five minutes of boiling. And talk about smooth.... Why Cream of Wheat hands you the smoothest, creamiest goodness that ever came out of a cereal package. So eat a better breakfast, feel better all day. Get a better start the Cream of Wheat way. And keep listening for our special Cream of Wheat game, that comes right after the first act of today's story, The Six Swans.

Then came the music and narration introducing the first scene of the story.

The middle commercial, the Cream of Wheat game, always included participation by the children in the studio audience, and Uncle Bill would rehearse them before the broadcast, with reinforcements from the cast in case the response was weak. The game would always require three responses—such as answers to a riddle, sound effects, animal noises, or giving the last word to a rhyme—always with a Cream of Wheat twist. Another sample:

SYBIL: Well, Uncle Bill, what's cooking in the Cream of Wheat game department?

UNCLE BILL: A rootin', tootin' game about the wild and woolly West, Sybil. Okay, let's shoot: What's the cowboy's name for food?

AUDIENCE: Chow!

UNCLE BILL: Chow it is, pardners. And you can bet your boots and saddles that the best all-fired breakfast chow on the whole range is smooth and delicious Cream of Wheat. Yes siree, it's right at the head of the herd for lip-smacking flavor.

and so on. The middle commercial would always end thus:

UNCLE BILL: It's wa-a-ay up in flavor...

SOUND: (SLIDE WHISTLE UP)

UNCLE BILL: It's wa-a-ay down in cost...

SOUND: (SLIDE WHISTLE DOWN)

UNCLE BILL: It's pa-lenty smooth.

                (Music playoff)

The closing commercial was only about 30 seconds long, and always ended with Gwen and Sybil singing the last two lines of the jingle:

> For all the fam'ly's breakfast
> You can't beat Cream of Wheat.

Then as Bill Adams announced each character's name, we in the cast would identify ourselves. There were closing credits for Maurice Brown, and for Nila Mack. There might be an offer of free tickets to a broadcast for those who sent for them (the closest thing to a premium offer Cream of Wheat ever made). The program ended with a teaser—some tantalizing facts about next week's story, with an invitation to tune in. Then Bill would sign off with: "Bill Adams speaking." And last the station break:[20] "This is the CBS Radio Network."

The comforting surety of this unvarying routine made everyone happy—the children listening, their parents, and the sponsor. And though the format did not vary, the stories of course did, and the excitement of each one kept everyone listening until the end of the broadcast, which of course included the commercials. Though those were addressed to children, their mothers could not help being aware of them too, especially as the youngsters were always urged to "Ask Mom to put it on her shopping list today!"

How many things can you say about farina, one might ask. It is a tribute to the ingenuity of the advertising copywriters that, though the answer is not many, they constantly devised new and sometimes entertaining ways for Uncle Bill to make a few more important points about their product. I can still hear some of them, almost in my sleep:

---

20. The station break was so that local stations would know when to cut away from the network and identify themselves, as required by the FCC. There would be only seconds for them to do that, and make local announcements, as the next network program would start in exactly 30 seconds. Only once in nine years did I see Bill Adams get rattled by this inflexible deadline. With his network cue coming up at the very end of the broadcast he was heard to mumble, "I'm sorry— I've lost my place." Jack Grimes bounded up to the microphone and said quickly: "This is the CBS Radio Network," thereby saving hundreds of stations across the country from utter confusion.

…Baby's best first solid food…

…Full of iron, niacin and Vitamin B_1…

…Make sure you have one hot dish for breakfast, even in summer…

People did not mind hearing these things over and over again. They were put in a good mood by the story, and the excitement of wondering how it would end. And that, of course, is part of the psychology of broadcast advertising.

Every sponsored radio program had to have an ad agency producer, even if the agency did not produce the program. Ours was Ed Marshall.

Edwin C. Marshall, who grew up in Chicago, had an extensive musical education, and became assistant to the stage director of the Chicago Civic Opera Company. He eventually went into radio work in New York during the Depression. Before joining BBD&O he worked for CBS, supervising many of their cultural broadcasts, including the New York Philharmonic concerts, and *Of Men and Books*, with Mark Van Doren.

Because of his background, plus the fact that he had a rather bookish mien—hair combed straight back, silver-rimmed glasses, and pencil-thin mustache, Nila apparently considered him a highbrow intellectual, and at first did not quite trust him. In any case, the commercials pretty much ran themselves. Bill Adams, being perfectly cast in his role of grandfather figure, storyteller and Cream of Wheat spokesman, knew exactly what to do. And part of the sponsorship arrangement for the program was that the network, meaning Nila Mack, was to retain complete artistic control over the story portion. So all in all there was not much for Ed Marshall to do except maintain pleasant relations with everyone—he was well-liked by all of us Pretenders—and act as diplomatic go-between if there should be any disagreements between CBS and the sponsor.

With sponsorship we now had the luxury of an extra hour's rehearsal, which took place at the 485 Madison studios at 5:15 P.M. on Thursdays. Nila would assign us our roles, and there would be a read-through, at which she would get a rough timing, and some idea of what special problems there might be for the Saturday broadcast. The scripts would be mimeographed at CBS, with the exception of the pages with commercials, which were mimeo'd at BBD&O and sent over to be collated.

The front page of the script, with BBD&O logo, would list the name of the program, the date, the broadcast time and the story's title, followed by the lyrics of the theme song. On one occasion the story was "Faithful John," below which the ad agency typist, evidently believing that he or she had a wicked sense of humor, had added:

(Or, The Plumbing That Never Broke Down)

As soon as Nila saw this, she gave all of us an order: "Get rid of that!" This was not amusing. She knew it was possible that *Let's Pretend* scripts might fall into the hands of people in the studio audience. Fun was fun, but where the public image of *Let's Pretend* was concerned, she would not stand for it to be cheapened or ridiculed.

Besides the improvements in the show which came with sponsorship, we now had more glamorous surroundings for our broadcasts. For a short time we were housed in CBS Playhouse 4, at 254 West 54th Street, which had recently been leased by the network. Built in 1927 by Fortune Gallo as an opera house (The Gallo Theatre), it eventually became Studio 54, a wildly successful discotheque in the 1970s and '80s. It was more recently restored to its former theatrical glory (ivory and cobalt colored arches, with white cherubs and gilt decorations) and the Roundabout Theatre's revival of *Cabaret* had a long run there.

By 1946 when I returned from service, the show had been moved to Playhouse 3, just around the corner, at 1697 Broadway, and there we stayed for the rest of our sponsored years. The theatre's auditorium was, and still is, behind a 13-story office building. Both were completed in 1927, the same year as the legendary Paramount Theatre on Times Square. The office building is in the shape of an "L." The inside of the L, the corner of Broadway and 53rd Street, was originally occupied by an ugly, nondescript four-story red brick building dating from about 1900. In 1960 that was torn down, and replaced by another ugly nondescript five-story *white* brick building.

The theatre's marquee, its rather ornate brass doors and its entrance lobby (and originally the box office), are on the Broadway side, while the building's lobby and elevators are on 53rd Street. When I first started working at Playhouse 3, I remembered vividly having gone up in those elevators to the top-floor studios of station WMCA, where in 1933 at the age of 11 I had done my first radio broadcasts on *Uncle Nick Kenny's Radio Kindergarten*.

The theatre was originally called Hammerstein's. It was built as a memorial to Oscar Hammerstein I, founder of that celebrated theatrical family, by his son Arthur, and the foyer originally contained a life-size bronze statue of the great man, dressed in a long frock coat. The house was ornately decorated inside in Gothic style, said a contemporary account, with "mullions of ornamented plaster reaching up to the point of the dome where a great lantern is the central source of illumination."

Along the walls were a series of ten illuminated stained glass panels, depicting scenes from operas produced by Oscar Hammerstein. As it was built by a Hammerstein, the theatre was designed for musicals. Its original capacity was 1,204, with 762 seats in the orchestra and 442 in the balcony.

Unfortunately, probably due to the Depression, the Hammerstein family was not able to hold on to the house, and it passed through several different ownerships. In 1931 it became the Manhattan, and then a theatre-restaurant owned by Billy Rose, who added a pipe organ, with console that rose from the orchestra pit. After one more brief, unsuccessful period as a legitimate theatre it was leased to Columbia Broadcasting in 1936.

By the time *Let's Pretend* moved there the theatre's former glamour had vastly diminished. The stained glass panels had been covered, the heavy leather upholstered furniture and individually lighted oil paintings were long gone from the downstairs lounge, and who knows what happened to the statue of Oscar Hammerstein? (A partial answer to that question, and a fuller history of Hammerstein's Theatre, are in the fascinating book *Lost Broadway Theatres* by Nicholas Van Hoogstraten.)

To me the theatre had vaguely the look of a Gothic European church, and the bronze chandeliers with their fake candles were somewhat reminiscent of *The Three Musketeers*, or *Cyrano de Bergerac*—not a bad atmosphere for some of the classic fairy tales of *Let's Pretend*.

On Saturday mornings when the doors were opened at 10:30, the theatre would fill with eager children, the girls usually wearing hats, and often gloves and patent leather shoes, and the boys jackets and ties. There were Girl Scout troops, teachers with their classes, as well as some older, middle-aged *Let's Pretend* fans trying to look inconspicuous.

Another audience group starting to appear was the second-generation *Let's Pretend* fans. By the late 1940s, some children who had grown up as our listeners were now married, and were beginning to bring their own offspring to the broadcasts. To all of these faithful devotees, radio was still king, and this was the big-time.

Thursday rehearsal at 485 Madison Avenue, circa 1947. Left to right, behind: Michael O'Day, Jack Grimes, Albert Aley, Rita Lloyd, Sybil Trent, Bill Adams, Gwen Davies, Arthur Anderson, and Maurice Brown. At table: Marilyn Erskine, Nila Mack (who has ditched her cigarettes for the picture), Bonnie Baxter, and Joey Fallon.
©1947 CBS, Inc. Used by permission.

It must have been rather confusing for some of the smaller children in the studio audience who had formed clear mental pictures of the stories being enacted as they were hearing them on the radio, to come in and see what was, after all, a group of actors standing in front of microphones, holding scripts. It was just before our broadcast one Saturday morning in 1952, our last sponsored year, that I had occasion to use the men's lavatory in the basement of Playhouse 3, the same one used by members of the audience. As I was leaving, I saw a father speaking to his little boy just before they went upstairs to take their seats in the theatre. "Now remember, sonny," he said, "it's only a radio show." I have always wondered since whether that child was expecting to see costumes, makeup and scenery.

For most children in the studio audience, the story's illusion was so strong in their own imaginations that the fact that we were in a radio studio did not matter. As Nila Mack was leaving the theatre one Saturday

Heroine worship, circa 1948: Brownies present a bouquet to Daisy Aldan.
©1948 CBS, Inc. Used by permission.

after we had done "Snowdrop and the Seven Dwarfs," she overheard a little girl talking to her mother on the street outside. "But she didn't eat the poisoned apple, Mother," the child was saying. "I was watching her!"

I suppose the thrill that most of the youngsters who came to the broadcasts felt was that of actuality: "There they are—that's what they look like—the actors I hear every week!" But the real excitement of radio drama is, or should be, what comes out of the speaker and goes into your ears, and imagination.

As a stage presentation, a *Let's Pretend* broadcast was of distinctly uneven quality. The actors, nearest the audience, were well lit, but both the sound effects (the most physical action there was on the stage) and the musicians were upstage, in rather dim light. Stage left (the audience's right) just in front of the proscenium was the control room, in which could be seen Nila Mack, giving cues, the production assistant Gene Hight, keeping track of time, Ed Marshall, the ad agency producer, and the engineer, who sat impassively through it all, no matter what the excitement.

Stage right, opposite the control room, was another glassed-in soundproof room, the client's booth, in which sponsors, VIP's and relatives and friends could watch the show, and smoke and converse if they liked. The only stage setting was two large ten-foot-high cutouts designed by Ed Marshall, on either side of the stage—on one side a fairy tale castle with soaring towers, and on the other a huge box of Cream of Wheat, with its picture of the smiling black Cream of Wheat Chef holding a steaming bowl of the sponsor's product. These were bathed in subdued pink and blue light when the audience entered, and all the lights came up when the broadcast started.

The show began for the studio audience with Bill Adams' warm-up. He would welcome them, and say, "Now you know, you're all part of this broadcast. We couldn't do without you." And he would then coach the children in their responses for the Cream of Wheat game during the middle commercial. He would finish with one last admonition: "Now you've got to be very quiet during our broadcast, so I want you to get all those coughs, and yawns, and sneezes, and foot-stamps out of your system right now. Come on, everybody—let's hear it!" And a theatre full of children would all delightedly cough, yawn, and stamp their feet. Then would come momentary silence as the hands of the clock neared 11:05 A.M.

Though we *Let's Pretend* veterans had by now all become supposedly mature and sophisticated, involved as we were in the glamour world of network radio, I do not think any of us failed to get a thrill when the lights came up, the show went on the air, and the audience's enthusiastic yells and applause filled the theatre as Bill Adams said: "Cream of Wheat, the g-r-e-a-t American family cereal presents...*Let's Pretend!*"...Because of radio, the Hammersteins' theatre had gained yet another new life. Audiences were still enjoying themselves there, in a way that family could never have foreseen.

What was then CBS Playhouse 3 has had several other lives since its radio days. For several years it housed *Toast of the Town*, starring Ed Sullivan, among other night-time audience television programs, and in 1963 I found myself back there doing silent comedy bits on *The Jackie Gleason Show*.

During its early television days the theatre was simply CBS's Studio 51. It was renamed The Ed Sullivan Theatre in 1967, in honor of the host of that phenomenally successful Sunday night variety show which had a 23-year run. It was used less and less by Columbia, however, as its big name night-time audience shows were emanating more and more from the West Coast, and the lease was finally allowed to expire in 1981. The situation was dramatically reversed in late February 1993 when, to keep its new acquisition *The Late Show with David Letterman* in New York, the network bought both the office building and the theatre, for a sum of $4,000,000. Completely refurbished, repainted and rewired by Columbia, under the watchful eye of the New York City Landmarks Commission, it became as much a high-tech television studio as a theatre, and was ready just in time for Letterman's first broadcast on August 30. (Columbia also announced that those ubiquitous Hammerstein illuminated stained-glass panels had been uncovered, carefully removed, and safely stored away.) What we Pretenders had known as Playhouse 3 thus began yet another chapter in its varied history, in which our program was by then almost a forgotten page.

Besides fond memories of many Saturday morning radio broadcasts from Playhouse 3, one particular incident which took place there later comes to mind which has a *Let's Pretend* connection. One of our sound men, Vic Rubei, heard that cameramen were needed in the CBS Television division, and switched to the new medium. He was operating a camera on the stage of the theatre during an important night-time audience show—live, of course.

"Camera 2, dolly back," came the instructions on his earphones. "Dolly back...dolly back...," so Vic and the camera kept backing downstage, off the edge and into the audience. Luckily, a carpeted floor now covered what had been the orchestra pit—otherwise he might have been killed. But I have always imagined what a weird picture must have appeared on thousands of home TV screens as the camera, and Vic, careened crazily off the edge of the stage.

It was also in our beloved Playhouse 3 that another television disaster took place, which I saw myself on the air. It was on *The Red Buttons Show* for Maxwell House Instant Coffee. Every week there was a commercial showing a hand spooning some of the sponsor's product from the jar into a cup. Then steaming, boiling water was poured in, as the announcer talked about how delicious and satisfying it was. On this occasion the instant coffee was put in, but as the camera moved in for a tight close-up, and the boiling water was poured, the cup shattered in a dozen pieces, and the microphone picked up the sound. A shocked "Ooohh!" went through the studio audience.

Then Buttons, not willing to let it alone, came on and began his next comedy shtick with "Folks, this is the only coffee that can make this claim." The next week, and forever after, the spoon was always left in the cup as the water was poured in.

It was during the high-publicity glamour days of *Let's Pretend* that Columbia decided to put the show on phonograph records. Each story was in an album of three 10-inch 78 rpm discs—six sides, each lasting a maximum of three and a half minutes. This made a total of 21 minutes for each story, slightly more than we had on our Cream of Wheat broadcasts. As each record side had to end logically, and usually with a musical "button," this meant some minor rewrites by Nila Mack, but it all came out neatly, and was up to the usual high *Let's Pretend* standard.

We made six albums, done at Columbia's recording studios at 799 Seventh Avenue in June of 1946, and in June and December of 1947. For those sessions we had the benefit of a larger orchestra, with added reeds, brass and tympani to give the music more body. The records of course helped publicize the broadcast, and the broadcast helped sell the records, and so both worked together to make *Let's Pretend* even more well-known. It is surprising how many people today assume that the *Let's Pretend* broadcasts themselves were pre-recorded.[21] Neither our show nor any other on network radio, except for some on the Mutual Broadcasting System, were pre-recorded until 1946. (Bing Crosby started the trend in that year by moving from NBC to American Broadcasting, because ABC was willing to accommodate his busy schedule by recording his show in advance.) Otherwise they were always "live from New York," or whatever the origination point. Stations in the Central, Mountain or Pacific time zones might not want an East Coast program at its original broadcast hour, due to the

---

21. Present-day radio and television programs are almost all pre-recorded, and so can easily be edited to fit time requirements. When radio was live, however, the editing all had to be done in rehearsal. Only minor adjustments could be made once you were on the air.

Though nothing could match the excitement of live radio, it was subject to human failings. Occasional "fluffs" could turn a director's hair grey overnight. Who can forget: "And now, the NBC Symphony, conducted by Artrusco Turanini," or, "Friends, be sure to get the breast in bed." Just as disastrous, and irretrievable in early live television were such things as doors that stuck, or corpses that got up and walked off the set.

time difference. For that reason in the early days of network radio, there was usually a "repeat for the Coast," which meant the cast would go back to the studio three hours later and do the entire program over again. The actors never complained about this, however, as it always meant an extra fee.[22]

As the networks began to relax their rigid rules on pre-recorded broadcasts, acetates would be used for the repeats, but this was never done with our show, except possibly by individual stations on the network. Though some people in the Pacific time zone were hardly out of bed at 8:05 A.M. on Saturdays, perhaps that was not a bad time for cereal commercials.

For the nine years *Let's Pretend* was sponsored by Cream of Wheat the company continued to be pleased with it. The whole package was a smoothly functioning blend—a good example of a radio program that was targeted for a particular audience, and gave that audience and the sponsor what they wanted.

---

22. In the days when programs were repeated for the Western time zones, horror stories abounded concerning actors who went home for a nap, out to dinner or to a movie, and completely forgot the repeat broadcast.

13

Nila's Family Grows Up

One immediate benefit of our being sponsored was that, beginning with our first Cream of Wheat broadcast ("Cinderella" on Sept. 25th, 1943), there was no further talk of any "children's program" waivers. All the *Let's Pretend* actors received the sponsored program fee, which at that time was $47.30, including four hours of rehearsal. As new union contracts were negotiated in succeeding years it finally rose to $71.25 in 1947. Maurice Brown and Bill Adams were paid more under their own negotiated contracts, and Gwen Davies and Sybil Trent earned additional fees because they were always in the commercials.

Agents' commissions were never deducted from our fees for *Let's Pretend* or for any other radio work, because rank-and-file performers in radio were not represented by agents. The reason was that AFRA when it was first organized had announced that it would grant agents franchises to represent its members only on condition that they not charge commissions on union minimum fees. If they wanted their 10% commissions, said the union, let them obtain 10% above union scale, or better, for their clients. However, producers saw no reason to negotiate with agents for fees above union scale, unless the performer had "name value."

Sponsorship as we have seen caused great changes in *Let's Pretend*, but another taking place at the same time, gradually and more subtly, was that Nila Mack's family of child actors had grown to adulthood. Indeed many of our male Pretenders were now beginning to be eligible for the military service. When our Cream of Wheat sponsorship started, this country was heavily involved in World War II. Don Hughes, in the Signal Corps attached to the Air Force and eventually sent to the combat zone in France and Belgium, was the first to leave in 1942, and he went the closest of any of us to the front lines. Bill Lipton enlisted in the Navy in 1943, and was stationed mostly at Dartmouth College, New Hampshire, in the V-12 program. Jack Grimes was in the Air Force briefly, using his knowledge of radio to produce broadcasts by Capt. Glenn Miller and his band. Kingsley Colton, younger than most of us, was in the Signal Corps Intelligence, and not sent overseas until 1946.

I was in the Air Force, too, supposedly repairing radios in P-47 fighter planes in Pocatello, Idaho, but due to an acute lack of mechanical aptitude was finally transferred into work I was suited for: writing, directing and announcing radio programs, writing newspaper columns, and putting on shows to sell War Bonds. Who would have thought that my Two-Man Band would one day help defend our country?

Returning to *Let's Pretend* early in 1946 I found many changes in the program, the much larger paycheck being among the most welcome. We had two new sound men—Art Strand, small and wisecracking, and Jimmy Dwan, large, with florid complexion, and fond of practical jokes—but in their work they were both up to the traditionally high CBS standards.

By then the second *Let's Pretend* wedding had taken place. In 1944 Albert Aley had married Maybelle Tunnicliff, originally from Florida, who was a New York Telephone Company operator. Before we were drafted, Don Hughes and I had joined Albert and Maybelle after the Saturday broadcasts, for bowling at the Roxy Bowling Center on 50th Street just east of 7th Avenue, which occupied part of the building that once was the huge Earl Carroll Theatre.

Neither Don nor I had steady dates at the time, and this unlikely foursome got along very well together, even on occasions when Don and Albert would position themselves on either side of me while we were walking along the street, and I would suddenly find myself deposited in the nearest trash basket.

Meanwhile Albert, deferred from the draft because of his heart condition, had begun to find success in his early '20s as a full-time radio writer, first for *Superstition* on the ABC network, in 1942 for *Don Winslow of the Navy* and more importantly for *Hop Harrigan*, who was a wartime flying ace. Albert took over the writing from Charles Stratton, then was made head writer.

Albert's personal life had meanwhile become very complicated. In May of 1945 a daughter, Suzanne was born to Albert and Maybelle. Five weeks later Maybelle tragically died of a brain embolism, and Albert was left with an infant to care for. Ivy Weston, a Canadian nanny who had been recommended to him by Austin Beardsley of The Young Professionals then moved into their apartment on East 49th Street to care for Suzanne. One day in 1946 Albert met Elaine Firestone, a tall attractive brunette. Elaine and Albert were mutually attracted, and she was willing to take on the double responsibility of a husband and a baby, and they were married several months later, when Suzanne was 15 months old. In 1947 Albert and Elaine's daughter Christopher was born.

It was a busy life for Albert. He would write the next day's *Hop Harrigan* script after Elaine had gone to bed, deliver it at 2:00 A.M. to the doorman at the Beaux Arts Apartments, where lived the show's producer Robert Maxwell. He would go back home to sleep until 11:00 A.M., then rise and go to the studio for that day's recording. In 1952 he began what was to be a five-year association with Rockhill Productions, and became head writer of *Mark Trail*, a half-hour, three-a-week broadcast based on the comic strip by Ed Dodd. Mark was an outdoorsman—a man of the woods who fought the crooks, badmen and bullies who would destroy nature. Albert encouraged Don Hughes, who sold several scripts to the show. *Trail* started on the Mutual network, shifted to ABC in 1951 as a five-a-week serial, and lasted until late in 1952. It was also in 1952 that Rockhill introduced *Tom Corbett, Space Cadet* on radio. Albert was Executive Producer. Before long, *Corbett* was being broadcast three times a week on radio, and two on television. Albert Aley had now become the most successful of all the Pretenders.

Though the original Pretenders were now all grown, our feeling for Nila as a mother and confidante did not cease. It was if anything stronger, especially among the girls, now women, who were coming to her for advice not only about careers, but also boyfriends and romances. One of our newer cast members, Marilyn Erskine, who had been in radio for some time and was now playing adult roles on the show, told Nila that she was thinking of marrying a much older man.

"It's not going to work, kid," said Nila, looking at Marilyn over her glasses with those large, blue, slightly bulging eyes. Marilyn assured her that this was different. Nila told her that no, it wasn't, with words to the effect that she should not marry the man, and that if she did, to remember that she had told her not to. A few years later, when the divorce came, Marilyn did remember.

Nila Mack, circa 1947. ©1947 CBS, Inc. Used by permission.

Gestures of respect and affection for Nila were given more freely by some of us than by others, but she had a real need of them. A "hello" kiss at first rehearsal was expected from every one of us, as was a "goodbye" kiss and a thank you after the show. So strong was Nila's need to receive as well as give affection that it became increasingly obvious that the frequency with which you were called had a direct relationship to your response in this department. Marvin Silbersher (later a CBS Television director) recalled that back in 1937, as a new child in the cast, he was physically turned off by kissing Nila (she wore too much lipstick, he said), and showed it by squirming out of her grasp. He was never called again after that incident. Rita Lloyd, new in the cast in 1948, remembers seeing the effusive greetings before morning rehearsal at Playhouse 3. She sat there not knowing what was expected. Nila turned to her and said, "Well, what's the matter with *you?*"

Playhouse 3, being a Broadway theatre, had union stagehands. (At 485 there had been only John Hosty, a redheaded Irishman who could speak Gaelic, and one other set-up man, who for years had lugged heavy equipment up those ten steps to Studio 1.) One Saturday as we gathered at the control room door after the broadcast, one of the stagehands said to me disgustedly: "Now I suppose yez all goin' to kiss da director." It was certainly protocol to thank the director and say goodbye after a broadcast, but he had never seen anything like this.

Another part of the after-the-show ritual involved Don Hughes and myself. During rehearsals I had formed the habit of drawing a cartoon illustrating the week's story. I would hand it to Don, who, with grumbling expressions of reluctance, would on the spot compose a short poem to go with the illustration. Then after the show, as part of my goodbye, I would show Nila the picture and read her the poem, to which she always responded with a low chuckle.

Though Don's *Let's Pretend* verses were probably not of lasting value except as "in" jokes, they were never less than original and witty. I eventually traced the pictures and poems on heavy paper and put them in a loose-leaf book which I gave Nila one Christmas, titled *Fairy Tales Gone Modern*. Only one poem survives, and that through memory. I had drawn a picture of King Midas (of "The Golden Touch") counting his wealth, and this was Don's poem:

> There was a king named Midas,
> So they say, in days of old,
> Who had the wondrous gift of turning
> All he touched to gold.
> And as the sad result of this,
> Most all the girls in town
> Made chiming sounds like golden bells
> Whenever they sat down.

In 1947 Gwen Davies married Larry Greenhaus, a good-looking young chemical engineer, and he became part of the *Let's Pretend* family. At Playhouse 3 on Saturday mornings there were poker games during rehearsal breaks, and sometimes after the show, upstairs in one of the dressing rooms, and Albert Aley, Jack Grimes, Don Hughes, Michael O'Day, Bob Readick, the two sound men and Larry were in on them. I was not interested in poker, though I am sure I would have been welcome to join the game if I'd wanted to.

August 1948: Another party, celebrating Nila Mack's 18th anniversary with CBS. Back row: Anne-Marie Gayer, Maurice Brown, Kingsley Colton (hidden), Donald Buka, Donald Hughes, Sybil Trent, Arthur Anderson, Albert Aley, Bill Lipton, and Bob Readick. Front row: Gwen Davies, Nila Mack, Patricia Ryan, Betty Jane Tyler, Miriam Wolfe, and Jack Grimes. ©1948 CBS, Inc. Used by permission.

Some of the Pretenders socialized with each other individually, such as Albert and Gwen and their spouses, Jack Grimes, Bill Lipton, and some of the actresses with each other. There were also two occasions when the entire cast charted a party boat, the Klondike IV, in New Rochelle, N.Y., for a day's sail on Long Island Sound, including a beach picnic, and swimming. I was the organizer of these jaunts, buying the food and drinks, and keeping track of the money. Every Christmas we were all invited to Nila's house, and the cast would always bring her a collective present. The family feeling was indeed strongest during the Cream of Wheat years.

Meanwhile Mae McNair, formerly receptionist on the 18th floor at CBS, had become good friends with Nila, and finally moved into her apartment. She was also promoted to assistant casting director, under Marge Morrow. Another change was that Lois McQuitty, Nila's secretary, was hired away from CBS by BBD&O, our Cream of Wheat advertising agency, and became assistant to Ed Marshall, the agency producer of *Let's Pretend*.

Nila meanwhile had become close friends with Sandra Levy, Gwen's mother, and was often invited to their apartment for dinner. After Gwen was married, she and her husband Larry would usually take Nila to dinner at Colbee's after Thursday read-through rehearsal. It may have been partly that they realized she was lonely, but she was always witty, and good company. I think that Nila's respect for Larry grew after one of those dinners, at which she apparently spoke to him in a way that to him resembled scolding. Larry said to her, "You can't frighten me, Nila. I'm not one of your kids." Their relationship was better after that.

One of the *Let's Pretend* actors' most memorable Christmas presents to our director was in 1945. It was a ten-minute take-off on the show, written by Don Hughes and entitled "Snow White Cinderella, or Sleeping Beauty and the Beast." It was recorded in Studio 1, on both sides of a 12-inch acetate.

It opened with Sybil and Gwen singing this version of the theme, in New Yorkese accents, with Mickey O'Day at the piano:

> Cream of Wheat may be good to eat
> But we really couldn't say,
> We've sung this song for so damn long
> That it makes us shout, "Oi veh!"
> Perhaps the babies love it,
> The sponsor does, we know,
> So on and on we sing it,
> We must-a stay on-a show.
> (We need the check!)

Uncle Bill tries to get the audience to shout out the name of a cereal they all love, but all he gets is "Wheaties!" and "Ralston!" He gives up and says, "All right, you little bastards. Just for that, no commercial!" (Cheers.) Don Hughes is asked how we should travel to the Land of Let's Pretend, and replies, "I do enough commuting as it is. Let's stay here."

We then meet Snow White Cinderella (Gwen Davies), who wants to go to the AFRA Ball. Her Fairy Godmother (Miriam Wolfe, sounding very much like Mrs. Nussbaum from Allen's Alley) makes her a coach from a tin can, and a coachman from a cockroach on the wall. At the ball she meets her dream man Hophead Harrigan (Albert Aley) but disappears at midnight, leaving Hophead holding her nylon stocking. He promises his sidekick Tank (Bob Readick) that he'll find the girl, and the mate to the stocking, by putting it in his radar detector.

Meanwhile, Snow White Cinderella left a little too late, and is condemned to live with a Beast (Jack Grimes) in the wilderness of New Jersey. She asks him why he has green skin, a tail, and two heads.

BEAST: Do I have two heads? Duhhh—I wondered why that guy was always lookin' over my shoulder.

We meet The Queen (played like Mae West by Betty Jane Tyler), who takes the advice of The Mirror (played by Pat Ryan with a Cockney accent), and slips her rival Snow White Cinderella a Mickey, which sends her into a deep sleep.

Hophead finds her with the aid of his radar detector. "What beautiful bumps she makes in the sheets," he murmurs. Snow White Cinderella awakes and says indignantly, "Were you tryin' to climb into bed with me? Takin' advantage of a poor sleepin' girl!" "Forgive me," says Hophead. "Well—I'm awake now," she replies. "Whatcha waitin' for?" And the cast all yells, "MERRY CHRISTMAS, NILA!"

Don had many other facets to his writing talents. Besides *Mark Trail* scripts, he also wrote several episodes of *Tom Corbett, Space Cadet* for Albert, at Rockhill Productions. Don and I had already been co-authoring a project for television called *Date for Three*, with a cast of three, including myself and Sybil Trent. The 15-minute show included songs, some of them originals written by Don, but nothing ever came of it.

Though Nila continued to audition child actors from 1943 onwards, the cast was now basically adults, and replacements had to be made from time to time as people became unavailable for various reasons, the most common of which seemed to be having moved to Hollywood. With adult performers, as with the children who had been her original cast, she continued to look for people who were not only good actors, but who could project the belief that fairy tales were real.

One of these was Marilyn Erskine. Marilyn called herself a "character leading lady." Blonde, with a sympathetic and appealing voice, she was able to play highly emotional parts as well as comedy. She came to *Let's Pretend* as a teenager, after doing children's parts on *Young Widder Brown* and other daytime serials. By 1950 she had left New York to do a stage play with Cesar Romero in California, and from then on only returned to the East occasionally. She later played Ida Cantor in *The Eddie Cantor Story* and did many other films. After playing Tom Ewell's wife on his TV sitcom series, she left show business in 1962, and still resides happily in California.

Anne Francis, blonde and fragile-looking, was cast by Nila in romantic heroine roles, but left for the film capital in 1947, where she became very successful in adventure and sci-fi films for 20th Century-Fox, in roles ranging from frail young things to hardened broads.

Florence Halop had been on *Let's Pretend* as a child, with her brother Billy. After he went to the Coast she did adult leads on our show until she too went west. She later made a great success in Hollywood, more in television sitcoms than in films. She was the hypochondriac patient Mrs. Huffnagle in *St. Elsewhere* and was "killed off" for an even better role as Florence Kleiner, the wisecracking bailiff in *Night Court*, which she played until her death from cancer in 1986.

Rosemary Rice had a long background of daytime radio serials, including *Archie Andrews*, as a teenager, then as an adult in *The Right to Happiness, Young Dr. Malone* and a run of twelve years on *When a Girl Marries*. Nila used her in leading roles such as fairy godmothers during the Cream of Wheat years. Rosemary later created the role of Katrin on television in *Mama*. She then launched a separate, and very successful career as a writer, producer, and singer in children's records.

Joan Shepard emigrated to the U.S. as a British war refugee child in 1939. By 1943 she was a panel member of the highly popular "Quiz Kids" on radio. Though Nila only used her on our show a few times, *Let's Pretend* helped launch Joan on a busy career in radio acting. She also appeared on Broadway as Tallulah Bankhead's adopted daughter in *Foolish Notion* in 1945, and in *A Young Man's Fancy* in 1947. She and her husband, actor Evan Thompson, formed Fanfare Theatre Ensemble, a children's theatre company, in partnership with John Clifton, in 1970, and since 1987 they have operated a successful summer theatre, the River Rep, in Ivoryton, Conn.

Another of our new adult actresses was Anne-Marie Gayer. Anne-Marie, tall, slim and blonde, and with a ready smile and great versatility, was born in the Midwest. She became active in theatre, then radio, in and near Chicago, as an ingénue and young leading lady. Then, in the late 1930s, so many Chicago radio shows had shifted to New York that she moved too, to be where the work was.

Postwar, Anne-Marie was very successful in New York radio, including night-time shows like *Gangbusters*, and daytime serials. She also did three Broadway plays, but only one, *The Desk Set*, enjoyed a run.

She remembers Nila Mack as "our earth-mother—like a benevolent dictator." Our director cast her as The Red Queen in "Alice In Wonderland" and in a great variety of roles. Her only negative experience with *Let's Pretend* was getting stuck in one of the cubicles in the ladies' room at Playhouse 3 just as we were about to go on the air. Jack Grimes heard her screams and yanked the door open just in time for the broadcast.

(Daisy Aldan had encountered exactly the same problem years earlier on the 21st floor at CBS. Alone in the lavatory, she had desperately tugged on its door, which was stuck, until it finally opened, then rushed up a flight of stairs to the studio just as we were going on the air, to be met by Miss Mack's baleful glare from the control room. She was not able to explain what had happened until half an hour later, when the broadcast was over.)

There were many other actresses who helped bring excitement to our show during the Cream of Wheat years. One was Susan Douglas, born in Czechoslovakia in 1926, quite active on *Let's Pretend* and other New York radio programs until she began to make a name for herself on the stage in 1946.

RITA LLOYD

Rita was the last of the long-term Pretenders recruited by Miss Mack. She joined the cast in 1948. As a child she had progressed from doing imitations of Greta Garbo and Margaret Sullavan to doing the leads in school plays in her Brooklyn neighborhood, then joining *The All-City Radio Workshop* on New York's municipal station, WNYC. She studied drama under Wilson Lehr at City College, and at the age of 18 decided to become a professional.

Rita had a mature voice, good speech and the ability to play emotional parts. She passed both the general audition at CBS ("Bring five minutes of your own material") and the *Let's Pretend* audition. Rita had for years listened to our show, but had never dreamed of actually being on it. At her first Thursday read-through she was so nervous that she dropped her script on the floor under the table, and when she bent down to pick it up, saw everybody's feet.

"Stars have small feet," thought Rita. She was taller, bigger than most of the girls, and felt terribly intimidated. But with their help and with Nila's she overcame it, and grew as an actress. Shortly after becoming active in radio, Rita obtained a scholarship in the American Theatre Wing's Professional Training Program, and got several jobs as a result of working with directors who had volunteered to teach radio and television classes. She did *Suspense, The Eternal Light* and running parts on *Backstage Wife, The Romance of Helen Trent* and several others. There was only one catch: as Rita's career was blossoming, so was television, and one by one, these radio shows started to go off the air.

Rita admired and was fond of Nila, but she did have two confrontations with her. The first was when she paid a casual visit to her office. Nila got up from her desk, shut the door and said, "I'm not going to let you leave here until I find out what makes you tick." Nila was exasperated because Rita had such a cool, unflappable exterior, and did not show any nervousness. Rita explained as best she could that she had as much insecurity as the rest of us sometimes did, and that the coolness was her way of handling it—a cover.

The other run-in was when Rita had landed a non-principal part on *You Are There* for Robert Louis Shayon—a prestige show which all actors felt was a privilege to be called for. At next Thursday's rehearsal Nila said, "Rita, I heard you did an extra on *You Are There*." "Yes," said Rita. "Isn't that wonderful?" "No," said Nila. "Let's Pretenders do not do extras. Do not do an extra again, or you will never do this show again." Nila was still fiercely jealous of her own program's position in the pecking order at CBS and in radio.

On the other hand, our director was just as capable of the warmth and kindness she had always shown. Once Rita showed up at rehearsal by mistake, as a result of a mix-up by her message service. "What are you doing here?", asked Nila. When Rita explained, Nila wrote in a part for her to save her the embarrassment and the disappointment, and Rita got a check the next week anyway.

Rita found her six years on *Let's Pretend* very happy ones. She gained experience in our company playing witches, wicked queens, other character parts, and leads as well. Though on the show less frequently after Miss Mack's death, she remained a member of the family.

Later she continued as a successful working actress. She had running parts, mostly as conniving women, on daytime television in *Edge of Night, Guiding Light* and *As The World Turns,* and appeared on the stage in such leading roles as Lady in Tennessee Williams' play *Orpheus Descending* off-Broadway and at the Bucks County Playhouse. She also learned how to lip-sync[23] for foreign films, speaking English for Giuleta Massina In *Juliet of the Spirits.* Her rather smoky voice and incisive delivery were heard more recently narrating some episodes of the National Geographic TV *Explorer* series.

There were many male actors, too, who Nila Mack either recruited during the Cream of Wheat years, or who had been on *Let's Pretend* only occasionally as children and were now called more frequently.

The best known of these, and the Pretender with the most enduring success of any of us is Dick Van Patten, called Dickie when he was a child. Never used much on our show before he was grown, he had an enthusiasm and an ingenuous charm which showed more during his adult years. Besides "Let's Pretend," Dick counted 600 other radio performances, and opened in a total of 27 Broadway plays. His days on our show probably ended in July 1949, when he began a seven-year television run as Nels, Rosemary Rice's brother, in *Mama.*

When he moved to the West Coast, Dick started a string of what is so far 34 feature films. Four have been for Mel Brooks, including *High Anxiety* and *Space Balls,* in which he is starred. Of his TV series, the best known is *Eight is Enough.* Another was *WIOU.* He married his former Professional Children's School classmate Patricia Poole, a dancer, and they have raised three sons. Dick remembers being in great awe of Nila (most of us were), as well as learning a lot from her, including an actor's discipline: "Never be late!"

Larry Robinson was another who had been on the show since childhood. At the age of nine he was also playing Harlan, the youngest of the Day family, in *Life with Father,* the second of his nine Broadway plays. He remembers Nila as a gruff but affectionate disciplinarian (he once got a lecture from her when he was twelve for not wearing a necktie). Not until he was 21 and had been on the show for twelve years did he feel he could call her by her first name. When in his teens, Larry created the role of Sammy for Gertrude Berg in the television version of her radio classic *The Goldbergs.* It had almost a six-year run, from 1949 to 1954. Larry remains

---

23. A lip-sync actor records words which have been specially written to match the lip movements of a character on the screen, who is usually speaking a foreign language. Lip-syncing is also used to re-record speeches which have been marred by unwanted noises such as passing airplanes. The film or video is replayed, sentence by sentence, until the performer has achieved perfect synchronization with the whole scene.

a successful New York actor. In the movie *Serpico* he played the Mayor's Press Secretary. He continued to do radio and television voice-over[24] commercials, and during a span of 25 years recorded over 200 books for the American Foundation For The Blind, including one on the history of radio.

Skippy Homeier, born in 1930 in Chicago, was only a Pretender for a short time. At age thirteen he appeared as a Nazi brat in *Tomorrow the World* on Broadway, and left for Hollywood in 1944 to repeat his role on film. He continued to work in the film capital, in such films as *Boys' Ranch* (1946) and adventure stories such as *Halls of Montezuma*.

Donald Buka, a teenager just arrived in New York from Pittsburgh, auditioned for Nila Mack in 1940. She found that he had an interesting character voice, with a slight "edge" to it, and he became a frequent Pretender. Starting in 1945 he was featured in *The Sparrow and the Hawk*, a CBS adventure series about a teenage aviator (Donald) and his uncle, a retired U.S. Air Force Lieutenant Colonel, played first by Michael Fitzmaurice, then by another Pretender, Lamont Johnson. Meanwhile Donald had started to acquire what is now a long list of Broadway, television and film credits. He later became an active director and teacher.

Peter Fernandez, having served his apprenticeship in radio on Madge Tucker's *Coast To Coast On A Bus*, appeared on *Let's Pretend* as a teenager during the Cream of Wheat years, while he was in the third of his seven Broadway plays, *Watch on the Rhine*. He also had the lead in a New York-made film, *City Across the River*. Peter remains busy in radio and television voice-over work, both as actor and director, also producing English-speaking soundtracks for foreign-made films. He was the original voice of Speed Racer in that cartoon series, and still autographs *Speed Racer* books for its fans at memorabilia conventions.

Bob Drew, born in 1936, auditioned for Nila when he was 15 years old. The audition was recorded on acetate. She played it back for him and said, "You're obviously very talented, but your speech is terrible. Come back in a year and let me hear you again." Bob, who grew up in the East Bronx, says he did indeed have a Dead End Kid accent. A year later he had improved his speech, and was on *Let's Pretend* often from then on, as well as many other radio shows. He eventually became a successful spokesman for large industrial firms at conventions and sales meetings.

---

24. "Voice over" is an abbreviation of the term from the film industry, "voice over film." As action takes place on the screen, you are hearing a voice but not seeing its owner.

There were many Pretenders during the 1943-1952 Cream of Wheat period who at one time or another decided that being performers was not going to be part of their futures. Some of them have since become very successful as executives, either in the creative end of show business, or in entirely different enterprises. One child actor briefly on the *Let's Pretend* scene at that time was Robert Evans. He eventually became head of Paramount Pictures, and returned there more recently as a producer. Another was Harlan Stone, who adopted that name professionally when he played Harlan in the Chicago company of *Life with Father*. At age 13 took over the role of Jughead on *Archie Andrews*. He grew up in radio, on the stage and in early television. After the Korean conflict and attaining a B.A. degree he was a successful director and producer at TV stations, and then became a major producer of television commercials. He became good friends with another Pretender, Charles Mullen. After some brief stints as a Pretender Charles took over the title role on *Archie Andrews* in mid-April 1945, and due to the time conflict, it being a mid-day Saturday program, that was the end of his *Let's Pretend* days. After a busy acting career as a young adult, he was in uniform as an Armed Forces Radio Service producer and writer. In 1950 he started to phase out of show business and joined the sales staff of the American Tobacco Company. When he retired 42 years later he was Chairman, CEO and vice-president for American Brands, American Tobacco's parent company. Acting being basically a freelance profession, he agreed with Pretender Eddie Ryan by saying that "actors and salesmen are one and the same."

Lamont Johnson, we called "The Orson Welles of *Let's Pretend*" because of his commanding vocal presence. A rather tall young man with wavy brown hair and deep-set eyes, he became a Pretender in 1943, at age 20, and remained for seven years, with time out for a USO tour of the European war theatre. His voice made him a very good leading man/hero type, but he also had the fun of playing, as he described it, "old trolls, with a scattering of elves, giants and ogres, sometimes mixed in all in the same broadcast." Though Lamont felt somewhat self-conscious when first on *Let's Pretend* because he was a comparative newcomer, as time went on he enjoyed more and more of what he called "a special camaraderie." He had fond memories of Nila Mack. "I loved her on sight," he said later, "particularly when she tried to get tough with her unruly brood, hacking into the (talkback) microphone with her nicotine-bronchitis-tinged basso and doing her best to terrorize us into order, decorum and serious work, when we were all such hellraisers at base." As Lamont could see, Nila's family had indeed grown up.

When Lamont Johnson moved his growing family to the west coast in 1950, his greatest successes were to be as a director, not an actor. From live television in Hollywood he shifted to filmed and taped television, including Gore Vidal's *Lincoln*, for which he won one of his four Directors' Guild awards, "Wallenberg" with Richard Chamberlain, and a later semi-documentary *Crash Landing*. He has also directed 27 important feature films.

* * *

After seventeen years of writing and directing *Let's Pretend* and its predecessor *The Adventures of Helen and Mary*, Nila Mack had grown used to losing good child performers, and replacing them with just as good, or better ones. But she was to find that losing people whom she had grown to depend upon emotionally as well as professionally would be tougher. The loss of Miriam Wolfe, even though it was a gradual departure, was the first.

In April 1947, Marge Morrow, CBS casting director, had introduced Miriam to Fletcher Markle, a young Canadian who had been hired by the network to write, produce and direct a new radio series, *Studio One*. Miriam's first job on it was a brief appearance in *Ah, Wilderness!* From then on she worked steadily with Markle, and graduated to playing leading roles, such as Cathy in *Wuthering Heights*, for which she got a rave review in *Variety*. Markle had previously offered her ingénue leads, but she refused, saying that the character roles she played were more interesting and durable.

After a year, during which she was on the show constantly, *Studio One* became *The Ford Theatre*, and Fletcher Markle moved it to the West Coast, taking with him only three New York actors: Mercedes McCambridge, who was his leading lady and new wife, Bob Dryden, and Miriam.

Until then Miriam had been able to continue on *Let's Pretend*, but now it was obviously impossible. She would later return to the East when *The Ford Theatre* went off the air, but for the time being Miriam Wolfe was a continent's width away, and unavailable in New York. Nila Mack was a loving mother and advisor to us all, besides being our employer, but in return for this she had been expecting, more and more, some degree of

Michael O'Day, Florence Halop, Arthur Anderson, and Patricia Ryan at the microphone. ©CBS, Inc. Used by permission.

control over our lives, especially those of her young actresses, and Miriam found it necessary to rebel, in order to establish her independence as an adult as well as to expand in her career.

There was in this case not much our director could do, except be angry and hurt. But two years later, in the case of Daisy Aldan, things were different. When Daisy left on her first trip to Europe in 1949, she did not realize that the rules of relating to Miss Mack had subtly changed. After she returned, she was puzzled at not having gotten any *Let's Pretend* calls for some time. She finally went and talked to Nila, who told her that she had expected that Daisy would ask permission to take the trip. Daisy apologized. There was a tearful embrace, and her *Let's Pretend* calls resumed. Nila Mack was a person who had a great need to be needed.

In 1949, Nila and the program suffered another loss. Patricia Ryan had been there before Nila was, as Mary in *The Adventures of Helen and Mary*. A rather plain little girl, she had matured into a lovely young woman, and a very good actress. Nila and all of us rejoiced with her as she won the female starring role in *Claudia and David* for General Foods in 1941. She also continued as a busy actress in many other radio shows.

In 1944 Pat was up for a Broadway play. Since she had no stage experience, Ed Marshall helped her write a resume featuring logical roles she might have done in a mythical stock company. (This is a practice not to be recommended for actors—one never knows when casting people may ask embarrassing questions about the mythical theatre, or the other actors the young hopeful is claiming to have worked with.) She got the part, and was featured in "Sleep No More," a three-act farce which opened at the Cort Theatre August 31st. Its chances were doubtful, said *Variety*. Pat was the heart interest, "a rather mild part," added The Bible of Broadway. *Sleep No More* closed after seven performances. So much for Pat's stage career.

Meanwhile, while a volunteer hostess at the Stage Door Canteen, as were several of our *Let's Pretend* actresses, she had met Bob Gibson, a British seaman. Bob was a good-natured fellow, rather short, with heavy eyebrows, blue eyes, and slightly protruding upper teeth. He bore no resemblance to the handsome Prince we Pretenders might have envisioned for Pat, but she loved him and was comfortable with him, and Bob was welcomed by the Pretenders at the studio, and when any of us gathered socially. Pat's mother hated him on sight. They were married in 1948, while Pat continued her busy radio career.

One of the things that endeared Pat Ryan to all of us was her complete openness and lack of guile, combined with a certain dignity and reserve that made her hard to know really well. In earlier years, when we adolescent boys started to exchange dirty jokes, we would never dream of letting Pat, or any of the girls hear them. And Pat refused to share in any of their female gossip sessions.

When Pat returned from her honeymoon, the girls all gathered around eagerly with "Well? Well?" Her answer was based completely on practicality. "Whatever you do, girls," she told them, "don't buy expensive lingerie for your honeymoon. The first thing that happens you take it off, and then what use is it? You don't keep it on that long." And having known

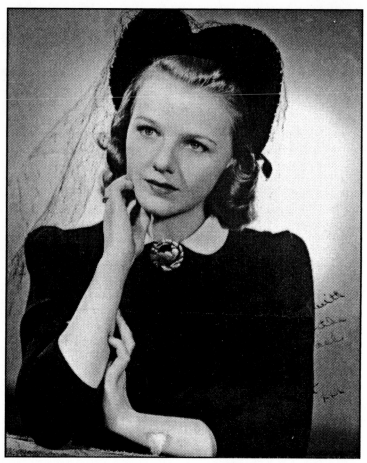

Patricia Ryan, circa 1944.

Pat, I would not be surprised if that bit of financial advice was all she revealed about her honeymoon.

When Pat found that she was pregnant, she became terrified. She came into the control room after the broadcast on February 12, 1949, and said to Nila, "I have something to tell you—just you alone," but she kept hold of Gwen Davies' hand while she said it. In a letter to Miriam Wolfe, who then was in California, Nila wrote, "Then she told me of being pregnant. And she was afraid I'd be mad. She was obviously frightened, and honest enough not to pretend she was in seventh heaven. Gwen (who had just given birth to her first child) was as usual wise beyond her years in saying that the ecstasy of motherhood was a lot of bunk, and it took time to get used to the idea, and many other things that were just what Pat needed to have said at that time, and it was so right that Gwen should be the one to tell her. We parted on a happy note as I thanked her for doing as I'd asked and 'staggered the Stork Derby' until Gwen was back in the cast."

The reader will note that this meant Nila was also timing her actresses' pregnancies so that only one at a time would be out for childbirth.

The following Monday night Pat had an important part on DuPont Chemicals' NBC program *Cavalcade of America*. Glenn Ford was starred, and Pat was playing opposite him. Others in the cast were Arlene Francis, Agnes Young and Barbara Weeks. Ed Marshall was the DuPont BBD&O agency producer.

After dress rehearsal, in NBC's Studio 8-H, there was a supper break before the broadcast, Pat returned from it early. Ed Marshall, who by now was Pat's surrogate uncle, was sitting onstage. She came and put her arms around his neck, unusual for her, and said, "Ed, I'm dying. I feel terrible." She told him she had gone home for supper break—her husband was out—and had a can of cold pork and beans. "That would make anyone feel terrible," said Ed. "Take it easy."

During the broadcast it became apparent that there was something seriously wrong with Pat. Ironically, this *Cavalcade* show was a special Valentine's Day broadcast entitled "Valentine for Sophie," and Pat played the title role—a girl who suffered from blinding headaches. After her biggest scene she staggered from the microphone, stricken with a blinding headache herself. Two of the other actresses filled in during the intervening scenes. Pat had the last line in the show, which was essential. As the cue came she got up to the microphone and said the line, mechanically.

A doctor was finally found, who gave her morphine for the pain, and said she should be taken to the hospital. Ed Marshall got hold of Pat's husband Bob, who insisted that she be taken home instead, which was done. Early the following morning Bob was awakened by the barking and whining of their little dog. Pat had died in the night...When Ed Marshall received the news in his office at BBD&O, he went into the lavatory, sat on the commode in one of the cubicles, and cried and cried.

An autopsy was performed, and the finding was that Patricia Ryan had died of a cerebral hemorrhage. She was 27 years old.

Walter B. Cooke's largest funeral chapel on West 72nd Street was filled the following Friday by the family, the Pretenders (we all contributed for a rose blanket for the casket), broadcast executives, and many other actors Pat had worked with. Her husband had decided that her body would be cremated, and the ashes sent back to England, the place of her birth, to be buried in Derby. It is easy to become maudlin, remembering our lovely blonde Pat lying there—the Sleeping Beauty whom no Prince would ever awaken.

Nila Mack's next loss was not in the *Let's Pretend* family but in her own household. She had now had Mae McNair sharing her apartment for some years. They needed each other's company, but there were frequent quarrels. Mae was not a particularly outgoing person ("I'm sure I don't know why I keep her. I should have turned her out long ago," Nila once told her secretary, Mary Ponterio), and Nila could not always have been easy to live with. In 1951 Mae died, of cancer, and Nila was again alone, with only her cats, and Maud Wilson part of the time, for company.

During the next year two more members dropped out of the solid framework of the *Let's Pretend* structure. First, Brad Barker died of a heart attack on Sept. 29, 1951. He had been a fixture on our program for over nine years, ever since Harry Swan had left New York, and radio. Brad had been more or less taken for granted, but was always there—for a kitten's mew or an elephant's trumpet, and just as creative an actor as any of us who expressed ourselves with words. His replacement was obvious. It had to be Donald Bain.

Donald had been Brad's only real competition in radio. He was not as versatile as Brad, but made up for this by enthusiasm and flamboyance. While Brad had been rather heavy-set, Donald, also in his 60s, was small and wiry. In fact, one radio wit said that he had seen Brad walking down Madison Avenue one day with Donald in his mouth.

Donald was a bit of a ham. When he did our broadcasts he always wore a handkerchief spread out over the top of his bald head to protect it from the sharp edges of the earphones, and rather enjoyed, I think, the bizarre visual effect this created for the studio audience.

It was in 1951 that Albert Aley, busy now as a producer for Rockhill Productions in both radio (*Mark Trail*) and television (*Tom Corbett, Space Cadet* in both media) made the decision that it was no longer suitable, or even humanly possible, for him to also be an actor on *Let's Pretend*. He came to Nila Mack's office one day and told her that he was going to have to resign from the program. Our director had now lost several important, and beloved members of her radio family.

Meanwhile, there was now a Shadow looming larger and larger on her horizon, and on that of every other radio producer. Its name was

Television. In 1948, network radio in this country was enjoying unprecedented popularity, and was bringing in record revenues. But it was also in that year that the first intercity co-axial cables were completed, meaning that network TV was now here, and had unlimited possibilities for expansion and profit.

First Cream of Wheat, then the CBS Network itself came to Nila, asking her to draw up budgets for putting *Let's Pretend* on television. The figure she gave the Cream of Wheat Company was $50,000 per show, and as far as is known, nothing further was heard from them on the subject. Then (exact time uncertain) the network practically ordered her to ready a video version of *Let's Pretend*. Her reply was that the show was unsuitable for TV. "When they show me how you can put a Prince on horseback climbing a glass mountain on the screen, I'll talk to them," she said to Mary Ponterio.

There were several reasons for Nila Mack's reluctance. To begin with, after twenty years, though she had an extensive and varied theatrical background, she was married to radio, and comfortable in the niche she had created for herself, and for the program. The fact that she was not in the best of health was probably of less importance to her.

Miss Mack was also resisting television for a much more personal reason. She was terribly afraid that if our program were televised it would be done by younger, video-wise people, and she would lose control of her show—her child—and with it the family of actors she had grown to love and depend upon. But anyone could see that the broadcast industry was changing, getting ready for the advent of an entirely new medium, and no matter what Nila Mack said, or did, The Shadow was not going to go away.

14

The End—Where Are They Now?

Let's Pretend did its last broadcast for Cream of Wheat on December 6, 1952, and reverted to being a CBS sustaining program. The cereal company had at last given in to what its advertising agency, BBD&O had been recommending for several years, and decided that its advertising money should go elsewhere.

Miss Mack, who had done most of adaptations and original scripts for *Let's Pretend* during our sustaining years, did only a few more during the Cream of Wheat period. They included "Alice in Wonderland" and "Alice Through the Looking-Glass," done on succeeding weeks, April 3 and 10, 1948, for which Maurice Brown wrote delightful musical settings to the poems, "Jason and the Golden Fleece" on November 10 of that year, and "The Song of Hiawatha," done in 1950.

There were a spate of *Let's Pretend* marriages during the later Cream of Wheat years. In 1948 Don Hughes married Ann Cushman, a fellow member of the Professional Children's School Alumni Association, and the next year their son was born. In 1949 Bill Lipton, out of the service and doing very well in radio, married Joan Abbrancati, and they too had a son.

Jack Grimes, who continued not only to be busy in radio but was now commuting to Hollywood for film roles, married Joan Farrell in 1949. When Jack asked Joan's father for her hand in marriage, Mr. Farrell wanted to know how much money he made. Jack, knowing that a non-performer would never understand our unpredictable incomes, quoted the AFRA overtime rehearsal rate, $6 an hour, which at that time was an excellent wage. Hearing that, Joan's father decided not to raise any objections.

Bill Lipton, circa 1946.

It was in 1950 that Betty Jane Tyler married Irwin Karp, who became a prominent copyright attorney, and later authored several books on the subject. They had two children, a daughter and a son. Sybil Trent also married an attorney, French-born Andrew Nieporent, and they later had two sons. Another of our *Let's Pretend* marriages was that of Daisy Aldan, who had become successful as a poet, teacher and lecturer. In 1954, she married a fellow poet, Richard Miller.

In 1952, our last Cream of Wheat year, the BBD&O agency started tinkering with the commercial format of the program. In November, with their sponsorship in its last weeks, and possibly feeling they had nothing to lose by experimenting, they had changed the program's opening by eliminating Gwen and Sybil's singing of the Cream of Wheat jingle, and

The End—Where Are They Now? • 175

the Komzak *Fairy Tale* theme was again being done instrumentally. After Bill Adams' introduction, a quartet now sang a new jingle, the music of which is lost to antiquity, and just as well. The words started with:

> Eat delicious Cream of Wheat,
> The hot fam'ly breakfast treat,
> Whose nourishment and flavor can't be beat...

In 1952, a new announcer, Peter Thomas, now did the commercials, while Bill Adams continued to be the host, and to do the narration. The idea no doubt was to liven up the show by providing a contrasting voice to attract more attention to the commercials. On one of our last commercial broadcasts one of them included the suggestion that you pour chocolate milk on your hot Cream of Wheat. No comment.

Peter Thomas, a slightly-built young fellow originally from Pensacola, Florida, fresh out of military service and new to New York, had auditioned for the agency and gotten the Cream of Wheat spokesman spot. He walked onto the stage of Playhouse 3 for his first Saturday rehearsal in tremendous awe at actually being on the legendary program he had heard as a child. He remembers his feeling of relief as Sybil Trent immediately walked over and said, "Welcome to *Let's Pretend*." Peter had bought for the occasion at Brooks Brothers a rather fuzzy, baggy, uncomfortable woolen suit, which he at once regretted, and a new pair of yellow shoes. "Suit's all right," said Bill Adams, "but get rid of those shoes." (He later relented, saying "Maybe they'll scuff up a bit.") Though no one knows what Nila thought of the new commercial format, she took an interest in Peter, and referred him to a special teacher to improve his speech. Peter remembers immediately being enveloped by a warm feeling of family on the program. It was a good introduction for him to New York radio.

He was for almost five decades very successful as an announcer, narrator and spokesman, both on and off screen. (P.S.: Brooks Brothers was very decent, and took the suit back.)

Meanwhile we continued to receive awards yearly from various organizations as the best children's program on the air. The fan mail continued, too, from children asking for stories, and from parents thanking us for giving their children entertainment and moral values as well.

Casey Allen, who had replaced Ed Marshall as our BBD&O agency producer, later relayed what might be thought of as a "harbinger of change,"

July 29, 1951: Sybil Trent Nieporent, married an hour before, visits Gwen Davies Greenhaus, who has just given birth to her second child. Left to right: Sybil's father, Nila Mack, Andrew Nieporent, Sybil, Miriam Wolfe, Gwen Davies Greenhaus, and Larry Greenhaus. Photo by Morris Jaffe.

not in *Let's Pretend* but in its audience. Nila arrived at the studio one Saturday morning chuckling, and told Casey of a fan letter she had received from a little boy, which said something like, "My mother asked me to write you and say how much we all enjoy your fairy tales every week," and so on. Nila, as always, was touched—until she happened to turn the letter over. In the same childish scrawl, evidently done when his mother left the room, the little boy had added his own P.S., a two-word imprecation starting with the well-known "f" word.

If some of our childhood audiences were becoming a bit cynical, our director herself was not immune. One day in 1952, Nila's secretary Mary Ponterio found in the morning mail almost the exact duplicate of that classic letter of some years before: "Dere Lespertend—please send me Free a Fairy." "How shall I answer this, Nila?" asked Mary. Her response was characteristically quick: "You tell that child to go to the third floor at NBC."

Meanwhile, *Studio One* had switched to television, and was being broadcast from New York. Miriam Wolfe, whose radio *Ford Theatre* engagement had meant a long stay in California, was back in New York, too. In 1952, she was cast as The Virgin Mary in a special *Studio One* Christmas program. Nila had also cast her as Mrs. Santa Claus, the part she had played for years, in our own special "The Night Before Christmas," and Miriam had thought she could do both broadcasts. Then she found that *Studio One* had scheduled both a rehearsal and a costume call on Saturday morning, a direct conflict with our broadcast time, and it was absolutely necessary that she be there. And so, the *Studio One* commitment having already been made, Miriam regretfully had to turn down *Let's Pretend.*

Nila was in a rage; disappointed over her lack of control over the situation she threatened, as she had done before, she would never call Miriam again. It was their worst disagreement, and it was never resolved. On the morning of Tuesday, January 20, 1953, just a few weeks after our last Cream of Wheat broadcast, Gwen Davies called Miriam, and all the rest of us, to say that Nila Mack had been found dead in her apartment of a heart attack. She was 62 years old.

That morning Dorothy Stickney had gotten a phone call from Maud Wilson saying that she could not get into Nila's apartment. Miss Stickney told her to call a locksmith, and that she would be right down (the Lindsays now lived on East 94th Street). Gwen Davies and her mother arrived at about the same time, and they found Nila's body.

None of us were prepared for this shock, although we knew Nila had not been in good health for some time. She had had a hospital stay the previous year, and was no longer able to function at her former pace. Both Jack Grimes and Albert Aley, though he was no longer on the show, would go to the office and help her edit scripts and make casting decisions for the next broadcast, while Mary Ponterio continued to loyally back Nila up, and protect her as much as possible from pressures and conflicts.

It is very likely that Nila, ever since Cream of Wheat had decided not to renew the contract, had been in a state of shock. At any rate, the severe emotional stress (not to mention her years of heavy smoking) must surely have affected her heart. Being a realist, she knew that CBS was not likely to find another sponsor for the show, nor was *Let's Pretend* likely to continue much longer as a sustainer. A sentimental verdict would be that her child was dying, and Nila Mack too died, of a broken heart.

Nila's funeral, which filled Frank Campbell's largest chapel, was a simple affair, but hardly somber. Several old friends spoke on her behalf, and the principal speaker was Howard Lindsay. In closing, he quoted the last lines from the letter of instructions which Nila had left for he and Dorothy Stickney:

> And if at last you should get
> To the Pearly Gate,
> Let me know you're coming,
> And I'll bake a cake!

At Nila's last appearance, she played to a full house, and exited to a laugh.

The Lindsays, as her closest friends, accompanied her casket on the train back to her birthplace, Arkansas City, Kansas, where she is buried next to her mother and father. The marker reads simply:

NILA MAC BRIANT

Nila's assets were valued by the executor at $64,193, leaving a net estate of $60,693 after the payment of her debts, which amounted to $3,500.

Among these debts the executor had listed this item: "$8.24 owed to CBS for Sand." An educated guess would be that, since the network bought the sand in large quantities for the ashtrays which stood near the elevators on each floor at 485 Madison, Nila had probably been in the habit of buying bags from them to use for her cats.

An appraiser's valuation of Nila's personal effects does not indicate a taste for luxury or high living. Her most valuable furniture item was a George Steck baby grand piano and bench, $150. Most furniture items were marked "poor" or "very poor" condition, and valued at $30 apiece, or less. She had a black seal coat with silver blue mink collar and cuffs, worth $300, and a 20-year-old black seal coat they valued at $15.

Nila had left a trust fund of $15,000 to Mae McNair (whose married name had been Mary Wiggin) if living with her at the time of her death, and a lesser sum if no longer living with her, but this was meaningless since Mae had already died. She left $5,000 to Maud Wilson, payable at $1,200 annually. She also left $5,000 to Sandra Levy. Nila had telephoned Gwen Davies as the will was being drawn in October 1951, and told her,

"I am giving you peace of mind." This meant that the $5,000 was to prevent Gwen from worrying about her mother's old age. However, Mrs. Levy had done very well for herself in business since her husband's death, and so she used the $5,000 for a trip to Europe. So much for peace of mind. Any cash remaining in Nila's estate was to be given to The Salvation Army...

An earlier biographer wrote that Nila had left money to her childhood friend Bonnie Nix to care for her handicapped son, but there was no mention of it in Nila's final will. Arkansas City historian Betty Sybrant guesses that she had already turned the money over to Bonnie so that it could be given to the institution where her son resided.

The Lindsays received all of Nila's books and theatrical memorabilia. They were also named as remaindermen to dispose of all her other personal effects, according to a non-binding letter of instructions. Her closest living relatives were first cousins, apparently on her mother's side, whom she had not seen for years. There is no indication of whether any of them wanted or were given anything, but some record does exist of things which went to various Pretenders.

Dorothy Stickney wrote to Sybil Trent on February 14th, after she and her husband had returned from Arkansas City, and had begun the task of getting Nila's personal possessions moved out of her office. Miss Stickney told Sybil that Nila had wanted her to have her little mantel clock, and any costume jewelry she might want. Miriam Wolfe and Gwen Davies received other personal items from our director's possessions. Daisy Aldan was left Nila's collection of chinaware and crystal cats, and a sterling silver pin in the shape of a little angel went to Betty Jane Tyler. Nila Mack's most important heritage, of course, was the *Let's Pretend* program itself, and the scripts, all of which remained the property of the Columbia Broadcasting System.

As "the show must go on" in radio as well as in the theatre, her immediate supervisor at the CBS network, Zack Becker, made sure that it did. Our former *Let's Pretend* production assistant Jean Hight was promoted to full director, and staff writer Johanna Johnston was assigned to take care of the scripts.

The biggest change in the program when it again became sustaining had already taken place. We were back in the studio building on East 52nd Street, in Studio 21, and had been shifted from 11:05 A.M. to 2:30 in the afternoon, Eastern time. Our checks, of course, were smaller, as we were now under the union's Sustaining Program code, and the actors' fee was $43. Under this contract two actors were allowed to double without additional fee, and I was usually one of them, as I had now taken over doing the animal sounds. The Cream of Wheat jingle was replaced by a new one Nila had written for Gwen and Sybil to sing, to the same Komzak *Fairy Tale* music, as follows:

> Hello! Hello! Come on, let's go!
> It's time for LET'S PRETEND!
> The gang's all here, and standing near
> is Uncle Bill, your friend
> The story is exciting
> From start to the end…
> So everyone come join the fun
> Come on and LET'S PRETEND.

Though Cream of Wheat was gone from our lives, the program retained some of the improvements that had been made under their sponsorship. We still had Bill Adams as our storyteller. Maurice Brown remained as conductor and writer of original music. We also retained our hour's rehearsal on Thursday, which meant a much smoother show. One thing we now lacked, which we had never realized we would miss, was the Cream of Wheat commercials. With their quizzes, rhymes and word games, they were lively, and fun for children, even if they did lessen the time available for the story. The commercials were now replaced by public service spots done by CBS staff announcers Jim Campbell or Warren Sweeney, on subjects such as "Don't start forest fires," or "Be careful with electricity," while the show's ending always included a plug for some other CBS radio program. These spots ranged from mildly to deadly dull, and were also depressing because they were a constant reminder that we were no longer sponsored.

Obviously, the biggest change in the program was the loss of Nila Mack. Most of us already knew Jean Hight, who was a veteran CBS production man, having started with station WABC as an announcer in the early 1930s. He came from an old New Jersey family which had founded the town of Hightstown. We all thought Jean was a pleasant enough fellow, but he had one obvious flaw: he was not Nila Mack.

Jean did not have an easy job. He was, after all, stepping into a very large pair of shoes. Each one of us, though we felt Nila's loss keenly, wanted the program, as we knew she would have, to continue to be its excellent self, and so we tried to help him especially when there was a complicated sound effects sequence which was not obvious from the directions in the script. Also, we wanted to continue getting called. Jean, being director, now had full control of casting, and could call whomever he wanted.

Johanna Johnston, the new writer, had more script time available, as we were now restored to being a half-hour program. Also, she did exactly what Nila Mack had done, confronted with Yolanda Langworthy's *Let's Pretend* scripts—she made changes. I was not able to be objective, having been with the program for so long, but to me the scripts now had a slight tinge of dullness. And it did not increase my feeling of good will when the closing credits were changed to: "originated by Nila Mack, and written by Johanna," with no last name. This I suppose was because it was a children's program, and you're supposed to talk down to children, so you only give your first name. I was disgusted. When I gave my name in the cast credits at dress rehearsal one week soon after, I simply said, "Arthur." "What's the matter, Arthur?" asked Jean after the dress. "Don't you have a last name?" I apologized. However, the cutesy "Johanna" was replaced by her full name soon after.

CBS sustained Let's Pretend for a year and nine months after Nila Mack's death. It was still an excellent children's program, but it now lacked adequate publicity exposure, and a stable time period. In 1954 the program was tossed around between several spots on the schedule, which made it harder for listeners to find. Jean Hight kept most of the original Pretenders, but added as well several of his own choices of actors, including Roger Sullivan, Robert Morea, Marian Carr, Cameron Andrews, Ruth Last, Stanley Martin, Hal Studer and Donald Madden. Donald was one of the best of the latter-day Pretenders. He had been highly recommended to Jean by Rita Lloyd. Donald later built an important stage career, playing 114 performances of *Hamlet* for the Phoenix Theatre, an American record. He replaced Kenneth Haigh in *Look Back in Anger* on Broadway in 1959, won a Tony nomination for *Black Comedy* in 1967, and later played Dickinson in the motion picture version of *1776*. He unfortunately died at the age of 49, of cancer, in 1983.

Johanna Johnston, to her credit, created some new adaptations which were good children's radio fare. They included "King Arthur and How He Won the Sword," "Ondine" and "Hans, Who Made the Princess Laugh." No doubt her best, though, was an adaptation of E.B. White's

Charlotte's Web, the story of the generous-hearted spider, done in two parts, which got a rave review from *Variety*.

One indication of the status of New York radio production during the last two years of *Let's Pretend* was that during that time we received our casting calls and our checks from the CBS Television Production Center at 524 West 57th Street. By then 485 Madison Avenue was only a minor part of the growing CBS empire. Bill Paley himself concluded his 1979 autobiography *As It Happened* by writing that running CBS had never been as much fun as it was in those early, great, experimental days.

The radio business had changed with the huge upsurge of television as the glamour kid of American entertainment, and the inevitable happened without much notice. At a Thursday rehearsal of "Jorinda and Joringel" we were informed that that Saturday's broadcast, October 23, 1954, one day before what would have been Nila Mack's 63rd birthday, would be our last. We were now broadcasting in the 2:00-2:30 P.M. (E.S.T.) time period. Football season had arrived, and *Let's Pretend* would interfere with the pigskin play-by-plays. The Let's Pretend Broadcast Log shows that the program had been pre-empted before during its sustaining days for various civic events and speeches. There had also been many a hiatus for football games, and now it was football that finally did us in. Obviously the network could not care less about a program that was not producing revenue and had no prospect of finding another sponsor, but many sponsors would come aboard for bowl games.

Our last broadcast was not one of our happiest or most "up" stories, but it was of course by chance—there had been no time to plan the last show. In the story of "Jorinda and Joringel" the happy couple (Robert Morea and Sybil Trent) announce their engagement, but are warned by their friend David (Michael O'Day) not to let Jorinda suffer the same fate that befell his beloved Robina. It seems that there is a Witch (Daisy Aldan) living in a nearby castle who likes nothing better than to capture unsuspecting maidens and transform them into lovely singing birds.

Jorinda and Joringel, now newly wed, walk through a mysterious forest and come upon a pitiful mewing kitten (that was me) and Jorinda, in spite of her husband's warning, goes into the bushes to pick it up. Once there she is caught by the Witch and transformed into a nightingale (the many bird calls were once more done by Henry Boyd). Joringel then makes it his life's work to rescue his beloved, and destroy the Witch and her power. An old man (my last role on *Let's Pretend*—a character man to the end) advises him of the best way to catch the Witch off guard. Jorinda finally does, thus freeing not only Joringel but all the other maidens from the Witch's spell, while the Witch herself falls from the castle's tower to a well-deserved death:

(Scream, fading off, but no body thump.)

At the end of the broadcast, in the spot where there was usually a teaser for the next week's show, Bill Adams said that CBS had decided for the time being to discontinue *Let's Pretend*, and that this would be our last show. There was an audible "Ohhhh" from the small audience in our upstairs Studio 28. When it was over Gwen Davies, Sybil Trent and I went across Madison Avenue to the Berkshire Hotel for a rather low-key lunch, and a drink. (Mickey O'Day had already left, to catch a train for New Jersey.)

In spite of that "for the time being" in the script, we had no illusions. Not only was this our last *Let's Pretend* broadcast; it was the end of a weekly association which had been a large part of the lives of each of us. More importantly, the program had been broadcast into American homes under that title 1,115 times, for 20 years and seven months. It was a well-beloved institution.

A necessary P.S.: For weeks after *Let's Pretend* was taken off, CBS received letters of protest. And early in 1955 we received, posthumously, two more awards as the best children's program in radio.

* * *

The reader who has followed the life of *Let's Pretend* and its cast thus far may be interested in knowing "Where Are They Now?"

The Columbia Broadcasting System, though not immune from the viewing and listening competition provided by other networks and other media, has continued to be one of the nation's entertainment giants. Long gone from 485 Madison Avenue, its corporate headquarters have since 1965 been in an imposing 38-story building at 51 West 52nd Street, New York. Designed by Eero Saarinen, it is known in the business as Black Rock, as it is sheathed in charcoal grey Canadian granite.

At 485 Madison Avenue there is still broadcasting. What was CBS Studio 7 on the third floor is now the home of WADO, one of New York's Spanish language stations, 1280 on your AM dial, owned by Telemundo. Across the street at the former studio annex, 49 East 52nd Street, there is silence—at least concerning broadcast. As the need for radio studios decreased, Columbia Records started to use the large studios 21 and 22 for recordings. Hit records were made there by Frank Sinatra, Paul Simon and Barbra Streisand. Then the space was used to store CBS business records, and in the glassed-in control rooms where Nila Mack and the other CBS radio directors once threw cues for coast-to-coast broadcasts, there were now typists and file clerks.

In 1988, Number 49 was leased to The Sony Corporation, which again used the large studios for recording, and needed office space as well, but that company vacated the building in 1992, and the following year CBS sold it to the Fischer Brothers real estate firm. The windows from the days of its Vanderbilt ownership have been restored, and it is now a handsome office building. And Studio 21, once the home of *Let's Pretend* for many of our sustaining years, has been made into a discount drug store.

As for the third floor terrace apartment at 55 West 53rd Street, it continued to have a history of its own after Nila Mack's death. In 1964 the then tenant made an arrangement with United Artists to film extensive location scenes on the terrace, by then bordered by an ornate white-painted trellis, for the Jack Lemmon picture *How to Murder Your Wife.* Under the opening titles the camera slowly pans left across the width of the terrace, and you can see quite clearly the Ziegfeld Theatre on 6th Avenue, still standing, and then the steelwork going up for the new CBS building. Seeing this as it was shown on television a few years ago gave me an indescribable feeling of nostalgia, excitement and sadness all at once.

Three years later, on May 1, 1967, the terrace attained another kind of notoriety. Nila's former apartment was now occupied by James Stephens, a pleasant, round-faced young actor 43 years old, and very successful mostly in television voice-overs and radio commercials. After a "Christmas in May" party given for clients of the nearby United Recording Studios, Jim brought an agency producer and two girls over for barbecue and drinks on the terrace. As the party got mellower, the four of them started singing, and swinging in a hammock, one end of which was attached to the trellis, the other end to a spike driven into a narrow, 15-foot-high chimney.

Suddenly, the ancient chimney toppled over from the pulling of the spike on its dried-up masonry. It was capped by a large granite slab, which crashed down on the two men, killing them, while the chimney's bricks fell on and around them. The girls were hysterical but relatively unhurt.

As this is written, the entire north side of that block between St. Thomas Church on Fifth Avenue, all the way to the American Broadcasting corporate headquarters on Sixth Avenue, once sedate brownstone row houses, has been replaced by high-rise office buildings. That includes numbers 45 and 47, once the home of the Rehearsal Club, which inspired the Edna Ferber-George S. Kaufman play, and later film, *Stage Door*, and, one of the last to be replaced, Nila Mack's home at Number 55, but as the steel went up, its outline could still be seen etched on the side of the ABC building.

As for Cream of Wheat, it has for years been part of corporate America, owned by Nabisco Inc. and distributed by Kraft Foods, and its business is still thriving. Besides regular and Enriched Five-Minute Cream of Wheat, there are now many instant varieties, and different flavors, which are microwaveable.

After *Let's Pretend*'s last broadcast, here is what has happened since in the lives of some of the surviving Pretenders:

Gwen Davies continued to do Casper the Friendly Ghost and other cartoon voices, and became very busy in singing commercials, including those for Mission Bell wine, Robert Hall clothes, and the "Sound Off" spots for Chesterfield cigarettes. In television, she had the lead in *The Boys From Boise*, the first original TV musical, done on the DuMont Network.

Gwen's husband Larry became Executive Vice-President of a large industrial firm, and her interest in him and in her three children eventually meant that she had no time for the rat-race of competing for jobs. Gwen has no regrets. A grandmother now, she occupies a big old stone farmhouse in Pennsylvania. She continues to live enthusiastically, and keeps in touch with the surviving Pretenders. Her telephone bill is tremendous.

Don Hughes, having found it impossible during his last years on *Let's Pretend* to make a living either acting or writing in radio to support a wife and child, started a new career in 1948, writing incisive summaries of new tax and other legislation for Commerce Clearing House. When he retired he was one of their most experienced and valued employees.

Don and I remained close, and our friendship was one of the greatest benefits I received from my years on "Let's Pretend." I felt a great loss when he died of emphysema in May 1990.

Albert Aley, aged 35 when *Let's Pretend* went off the air, was already very successful as a writer and producer in New York radio and television. In 1956 he and Elaine moved to California, where he soon sold scripts for

Cheyenne, Have Gun, Will Travel, The Rifleman, Rawhide and *Laramie*, among many others. They shared a private joke that writing all these Westerns was doing pretty well for a young boy who had grown up knowing only the streets of Manhattan.

Afterwards he wrote for Walt Disney Productions, including animal stories for *The Wonderful World of Disney*, and the screenplay for *The Ugly Dachshund*. He then went on to be producer and head writer of *Cimarron Strip*, and became producer of the Raymond Burr series *Ironside*, for which he won two Emmy Award nominations. He then produced *The Paper Chase*, for which he won a third.

During most of his Hollywood career Albert was very active on committees and on the Board of Directors of The Writers' Guild of America West. His special interest was guiding and teaching young writers. His career was cut short by cancer in 1986, when he was 66 years old. Nila would have been proud of Albert's achievements.

Michael O'Day was already in other kinds of work before *Let's Pretend's* demise. Radio acting jobs were drying up, and Mickey, his parents and his sister moved to what had been their summer home at Point Pleasant Beach, New Jersey. He soon had two jobs—as a Social Security representative weekdays and as a radio disc jockey on weekends, both in Asbury Park.

In 1965 Mickey and his parents moved to San Diego, California, where he continued to work for the government. He was offered work in voice-over commercials as well as voice dubbing at the film studios, but, as his sister Joanne explained, "he never wanted to do that kind of work anymore…He never really liked acting. He loved to draw, and art was the only thing he truly liked to do, along with playing the piano. Would have loved to have gone to art school. Never got the opportunity." Mickey, like Don Hughes, was another Pretender who never got to use more than a fraction of his talents. He died of a heart attack in 1982.

Miriam Wolfe was spending less and less time in New York when *Let's Pretend* was cancelled. She now had many contacts in California radio and television, but was not happy with what she found to be its aggressive commercialism. Friends then persuaded her to visit Canada, where 2½-hour dramatic radio shows with full orchestra were still being done. In 1956 she moved there permanently, and was soon working on radio and television in Toronto, some days from 7:00 A.M. until midnight.

In 1957 Miriam met Canadian John Ross. They were married, and moved to France after their son was born. There she developed a method of teaching communication skills with phonetic sound games. When she returned to Canada in 1980, she was by now more interested in teaching and writing than in acting. She wrote a book, *The Sounds of English*, as part of her *Listening to Language* series. She worked with students of the Ontario Gifted Children's Program, and with the Faculty of Medicine at the University of Toronto. Miriam credited her years of work on *Let's Pretend* under the strict tutelage of Nila Mack for her ability to successfully direct her pupils in good speech and group communication.

Miriam outlived her husband, to whom she was happily married, but was herself a victim of cancer in October 2000.

Daisy Aldan by the time of our last broadcast had developed a wide range of literary and artistic interests. While achieving her doctorate at New York University she was also teaching at New York's High School of Art and Design, was founding member of the Tiber Press, and was also starting *Folder*, an avant-garde magazine, which first introduced many later renowned poets and graphic artists. A major poet, she produced seven books of poetry, as well as translations of the works of major European poets. More recently Daisy launched herself into fiction, having written two novellas, *A Golden Story* and *Day of the Wounded Eagle*. Those and *In Passage*, her last book of poetry, were all nominated for Pulitzer awards.

In the 1980s Daisy started creating her own shows, doing readings of her own poetry, or of Shakespearean excerpts, at universities and other places, with another actor and musical accompaniment, or alone—performances that went far beyond the rather dry and analytical approach that academic audiences had learned to expect.

In 1993 she was introduced during an exhibit of her papers, manuscripts and photographs at Yale University's Beinicke Rare Book and Manuscript Library, and when her *Let's Pretend* affiliation was mentioned the entire audience, or at least its older members, spontaneously burst into a rendition of our Cream of Wheat theme song.

By the time of her death in 2001 Daisy Aldan had had a rich and varied career, of which *Let's Pretend* was only a part.

Sybil Trent had been married for three years when *Let's Pretend* went off the air. Meanwhile, she played Countess Marla Darnell, who stole the daughter of *Stella Dallas* shortly before that show went off the air—which she found a refreshing change from the sweet, virtuous parts she had played since the age of five. She played both comedy and dramatic parts on live TV shows, including *The Martha Raye Comedy Hour*, and closed out her acting career doing a Charmin Bathroom Tissue commercial ("Please don't squeeze the Charmin"). The following week she joined Fifi Oscard Associates as a talent agent.

In 1973 Sybil became a casting director at Young & Rubicam, one of the nation's largest advertising agencies, and was with them for 23 years, until that agency like most others eliminated its casting department to use independent casting directors. Sybil's younger son Drew is the owner of the Myriad Restaurant Group, which runs New York's Tribeca Grill, the elegant Montrachet, and Nobu, among others in New York and other cities, while her eldest son Tracy is Director of Marketing, and a partner.

Unable not to keep busy, Sybil in her last years worked at Montrachet, charming guests and handling reservations. As Ruth Reichl wrote in the *New York Times*, "The woman on the phone has the most delicious voice. Just calling for a reservation makes you want to eat at Montrachet." And so almost until her death from cancer in 2000, a tragic loss to her family and many friends, Sybil was still performing on mike.

Arthur Anderson, the undersigned, continued in radio, playing a talking parrot and a cat on "Mr. Jolly's Hotel for Pets" sponsored by Puss n' Boots Cat Food (another cereal maker, the Quaker Oats Company). Then early in 1955 I went into rehearsal for The Phoenix Theatre's production of *The Doctor's Dilemma* directed by another ex-Pretender, Sidney Lumet. I continued actively in live television, in theatre, and did several films in New York, including *The Group, Zelig* and *Green Card.*

Some of my theatre involvement during those years included a year off-Broadway as The Girl's Father in *The Fantasticks* and two years on Broadway in *1776*. Like many actors, I have also lived by doing commercials. For seven years I was Mr. Kuppenheimer, genial spokesman for Kuppenheimer Men's Clothiers. Much more long-lived, though, has been my work for yet another cereal. From 1963 through 1992, 29 years, I was the off-camera cartoon voice of Lucky the Leprechaun for Lucky Charms (General Mills).

In 1963 I married Alice Middleton, former actress, associate director in live television and later a commercials casting director, and we have a grown daughter.

During the last *Let's Pretend* years Jack Grimes, like Albert Aley, had become interested in producing. In 1962, he started doing children's stories for MGM Records, and several of us ex-Pretenders were on them. Jack also formed a film company with Peter Fernandez, and for seven years they produced educational films. In 1972, Jack met Norman Lear in Hollywood, which resulted in his playing Mr. Whitehead the Undertaker in 17 episodes of *All in the Family*. Meanwhile, he had been commuting to California for several years doing roles in feature films, including the murder mystery *Pendulum* with George Peppard, and the later production *Cold Turkey*.

In the 1980s, due to ill health, Jack had to give up acting, but continued his childhood tradition of being responsible for members of his family, and personally cared for his wife's aged father during his last years. Jack's son is president of a New York advertising agency, his older daughter is V.P. of a large publishing company, and his youngest is the mother of three children. Jack, now white-haired and a grandfather, has not lost any of his enthusiasm for his days in radio, and *Let's Pretend*.

By the time World War II was over, Kingsley Colton was no longer interested in acting. He was much too busy completing his B.A. degree at Columbia University. For employment he started in the messenger room at Young & Rubicam Advertising, later switching to Production Assistant on their television shows. In 1951, he terminated his union membership, which took him completely out of the performing field.

Kingsley married in 1951, and he and his wife raised a boy and two girls. Meanwhile he had switched to the business side of TV advertising, then the administrative, meanwhile achieving an M.A. degree in 1969. When he retired in 1987 he was a Vice President and Benefits Administrator at Y & R. The sincerity and honesty that marked his acting on *Let's Pretend* had carried Kingsley to great success in an entirely different world.

Betty Jane Tyler was already into other things by the time of our last broadcast. When her two children were old enough she completed her work for a B.A. degree at Sarah Lawrence College. She had become a writer, and put this skill to work as Public Relations Director at the State University campus at Purchase, New York. Betty's performing days were by no means over, however. Now billed as Elizabeth Karp, in 1970 she started her own Monday-through-Friday radio show on station WGCH, Greenwich, Connecticut, interviewing many theatre celebrities educators, writers and Greenwich residents.

Betty became active as a playwright, joining New York's Ensemble Studio Theatre in 1979. One of her plays done there was *Ten Cents on the Dollar*, a partly autobiographical story about a little girl who becomes a child actress in radio. Betty had to give up her radio show in 1982 when she underwent surgery for cancer, and two years later succumbed to it. As a child actress, and into adulthood and two other careers, Betty Jane Tyler kept the spirit of gaiety, freshness and discovery that was always part of *Let's Pretend*.

After his discharge from the Navy, Bill Lipton went right back to *Let's Pretend* and to many other radio shows, including a part on *Road of Life*. Bill had also become interested in politics. In the 1960 campaign for the Democratic Presidential nomination, he was Stuart Symington's radio and television advisor.

At about this time he was diagnosed with Parkinson's disease, which made continuing as an actor impossible. His wife, who was in advertising, got a job in England, and the Lipton family lived there for five years, during which time Bill became a guinea pig for experimental treatments with L-dopa and other drugs. After returning to this country he and his wife were divorced, and he went to live with his brother and family in Michigan. In 1980, through the efforts of Betty Jane Tyler, he moved to housing for the handicapped in Greenwich, Connecticut, his former hometown. Though this eventually became too difficult for him, he never forgot her loyalty and friendship. In 1984 Bill moved to Portland, Oregon, where his son, now a judge, lives with his family. Bill kept active as a member of the Board of Directors of the Oregon Chapter of the American Parkinson's Disease Association, but eventually died of the disease in 2001.

Bob Readick was a very busy radio actor in the 1940s. Besides frequent *Let's Pretend* appearances, he had running parts on *The Second Mrs. Burton, This is Nora Drake* and later, in 1960, the lead on *Yours Truly, Johnny Dollar* on CBS. Then he, too, began to be plagued by a disability, but of a different nature.

During a rehearsal of *Aunt Jenny's Real Life Stories*, Bob complained that devils were after him. During a broadcast of *Café Istanbul*, on which he had the male lead opposite Marlene Dietrich, he starting throwing microphones on the floor. He received treatment for a mental illness, which Miss Dietrich paid for.

By the mid-1970s Bob was no longer working much. Rolly Bester, an ad agency casting director and a former actress herself, threw some radio commercials his way so that he could earn the minimum necessary to qualify for union medical benefits. She also recommended him to Himan Brown, whom all of us had worked for, who called him for his hour-long *CBS Mystery Theatre*. But this did not last long. He had become too unreliable.

Bob Readick, circa 1944. Courtesy of Anthony Tollin.

In the mid-1980s Bob disappeared several times, once turning himself in to the police and telling them that he was AWOL from the Army base at Fort Dix. It was on May 27, 1985, that his wife received a phone call from Cherry Hill, New Jersey. Bob had been killed there, trying to walk across an eight-lane highway.

* * *

As each of us Let's Pretenders went our separate ways, it is doubtful that any of us ever thought of the contributions we had made to the show. But every one of those I talked with had been touched in a positive way by the character of the program and of the stories we did, and the indelible personality of the woman who directed them.

None of us veteran Pretenders really had anything to feel sad about when the program went off the air. For a period of time ranging from six years for Rita Lloyd to 25 for Gwen Davies, we had had a security that was often lacking in radio—a business where most people were freelancers, and today's broadcast was your last…until some director called you tomorrow.

By the time of *Let's Pretend*'s demise, all of us had found success on other shows, in other media, or in other occupations, and none of us had been dependent for some time on the income from *Let's Pretend*. We had received as much as we gave, and we had had the creative joy of participating in a delightful program, under the loving, if strict, tutelage of a remarkable woman. The radio industry and CBS owed us nothing. In short: We were lucky.

15

After the Station Break:
Where Is Radio Now?

Just as we have followed briefly the lives of some of the Let's Pretenders since the program went off the air, it might also be useful to mention the later life of radio itself.

As *Let's Pretend* was dropped from the CBS roster, so were, one by one, the other dramatic programs on all the networks. Sponsors were not supporting them because listenership was falling off, and that was happening because there was more interesting programming available on television, and less on radio. And that in turn was because the networks were able to convince sponsors to spend their money in the new medium, and were using the large profits they had made in radio to finance the development of television programming, and the studios and equipment it needed. The decline of the Golden Age of Radio thus fed upon itself.

Though the last of the network dramatic programs disappeared from American radio in 1962 (*Yours Truly, Johnny Dollar*, Sept. 30), audio drama and comedy in the 21st century are very much alive. Audiences are now hearing The Theatre of the Imagination in new ways, sometimes from new sources not even conceived of in that Golden Age, and not necessarily broadcast on radio.

The best example of this is audio books and CDs, narrated by their authors, by well-known actors, and some by lesser known performers who have found it a welcome source of income. Others have even been dramatized, with full casts, music and sound effects.

The line between audio recordings and radio broadcasting is now being blurred. Carl Amari, founder of Radio Spirits, is as of this writing producing new aural episodes of *The Twilight Zone*, based on the 1960s video series, in Chicago and Los Angeles, syndicated to 100 U.S. radio stations and also sold retail in Barnes & Noble stores. In New York, Craig Wichman, an actor who has appeared in this series, produces Quicksilver Radio Theatre (email address: QuicksilverRT@aol.com). With director Jay Stern, Quicksilver has since 1995 adapted one-hour classics from authors such as Conan Doyle, Dickens, and Shakespeare.

Though new and original radio shows are no longer broadcast on coast-to-coast networks as in those olden, Golden Days, they are heard on commercial outlets, syndicated by many independent producers, and are carried by radio stations on a shared basis: that is, the producer gets income from its own commercials, and time is reserved for local spots which the station buying the program sells in its own listening area.

New radio creations, including those mentioned above, are also heard "streaming," as it is called, on the Internet, where producers are free to experiment, and new microphone acting talent is being developed. And new program ideas have for years now been tried out on listener-supported public radio and college radio stations, the best known of course being Garrison Keillor's *Prairie Home Companion* on NPR.

Besides the dramatic shows there is still incredible variety in present-day radio, but now each station usually has one single format, and listeners in each area have to roam the dial among many stations to get what they want, as detailed radio program listings are not carried anymore by newspapers. Indeed, many music stations do not have programs—just different personalities presiding in turn over one basic format for all of the broadcast day, which in many cases is 24 hours long. The only important exceptions are major sporting events. As for news and special events, radio still excels. Especially in on-the-spot coverage, radio gets there sooner, is more flexible, and, having only words and not pictures to rely on gives, at least from one point of view, more information than does television.

Radio music formats range from hard rock to classical with many others in between, including easy listening, hip-hop, country western, etc. There are also religious, multi-ethnic, all-news and all-talk stations. There was even at one time a station in Fort Myers, Florida, which was all-Christmas—all year.

Radio transmission itself has also changed. Frequency modulation stations started going on the air in 1948. FM means higher fidelity—a boon for music—and no static. Another development was that by 1990 all the long distance telephone lines for network broadcasting had been replaced by satellite. And we now have satellite radio direct to listeners, available by paid subscription. It has its own unique programming, beamed from above, which means that car owners will never hear it fade out when they drive to other areas.

Though radio creativeness obviously has not ceased, there is one interest which has been largely forgotten, at least in American radio—that of children. The fantasy world which pre-teens delight in is now occupied mostly by violent space monsters on television and in toy stores, and so radio's Theatre of the Imagination, which *Let's Pretend* typified for them, is no more.

One more sidelight on radio's transformation: On August 16, 1990, almost 60 years to the day after Nila Mack directed her first broadcast at CBS, that network announced that it had ended its operations at station WCAU-AM, Philadelphia, which had been the first station in William S. Paley's new network. About 35 employees were laid off. The station's talk show and local news format was replaced with "golden oldies" rock-n-roll programming, and its call letters became WOGL-AM.

Radio has re-invented itself, and created a new and quite profitable industry in the television age. Who could have foreseen such complete changes back when radio was king? But then, who could have predicted that man would walk on the moon—that people would have themselves frozen after death, leaving wake-up calls a century later—and no one would have guessed back then that Broadway shows would be mounted, not by David Merrick or even by the Brothers Shubert, but by the father of Mickey Mouse.

16

How Old-Time Radio
Is Heard Today

In spite of the new and creative programming on radio, there are thousands of Americans who remember and long for the excitement of the classic shows of the 1930s, '40s and '50s ("And now, live from New York, here is...!") and there are younger ones who are discovering them for the first time. Interest in nostalgia in this country is thriving, especially Old Time Radio (sometimes abbreviated OTR) nostalgia, and to mention the Kate Smith Fan Club, the Lum n' Abner Fan Club, the Abbott and Costello Fan Club and the International Jack Benny Fan Club is to only scratch the surface.

There are many ways in which those Golden Age programs can be heard today. One of them is a more recent invention—the Internet. Certain websites carry recordings of Golden Age radio, and people can call up on their computers not only pop or classical music, but can also hear *The Shadow, The Lone Ranger* or maybe even *Let's Pretend*.

Many U.S. radio stations regularly broadcast the old programs. It would take many pages to list all of them, and the list would undoubtedly be out of date by the time this book reaches print. Those I will mention can admittedly give only an idea of how ubiquitous are OTR broadcasts on our airwaves.

In New York City Max Schmid presides over two hours of *The Golden Age of Radio* on WBAI (99.5 FM) every Sunday at 7:00 P.M. Sunday nights at midnight station WFUV (90.7 FM) broadcasts an hour of *Radio Classics*. New York is also home of the Museum of Television and Radio, founded by William S. Paley, where listeners can hear hundreds of radio shows on earphones and attend special radio celebrations.

197

Elsewhere in eastern U.S., Washington, D.C. has *The Big Broadcast,* (WAMU, 88.5 FM) on which Ed Walker has presented vintage radio shows since 1964, and WVKR (91.3 FM) in Poughkeepsie, N.Y., has Bill Eberle's *Radio Show Time* on Sundays from 6:00 to 9:00 P.M. He even takes requests. Further upstate, Gary Yoggy talks about and plays those classic dramas and sitcoms at 6:00 P.M. every Sunday on station WCBA-AM, Corning, his 17th year. He also hosts A Visit to the Golden Age of Radio every April for the Elmira Little Theatre, starring a well-known radio personality.

In the Midwest, Chicago is a veritable beehive of OTR activity. Its Museum of Broadcast Communications has a replica of the junk in Fibber McGee's closet included in its wealth of radio material, and in its studio are regular radio re-creations by Chuck Schaden's Those Were The Days Players. Mr. Schaden's four-hour *Those Were The Days* program (WDCB, 90.9 FM) broadcasts radio classics on Saturdays from 1:00 to 5:00 P.M., also heard world-wide on the Internet (www.wdcb.org).

Los Angeles, always a major radio origination point has a branch of the Museum of Television and Radio, which like New York has listening consoles, and special radio events. Old-time radio is also on the air at midnight the first Monday of every month on KPFK-FM, (90.7 FM) where Bobb Lynes and Barbara Sunday have broadcast their *Don't Touch That Dial!* program since 2001, after a 27-year run on KCSN.

For people who are avid to hear again one particular program they have always loved, there are several companies which sell tapes and CDs of old-time radio shows, and have extensive mail order catalogs. The largest of these is Radio Spirits, P.O. Box 3107, Wallingford, CT 06492-1591. Though their printed catalog at present lists only comedy and crime shows, they will also take orders for tapes and CDs of many other Golden Age programs. Prominent among others is The Audio File, P.O. Box 93, Glenview IL 60025, which has its own large catalog of radio classics.

These programs were taken from acetates, recorded for reference by ad agencies, or sometimes by engineers at network member stations for rebroadcast at more convenient times. There were also pressings of transcribed radio programs on 16-inch discs, 15 minutes on a side. While hundreds of radio discs were thrown in trash cans when dramatic shows disappeared, others were saved by people who saw their historic value, and made copies. Their sound quality depends upon their sources, and the care with which they have been reproduced and handled. These recordings are not available in record stores, but only from companies like those mentioned above, and from individuals and dealers who specialize in OTR recordings and other memorabilia.

Though there is no single source of information on old-time radio broadcasts in one place (aficionado Charles Summers wrote recently that that would be like trying to herd a billion kittens), there is the very useful OTR Digest, a free daily publication whose website is www.oldradio.net. Internet users can ask questions and exchange information, and get as deep into this hobby as they would like.

Anyone interested can also join one of the Old-Time Radio enthusiasts' organizations. They publish periodic newsletters, and listings on OTR programs. In the East the largest is Friends of Old-Time Radio (website www.fotr.net). Their bi-monthly newsletter *Hello Again* is $15 per year (Box 4321, Hamden CT 06514.) The newsletter mentions other organizations in many U.S. cities, and gives details on collectors, traders, dealers and books about Old-Time Radio. FOTR holds its yearly convention opposite Newark Liberty Airport in New Jersey in late October. On the West Coast the largest OTR club is SPERDVAC, which stands for Society to Preserve and Encourage Radio Drama, Variety and Comedy (website www.sperdvac.org). First-year membership is $25, *Radiogram* newsletter only, $15, P.O. Box 7177, Van Nuys CA 91409-7177. SPERDVAC also has a members' lending library with hundreds of OTR programs on open reel and cassette tape. SPERDVAC's convention is held in the Los Angeles area in November.

In Seattle, Washington, REPS (Radio Enthusiasts of Puget Sound) also maintains a tape library, holds monthly meetings, and in June of each year recruits radio stars for its three-day Radio Showcase re-creations near the base of the Seattle Space Needle. Their website is www.repsonline.org.

Each organization does its best to get as many members of the original casts of the classic radio shows as possible to stride, or in some cases totter, up to the microphone and re-create actual broadcasts. There are also panel discussions, with guest stars, and dealers' tables. There are similar organizations in Baltimore (Golden Radio Buffs), and an annual OTR and Nostalgia Convention is held in Cincinnati, Ohio in April (email address: haradio@hotmail.com). Massasoit Community College in Brockton, Mass., also has "Radio Classics Live" every May to fund scholarships for its Communications School, and brings radio performers from Boston, New York and Hollywood.

Another source of radio Golden Age performances is do-it-yourself. Many radio devotees have formed clubs, and they re-create the old broadcasts for live audiences, and sometimes on radio stations or websites. One example is Steve Lewis' Gotham Radio Players in New York. Since 1992 they have performed radio classics and more recently, new scripts, with other organizations asking for the rights to reproduce them. With this club and with others, the line between amateur and professional is being blurred, as actors and directors become more skilled and experienced.

All of this should demonstrate that radio, known as The Theatre of the Imagination, fills a need which television cannot. If the writing is good, the mind's eye can see a lot, and the entertainment value of the comedy and drama on radio is beginning to be appreciated by an entirely new generation.

How *Let's Pretend* Is Heard Today

Where does this leave the fans of *Let's Pretend?* They can use the catalogs and dealers mentioned above, many of whom have *Let's Pretend* recordings to sell. Though it went off the air in 1954, such was the interest in and affection for the program that it has reappeared many times since then, and still does, via recordings, and re-creations of various kinds. It is among the many old-time radio shows resurrected, and occasionally broadcast today. There are good recordings of it, bad recordings, and pseudo-recordings. Here are some of the many ways our program has been heard since its last live broadcast:

Probably the best in sound quality, depending upon how they have been treated, are our 78 rpm phonograph albums, recorded in 1946 and 1947, which have become valuable collectors' items. Each story was complete on three ten-inch discs, and, except for the 3½-minute time limitation on each side, was done exactly as we had broadcast it. The story titles, and the Columbia album numbers are as follows:

Jack and the Beanstalk	Album MJ 31
Cinderella	Album MJ 32
Puss in Boots	Album MJ 33
Rumpelstiltskin	Album MJ 40
Sleeping Beauty	Album MJ 45
The Chinese Nightingale	Number unknown

Two of these, "The Chinese Nightingale" B/W "Rumpelstiltskin," were later transferred to a Columbia LP, JL 8502, and it is possible that others were put on LP records, too. For avid searchers, some of these may still be found in flea markets, yard sales, antique stores, or in a neighbor's attic or basement.

An LP pressing of our January 9, 1954, broadcast of "Robin Hood," a year after Nila Mack's death, on the Radiola label, might still be found in dusty corners of some thrift shops. In the cast list Robert Morea's name is misspelled, as is Betty Jane Tyler's name in the caption of the 1948 cover photo. The record's flip side contains excerpts from broadcasts by Smilin' Ed McConnell's Buster Brown Gang, and also a show called *Big Jon and Sparky*. These are for very young children, and are interesting only because they represent the insufferably cute "itty-bitty-kiddie" approach to children's broadcasting which Nila Mack never accepted.

Of greatest entertainment and historical value are recordings of the actual *Let's Pretend* broadcasts which were both written and directed by Nila Mack. The oldest (some do exist) were made in our original sustaining days in 1942. Recordings of our Cream of Wheat broadcasts would be those dated Sept. 25, 1943, through December 6, 1952. Our later sustaining broadcasts were from December 13, 1952, through the last show on October 23, 1954.

Of the *Let's Pretend* broadcast recordings available, the only ones to avoid are those which were re-edited for the Armed Forces Radio Service. Commercials, lead-ins and cast credits have been removed. There is an orchestra playing "Smiles," and a smarmy, patronizing announcer doing the lead-ins. Anyone judging *Let's Pretend* by these tapes might wonder why the show had ever received so much praise. The AFRS tapes can be identified by the fact that the others usually list the date of original broadcast, and these do not.

In 1970 CBS leased the *Let's Pretend* rights to a Canadian firm, which recorded 50 of our stories on the Stereo Dimension label, two on each of 25 LP records, done in Toronto by a cast of Canadian actors.

How to describe them? First, I must admit a built-in prejudice born of long association with the original. These actors are not bad—the whole result is simply rather bland. There is an Uncle Ted, who does not sound at all avuncular, and children who discuss how shall we go to the Land of Let's Pretend, but they sound rather uninterested in the whole thing. The main interest of these records, to an ex-Pretender at least, is that the scripts seem largely intact, and if the direction, and some of the performances can be discounted, the charm, originality and excitement of Nila Mack's radio adaptations still come through.

If there is anything else to be learned from these records it is something negative: that Nila Mack's impeccable taste, discernment and humor, and her unerring skill at working with child actors, were things which no amount of money paid by the Canadian firm could buy.

Seven of the *Let's Pretend* broadcast recordings, all done after Nila Mack's death, are also available for listening at the Museum of Television and Radio.

The Museum held a *Let's Pretend* reunion October 31, 1995, and 14 of the original cast members were there to tell about our lives on radio and on *Let's Pretend*. They were Arthur Anderson, Vivian Block, Donald Buka, Gwen Davies, Anne Francis, Jack Grimes, Lamont Johnson, Rita Lloyd, Dick Van Patten, Rosemary Rice, Larry Robinson, Arnold Stang, Sybil Trent and Miriam Wolfe. An enthusiastic audience filled the museum's largest auditorium, and their enduring affection for our program and the actors on it was touching. The interlocutor was the actress Anne Meara, never on the show but an enthusiastic listener as a child. The reunion was videotaped and is in the Museum's archives.

The program has been re-created several times by members of the original cast since its disappearance from the airwaves. All of the performances, directed by myself, were at annual conventions of Friends of Old-Time Radio. The first was in October 1980 at the Holiday Inn in Bridgeport, Connecticut, where we did "Cinderella."

Betty Jane Tyler played the lead, Sybil Trent and Gwen Davies were the nasty Sisters, and Rita Lloyd the Stepmother. I played The Prince, a part in which Nila would never have cast me, but this was necessity. All our regular Princes had either died or were unavailable by then.

Three years later FOTR had moved to Holiday Inn North opposite Liberty Airport, Newark, New Jersey. There we did "The Brave Little Tailor, Or Seven At One Blow" with Larry Robinson in the lead, Sybil Trent as the Princess and Donald Buka as the exasperated King. Jackson Beck, a seasoned radio performer but never on *Let's Pretend*, and I played the two Giants. The next *Let's Pretend* re-creation was in 1988 at the same location, where we did "Beauty and the Beast." Beauty was Sybil Trent, I was the mysterious Butler, and The Beast was Don Hughes, by then wracked with coughing and not sure he could get through the performance, the last before his death, and done as a favor to me. He did get through it, and was excellent, as he had always been. Miriam was there to do not a witch, but her old part as The Voice in the Wind.

The amazing, and touching thing about these *Let's Pretend* reunions was that the first took place 26 years, the second 29 years and the third 34 years after our last broadcast, and yet as we sat at a table each time for our read-through rehearsal, it was as if the previous show had been just the week before, so smoothly and almost effortlessly did everything go. It was not as if we had all maintained intimate friendships. Indeed, some of us had not seen or heard from the others once in all that time. But we had been, after all, a radio repertory company, under a director whose feeling of caring for her actors and for her material united us still.

Another *Let's Pretend* re-creation of a different sort took place in January 1990 at the Museum of Television and Radio (then called The Museum of Broadcasting). It was a Saturday workshop for children called Re-Creating Radio, which the museum still continues. The children are given scripts, and they rehearse and perform classic radio programs, playing all the parts, and operating manual sound effects, and each child receives a recording of the performance afterwards. I was asked to come and tell a little about children's programs on radio, and to participate in a performance of "Aladdin and the Wonderful Lamp." I played the evil magician Magi Tapha.

The children, who ranged in age from 8 to 12, took to it enthusiastically, and there were remarkably few stepped-on cues and muffed lines. There were only two microphones on the tiny stage of the auditorium, for both actors and sound effects, and I was reminded that during our radio days there had been a mystique about Microphone Technique—a skill that only old, experienced radio pro's were supposed to know. I came to the conclusion that Microphone Technique could really be expressed in one sentence: Don't forget to stay close enough to the microphone.

The children doing the Aladdin story had a fine time. Though there was little resemblance between them and professional actors, it did not matter. They were participating in a ritual as old as civilization—telling a story. That was part of the fascination of *Let's Pretend*—a good story, for both its actors and its listeners—and telling a story, after all, was how theatre began.

These children's pleasure in what they were doing suggests that, in spite of the latest fads in violence, cruelty and destruction as seen on our screens and heard in our loudspeakers, the beauty and the adventure expressed in older forms of narrative are still attractive to children, and the old-fashioned virtues possessed by their heroes and heroines can still be exciting, without being stuffy.

Some might consider the praise I have given Nila Mack as excessive. After all, many others have been successful in writing for and working with children. She did, however, have a kind of genius, made up of show business savvy, a sense of humor and a genuine respect for values, which she was able to express clearly in the medium of radio. To put it simply: She knew what she was doing. In spite of the enthusiastic fan mail she used to receive from parents as well as from children, Nila could have had no idea then of the influence which her creation would still have today in the minds of those same children who survive, and how strong would be their memories of it. Here are a few examples of that:

While I was working on the first edition of this book *Variety* published a letter of mine, asking anyone who had been on *Let's Pretend* or who had known Nila Mack to please get in touch. Part of my responses were from several *Variety* readers who were not in show business, and had no hard information to add, but who simply wanted to express their own fond memories of the show.

One day in the 1980s Jack Grimes, who was then employed in the Queens, New York District Attorney's office, was conversing with a co-worker, when a woman's voice spoke to him from behind. He turned to find a lady aged in her 70s, who asked hesitantly, "Were you ever on a program called *Let's Pretend*?" Almost three decades had gone by, but Jack's voice had formed an indelible impression in her memory. Besides being a compliment to Jack and to our program, it was also a tribute to radio. There were no pictures to watch. The sound was all, and it stimulated the imagination in a way nothing else could.

More recently Jack received a letter, forwarded by our union, AFTRA (the union's name was changed in 1952 to the American Federation of *Television* and Radio Artists), from a man who had grown up in Philadelphia. He had just recognized Jack's voice when playing a radio buff collector's tape of *Let's Pretend*. "Coming as I did from a working-class background, from 1940s radio I learned to speak well, without the curse of my family's typical Philadelphia accent," he said. He went on to thank Jack for the many hours of radio entertainment he had provided him, both on *Let's Pretend* and on other programs. Nila would have been pleased—especially at the mention of good speech.

While Miriam Wolfe was living in France, a good friend who was a psychotherapist met her on a Paris street one day. "I shouldn't tell you this," she said to Miriam. "I'm supposed to keep everything my patients tell me confidential, but this American lady had her first session with me today," she went on, "and practically her first words were that, as a child, one of the most important influences in her life was a children's program called *Let's Pretend,* and that she was terrified by the actress who played the witches, Miriam Wolfe."

Francis Ford Coppola, the celebrated film director, mentioned in an interview how as a child he had spent long hours confined to a sickbed with polio. He passed the time by reading James Joyce, playing with his puppets, listening to *Let's Pretend* on the radio, and beginning to fantasize stories he might tell—another example of how the classic fairy tales, which after all came from European folklore centuries old, still had the power to stimulate a young imagination in the late 20th century, through the medium of our program.

Sybil Trent one evening visited her son Drew Nieporent's Tribeca Grill. Drew steered his mother to a table where sat Robert DeNiro, another Tribeca owner, Dustin Hoffman and their party. As she was leaving the building, she felt a hand on her shoulder. Dustin Hoffman had run to catch up with her. Someone at the table had apparently told him of her background. "I used to listen to you every Saturday morning on *Let's Pretend!*" he said excitedly. "I grew up in Los Angeles, and every Saturday morning I would be glued to the set." And he continued happily rambling on about how he had enjoyed Sybil, and the program, as a child.

In an old *Saturday Evening Post* cartoon, a wife asks her husband if he by any chance remembers the *Let's Pretend* theme music. And in the Broadway play "6 Rms Riv Vu" a couple who are trapped in a vacant apartment with a missing doorknob pass the time waiting for rescue by singing old radio and television theme songs: *Your Hit Parade, Your Show of Shows* and *Let's Pretend.*

"Long ago, when radio mattered, *Let's Pretend* was a good entertainment for children," wrote Russell Baker, beginning one of his syndicated columns. His subject was not our program, but the fairy tales he felt the first Bush administration was telling the American public at the time.

All of these examples taken together suggest that if the Golden Age of Radio, as it existed in the 1930s, '40s and to some extent the '50s, has become a chapter of our American folklore, then *Let's Pretend* must surely be included as an important page.

* * *

Nila Mack once told an interviewer how as a little girl in Arkansas City, in the garden beside the white house with green shutters, she had tied her mother's apron around her waist for a train, pretending that she was a beautiful princess, and that her audience of geraniums had shown appreciation by nodding their heads in the breeze.

The imagination starting to grow in her then was to bear fruit years later in radio—a medium that had not yet been invented.

Appendix A:
Long-Term Let's Pretenders

	Born	Joined Cast	
Davies, Gwen (originally Estelle Levy)	1922	1929	
Ryan, Patricia (Pat)	1921	1929	Died 1949
Hughes, Donald (Don)	1917	1929	Died 1990
Block, Vivian	1922	1931	Resigned 1944
Aley, Albert	1919	1932	Resigned 1952 Died 1986
O'Day, Michael (Junior/Mickey)	1920	1933	Died 1982
Wolfe, Miriam	1922	1933	Died 2000
Aldan, Daisy	1923	1933	Died 2001
Trent, Sybil	1926	1935	Died 2000
Anderson, Arthur	1922	1936	
Grimes, Jack (Jackie)	1926	1937	
Colton, Kingsley	1924	1937	Resigned 1951
Tyler, Betty Jane (later Elizabeth Karp)	1928	1937	Died 1984
Lipton, Bill (Billy)	1926	1938	Died 2001
Readick, Bob (Bobby)	1926	1939	Died 1985
Lloyd, Rita	1930	1948	

(All were on the program until 1954 unless otherwise noted)

Appendix B:
The Let's Pretenders

Time Periods:

O = Original *Helen and Mary*   (sustaining, 9/29-3/34)
E = Early *Let's Pretend*   (sustaining, 3/34-9/43)
CW = Cream of Wheat   (sponsored, 9/43-12/52)
L = Late, through last bcst.   (sustaining, 12/52-10/54)

Abel, Edmund	E
Adams, Barbara	CW
Adams, William P. (Bill)	E CW L
Aldan, Daisy	E CW L
Alexander, Denise	CW
Alexander, Janie	CW
Aley, Ablert	E CW (& Director)
Altman, Elmer	O E
Altman, Julian	O E
Anderson, Arthur	E CW L (& animal sounds)
Anderson, David	CW
Andrews, Cameron	L
Artist, Michael	E
Ashley, Mary Ellen	CW
Ayers, Jack (Jackie)	CW
Bain, Donald	CW (animal sounds)
Barker, Brad	E CW (animal sounds)
Barker, Ethelmae	CW
Barry, Lloyd	E

Bashner, Lila	O E
Bauer, Charita	E
Baxter, Bonnie	CW (Phyllis Chalzell's daughter)
Bellin, Charles	E
Benkoil, Maury	E
Bishop, Adelaide	E CW
Blakeman, Robert	E
Block, Vivian	E CW (& baby cries)
Blume, Ethel	O E
Boyd, Henry	O E CW L (bird whistler)
Breyer, Bert	E
Bruce, Edwin	CW
Buka, Donald	E CW
Cameron, Marlene	CW
Carney, Art	CW
Carr, Marian	L
Case, Richard	L
Cavell, Maurice (Butch)	CW
Chalzell, Phyllis	E
Chapman, Pattee	E CW
Collins, Lillian	L
Colton, Kingsley	E CW
Cooper, Ben	CW
Cort, Bob	E
Cort, Harvey	CW
Cury, Ivan	CW
Dante, Jean	E
Danton, Ray	CW
Davies, Gwen (Estelle Levy)	O E CW L
Dayton, Jean	E
DeGore, Janet	E
Dengler, Ronnie	CW
Diem, Peggy	CW
Donnelly, Andy	E
Donnelly, Jimmy	E
Donnelly, Tommy	E
Douglas, Susan	CW
Drew, Bob	CW L

Dreyfuss, Michael	CW
Eaton, Evelyn	E
Eaton, Warren	E
Englander, Alec	E
Engler, Elaine	E
Erskine, Marilyn	CW
Etlinger, Dick	E
Evans, Robert	CW
Fallon, Joey	CW L
Fernandez, Peter	CW
Fields, Elvin	E
Flicker, Joan Patsy	CW
Francis, Anne	CW
Gates, Joyce	E
Gayer, Anne-Marie	CW
Gilman, Toni	E
Glass, Mary Ellen	CW
Goodwin, Patricia	E CW
Gordon, Dorothy	E CW
Greenhouse, Martha	E
Grimes, Jack (Jackie)	E CW L(& vocal horse effect)
Hagen, Edna	E
Hale, Diana	L
Halop, Billy	E CW
Halop, Florence	E CW
Homeier, Skip (George)	E CW
Hughes, Donald (Don)	O E CW L
Hughes, Tommy	CW
Ives, Burl	E
Jay, Lester	E
Johnson, Lamont	CW
Jordan, Jack (Jackie)	E
Jouvin, Regina	CW
Juster, Evelyn (Evie)	CW L
Kahn, Lillian	L
Kamen, Milton	E
Kane, Ronald (Ronnie)	L
Kane, Sugar	E

Karen, Barbara	L
Kassel, Arthur	L
Kelk, Jack (Jackie)	E
Kelly, Nancy	E
Last, Ruth	L
Lazar, Joan	CW
Lee, James	L
Lee, Madeline	O E
Lee, Robert (Bobbie)	E
Levy, Estelle (see Davies, Gwen)	
Lipton, Bill (Billy)	E CW L
Liss, Ronald (Ronnie)	E CW
Lloyd, Rita	CW L
Lockser, Judith	CW
Loring, Lynn	L
Lumet, Sydney	E CW
Lydon, James (Jimmy)	E
Lynn, Lorna	E CW
McCallion, James (Jimmy)	E
McGonagle, Robert (Bob)	E
McKee, Margaret	E (bird whistler)
McKenna, Robert	E
Mack, Nila	O E CW
Madden, Donald	L
Martin, Stanley	L
Mauch, Billy	E
Mauch, Bobby	E
Merrill, Howard	O E
Miller, Hope	E
Monks, James	E
Morea, Robert	L
Mullen, Charles (Charlie)	CW
Nelson, Bill	CW
Nye, Louis	CW
Ober, Muriel	E
O'Day, Michael (Junior/Mickey)	E CW L
O'Shea, Patsy	CW
Patterson, Patricia	E

Peardon, Patricia	E
Peterson, Nancy	E
Philson, Betty	E
Porter, Paul Jr.	E
Raphael, Gerrianne	CW
Readick, Robert (Bob)	E CW
Redfield, William (Billy)	E CW
Reed, Lydia	L
Remsen, Bobby	CW
Rice, Rosemary	CW
Robinson, Larry	E CW L
Roe, Raymond	E
Rose, Donald	L
Rose, Teddy	CW
Ross, Arthur	E
Ryan, Eddie	E CW
Ryan, Patricia (Pat)	O E CW
Schneider, Mildred	O E
Shay, Alan	CW
Shepard, Joan	CW
Silber, Roslyn	O E
Silbersher, Marvin	E
Somers, Jimsey	CW
Stang, Arnold	E
Stanton, Ed	CW
Starkman, Molly	CW
Stickney, Dorothy	E
Stone, Harlan (Hal)	CW
Studer, Hal	L
Sullivan, Roger	L
Swan, Harry	O E (& animal sounds)
Sydell, Amy	O E L
Taylor, Charles	L
Tetley, Walter	O E
Tetzel, Joan	E
Thatcher, Lynn	CW L
Thomas, Peter	CW
Thorne, Susan	CW

Trent, Sybil	E CW L (& baby cries)
Twamley, Mack	CW
Tyler, Betty Jane	E CW
Van Patten, Dick	E CW
Van Patten, Joyce	CW
Wallach, George	E
Warren, Nan	E
White, Robert	E
Wigginton, Sandra Ann	L
Wolfe, Miriam	E CW L
Worth, Diane	CW
Total as of 2004:	181

Let's *Pretend* Broadcast Log

by Martin Grams, Jr.
and Derek Tague

AUDIENCE RATINGS

(As reported on May 27, 1937) A.M. Crossley: 3.1
(As reported on December 7, 1937) A.M. Crossley: 4.5
(As reported on December 21, 1937) A.M. Crossley: 3.1
(As reported on January 11, 1938) A.M. Crossley: 4.5
(As reported on May 23, 1939) A.M. Crossley: 2.2
(As reported on September 1939) A.M. Crossley: 3.7
(As reported on December 1939) A.M. Crossley: 3.1
(As reported on January 1940) A.M. Crossley: 3.4
(As reported on January 1941) A.M. Crossley: 4.3
(As reported on February 1941) A.M. Crossley: 4.8
(As reported on July 15, 1941) A.M. Crossley: 4.8
(As reported on March 1942) A.M. Crossley: 6.0
(As reported on November 1943) A.M. Crossley: 6.0
(1944 to 1945 season) C.E. Hooper: 5.7
(1945 to 1946 season) C.E. Hooper: 5.6
(1946 to 1947 season) C.E. Hooper: 6.5
(1947 to 1948 season) C.E. Hooper: 4.1
(As reported on March 15, 1948) A.M. Crossley: 7.9
(1948 to 1949 season) C.E. Hooper: 4.8
(1949 to 1950 season) A.C. Nielsen: 9.9
(1950 to 1951 season) A.C. Nielsen: 8.4

"LET'S PRETEND" BROADCAST TIMES

CBS Network, Eastern Standard, Eastern Daylight or Eastern War Time
October 27, 1928 to August 10, 1929, Saturday morning, 11:30 a.m. – 12 noon
August 17, 1929 to December 7, 1929, Saturday morning, 11:00 a.m. – 11:30 a.m.
December 14, 1929 to October 18, 1930, Saturday afternoon, 12 noon – 12:30 p.m.
December 20, 1930 to October 31, 1931, Saturday morning, 11:00 a.m. – 11:30 a.m.
November 7, 1931 to December 19, 1931, Saturday morning, 10:30 a.m. – 11:00 a.m.
(The December 19, 1931 date is subject to correction, it could be Dec. 12, if not Dec. 5.)
December 26, 1931 to February 20, 1932, Saturday morning, 11:00 a.m. – 11:30 a.m.
February 27, 1932, Saturday morning, 10:30 a.m. – 11:00 a.m.

March 5, 1932 to November 5, 1932, Saturday morning, 11:00 a.m. – 11:30 a.m.
November 12, 1932 to March 18, 1933, Saturday morning, 10:30 a.m. – 11:00 a.m.
March 25, 1933 to December 2, 1933, Saturday morning, 11:00 a.m. – 11:30 a.m.
December 9, 1933 to February 24, 1934, Saturday morning, 10:30 a.m. – 11:00 a.m.
March 3, 1934 to September 29, 1934, Saturday morning, 10:35 a.m. – 11:00 a.m.
October 13, 1934 to October 16, 1937, Saturday morning, 10:30 a.m. – 11:00 a.m.
October 23, 1937, Saturday morning, 10:00 a.m. – 10:30 a.m.
October 30, 1937, Saturday morning, 10:15 a.m. – 10:45 a.m.
November 6, 1937, Saturday morning, 10:45 – 11:00 a.m.   (fifteen minute drama)
November 13, 1937 to January 15, 1938, Saturday morning, 10:30 a.m. – 11:00 a.m.
January 20, 1938 to March 31, 1938, Tuesday and Thursday evenings, 6:00 p.m. – 6:30 p.m.
April 5, 1938 to April 21, 1938, Tuesday and Thursday evenings, 5:00 p.m. – 5:30 p.m.
April 26, 1938 to September 8, 1938, Tuesday and Thursday evenings, 5:30 p.m. – 6:00 p.m.
September 13, 1938 to October 6, 1938, Tuesday and Thursday evenings, 5:00 p.m. – 5:30 p.m.
October 10, 1938 to December 29, 1938, Monday and Thursday evenings, 5:00 p.m. – 5:30 p.m.
January 5, 1939 to April 13, 1939, Monday and Thursday evenings, 5:15 p.m. – 5:45 p.m.
April 22, 1939 to February 3, 1940, Saturday afternoon, 12:30 p.m. – 1:00 p.m.
February 10, 1940, Saturday afternoon, 12:45 p.m. – 1:00 p.m.   *
February 17, 1940 to January 11, 1941, Saturday afternoon, 12:30 p.m. – 1:00 p.m.
January 18, 1941 to April 19, 1941, Saturday afternoon, 1:00 p.m. – 1:30 p.m.
April 26, 1941, Saturday afternoon, 1:05 p.m. – 1:30 p.m.
May 3, 1941 to January 24, 1942, Saturday afternoon, 1:00 p.m. – 1:30 p.m.
February 7, 1942 to April 11, 1942, Saturday morning, 11:30 a.m. – 12 noon
April 18, 1942, Saturday afternoon, 1:00 p.m. – 1:30 p.m.
April 25, 1942 to March 27, 1943, Saturday morning, 11:30 a.m. – 12 noon
April 3, 1943 to December 6, 1952, Saturday morning, 11:05 a.m. – 11:30 a.m.
December 13, 1952 to May 23, 1953, Saturday afternoon, 2:30 p.m. – 3:00 p.m.
May 30, 1953 to October 17, 1953, Saturday morning, 10:30 a.m. – 11:00 a.m.
November 7, 1953 to February 6, 1954, Saturday afternoon, 2:05 p.m. – 2:30 p.m.
February 13, 1954 to June 12. 1954, Saturday afternoon, 2:00 p.m. – 2:30 p.m.
June 19, 1954 to October 23, 1954, Saturday afternoon, 1:35 p.m. – 2:00 p.m.

*   The program of February 10, 1940 was broadcast from 12:45 p.m. to 1:15 p.m. instead of
12:30 p.m. to 1:00 p.m. because of President Roosevelt's speech earlier in the afternoon.

ASSORTED TRIVIA ABOUT THIS BROADCAST LOG

The Adventures of Helen and Mary was the forerunner of *Let's Pretend*. Its first broadcast was
June 29, 1929. For a very brief time during December 1930 and January 1931, the name of the
program became *Land O' Make Believe*. This was no doubt an experiment on Nila Mack's part,
which she decided did not work out.

Nila Mack wrote numerous scripts for other radio programs such as an adaptation of the classic
novel, "Little Women" for the November 16, 1932 broadcast of *The American School of the Air*. She
also wrote scripts for *The Columbia Workshop* including "A Letter from Home" (March 20, 1939),
"The Reluctant Dragon" (April 20, 1941), "Good Morning, Mr. Crumb" (May 17, 1942), and "And
to Think That I Saw it on Mulberry Street" (December 1, 1940), based on the Dr. Seuss book of the
same name. She even played an acting role on the February 29, 1940 broadcast of *The Columbia
Workshop* entitled "The Great Microphone Mystery."

The radio script "Rapunzel" was first dramatized on *The American School of the Air* on January
28, 1931 with an all-adult cast. Afterwards, the same script was performed at least fifteen times for
the *Helen and Mary* and *Let's Pretend* broadcasts.

There is some evidence suggesting the possibility that the April 14, 1932 and January 21, 1933 broadcasts of "Goody Two-Shoes" were dramatized in fifteen-minute time slots instead of thirty-minute time slots.

The broadcast of November 19, 1932 entitled "Junior Meet the Artist" was a special Thanksgiving drama that was dramatized only once. Other holiday dramas, however, were broadcast year after year such as the Christmas classic "The House of the World," initially broadcast on December 23, 1933 and traditionally presented every year for the holiday season.

"The Rusted Knight" (April 20, 1935) was a special Easter broadcast, but eventually "Heavenly Music" became known as the annual Easter story for the series.

The January 18, 1940 broadcast of *The American School of the Air* featured an adaptation of the children's book "The Five Hundred Hats of Bartholomew Cubbins" by Dr. Seuss. Mack's script was dramatized on the August 18, 1940 broadcast of *The Columbia Workshop*. The same script was performed a third time on the September 25, 1948 broadcast of *Let's Pretend*.

The drama "Little Red Riding Hood" was dramatized at least four times, twice on *Helen and Mary* and twice on *Let's Pretend*. The *Helen and Mary* broadcasts (November 28, 1931 and July 1, 1933) were treated like a vaudeville show, presented as a musical comedy. The two *Let's Pretend* broadcasts of the 1950s were played straight with no music.

The broadcast of March 16, 1946 entitled "Old Pipes and the Dryad" was presented only once on *Let's Pretend*. This dramatization was based on the short story by Frank R. Stockton. The November 22, 1947 broadcast of "Rumpelstiltskin" was presented in the form of a reading rather than a drama. The broadcast of April 16, 1949 was originally intended to be "Snowdrop and the Seven Dwarfs" but just before the broadcast (for reasons unknown) it was decided to act out the drama "Heavenly Music" instead.

"Fairer Than a Fairy" was considered the "Halloween" broadcast, always dramatized on the last weekend of October in 1931, 1932, 1937, 1938, 1939, 1947, 1948, 1950, 1951 and 1952. A slightly revised version of this script with many noticeable differences was dramatized for Halloween of 1936 and 1943.

The April 21, 1934 presentation of "Rumpelstiltskin" did not originate from the radio studios at CBS in New York. Instead, it was performed on stage at the Hudson Theatre located at 141 W. 44th street in New York City. The November 7, 1936 broadcast of "The Nuremburg Stove" was performed on stage at the Avon Theater in Decatur, Illinois. The July 12, 1938 broadcast of "Snow Drop and the Seven Dwarfs" originated from the Montefiore Hospital, Bronx, N.Y. The August 8, 1942 broadcast of "Prince Darling" was performed on stage at the Mauch Chunk Opera Playhouse in Jim Thorpe, Pennsylvania.

Every attempt has been made to insure the accurate spelling of the script titles:

"How Six Traveled Thru the World" is the correct title, not "How Six Traveled Through the World."

"Why the Sea is Salt" is the correct title, not "Why the Sea is Salty."

"Childe Roland" is the correct title, not "Child Roland."

"The Magic Carpet of Baghdad" is the correct title, not "The Magic Carpet of Bagdad."

"Puss in Boots" is the correct title, not "Puss 'n' Boots" or "Puss 'n Boots."

Cream of Wheat began sponsoring the program on September 25, 1943. The broadcast of December 6, 1952 marked the end of the Cream of Wheat sponsorship. The program reverts to sustaining. Nila Mack died January 20, 1953. The new CBS director was Mr. Jean Hight. The new writer was Johanna Johnston.

There are a few dates that offer conflicting titles. The broadcast of May 9, 1936, for example, is either "The Bremen Town Musicians" or "King Thrushbeard" but it has not been determined which of the two scripts was broadcast. Throughout the broadcast log you will find entries (like May 9, 1936) where two titles are listed. This does not mean that two scripts were broadcast (that remains an open possibility, one for the East Coast and one for the repeat performance for the West Coast). This only means that we have two titles for the same date and we were unable to determine which script was dramatized on that particular date.

PRE-EMPTIONS

Due to the New York Philharmonic Symphony Society Children's Concert, an almost weekly musical presentation broadcast on Saturday morning, *The Adventures of Helen and Mary* was not broadcast on the following dates: October 25, 1930 – November 8, 1930, November 22, 1930 – December 13, 1930, December 27, 1930, January 3, 1931, January 17, 1931, February 21, 1942 and February 13, 1943.

The broadcast of April 4, 1931 was pre-empted due to the remote description of the arrival of Lord Bessborough, new Governor General of Canada at Halifax. The broadcast of May 30, 1931 was pre-empted due to Memorial Day Services at Washington Cathedral. The broadcast of July 11, 1931 was pre-empted due to a rebroadcast from London, the mass meeting at Royal Albert Hall. The broadcast of July 18, 1931 was pre-empted due to a rebroadcast from London, an address by King George V at the opening of the New Ilford Hospital. The broadcast of October 17, 1931 was pre-empted by a special broadcast of the Yorktown Sesquicentennial with General John J. Pershing as the speaker.

The broadcast of April 30, 1932 was pre-empted due to a pageant depicting Washington's farewell to his officers at Fraunces Tavern. The broadcast of March 4, 1933 was pre-empted due to coverage of Roosevelt's Presidential Inauguration which was featured on all the major networks. The broadcast of September 30, 1933 was pre-empted due to Jewish High Holiday Services broadcast via remote from Carnegie Hall. The broadcast of October 7, 1933 was pre-empted due to a dedication of a memorial to Samuel Gompers in Washington, D.C. The broadcast of October 21, 1933 was pre-empted due to the Conferring of an Honorary Degree of Doctor of Laws to President Roosevelt, and the Inauguration of Dr. Gilbert W. Mead as President of Washington College. The broadcast of November 11, 1933 was pre-empted due to an American Legion Armistice Day Memorial Service.

The broadcast of October 6, 1934 was pre-empted due to coverage of Premier Benito Mussolini addressing the people of Milan on foreign and social policy. This program actually originated "live" from Italy. The broadcast of February 22, 1936 was pre-empted due to President Roosevelt's speech to the nation. The broadcast of April 25, 1936 was pre-empted due to coverage of Professor Stephen P. Duggan at the Meeting of the American Academy of Political and Social Science in Philadelphia. The broadcast of July 4, 1936 was pre-empted due to President Roosevelt's speech to the nation at an Independence Day ceremony.

A musical/variety program was responsible for *Let's Pretend* not being broadcast on July 31, 1937. The broadcast of September 20, 1938 was pre-empted because of a special broadcast featuring President Roosevelt at the Chickamauga celebration at Chattanooga. The broadcast of January 2, 1939 was pre-empted because of a special broadcast entitled "Forecasting 1939: Opinions on the New Year" which was sponsored by King Features, and featured radio news authorities as the guest panelists. The broadcast of June 3, 1939 was pre-empted because of a special discussion broadcast about the aims of National Organizations for Decent Literature. The broadcast of November 11, 1939 was pre-empted because of a special broadcast entitled "The Carnegie Endowment for International Peace Program."

The broadcast of January 31, 1942 was not heard in New York due to a special Red Cross War Fund Campaign Talk hosted by actress Gloria Swanson. The *Let's Pretend* drama of that weekend, "The House in the Wood," was heard over other CBS affiliates in other areas of the country.

Football coverage was responsible for *Let's Pretend* being broadcast at a later time (or in most cases, not broadcast at all) including November 1, 1941, November 29, 1941, October 24, 1953, October 31, 1953, November 14, 1953, and November 21, 1953. The Palm Beach Golf Tournament was the cause for the pre-emption of *Let's Pretend* on May 16, 1953. Wimbledon coverage originating from England was responsible for *Let's Pretend* being pre-empted on July 20, 1935, July 27, 1935 and July 17, 1937.

Let's Pretend was not broadcast on April 14, 1945 due to the recent death of President Roosevelt. Networks and independent stations publicly announced the day before the cancellation of all regularly scheduled programs through Sunday evening, with normal operations not being resumed until

Monday, April 16, 1945. Broadcasts throughout the weekend consisted of news broadcasts, appropriate music, memorial services, eulogies and other special tributes to the late President.

Let's Pretend was not broadcast during much of October and November 1953 due to coverage of football games. The broadcast of November 7, 1953 was not broadcast in certain areas along the East Coast.

The following broadcast dates have no known titles: January 25, 1941, June 14, 1941 and August 30, 1941. Although best attempts have been made to verify what drama was broadcast on these particular days, the following scripts remain the only possibilities: "The Enchanted Frog," "The Castle of Hatred," "The Princess and the Pea" and "The Maiden Without Hands."

RETITLED SCRIPTS

Many of the scripts were retitled throughout the years. This confuses some fans of the program, who occasionally wonder why the same story was given two different titles. "The Winged Princess of Bronze Mountain" was later retitled "The Bronze Mountain." "The Enchanted Stag" was the same as the script entitled "Brother and Sister." The story entitled "Fur Ball," based on the classic fairy tale and on occasion rewritten was blended with the story "Donkey Skin." "Babes in the Wood" was also dramatized under the title "Babes in the Woods." "The Six Swans" is the same as "Fantasy of the Six Swans."

The script entitled "The Fisherman and His Wife" was also dramatized on the *Helen and Mary* and *Let's Pretend* program as "Flounder, Flounder in the Sea" for many broadcasts. "The Ferryman and the Mermaid" is the same story but once again, a different title. All three titles were used during the course of the 20+ years on the air, but it is unclear which broadcast used which title.

The April 14, 1934 and June 22, 1935 broadcasts of *Let's Pretend* were the only two broadcasts on which "The Golden Blackbird" was entitled "The Golden Bud." "The Snake Leaves" was the same script as "The Three Snake Leaves." "The Tinder Box" was blended with "The Blue Light" for some of the later presentations. "The Giant Who Had No Heart" was also dramatized at least eight times during the program's run. For the final dramatization, the broadcast of May 22, 1954, the same script was retitled "The Giant Who Had No Heart In His Body."

The May 15, 1937 and June 28, 1941 broadcasts featured "The Little Black Pot" written by seven-year-old Jean Barhydt, which was only 150 words long. It was naturally followed by a full-length story by Nila Mack, usually "The Princess and the Pea" or "The Little Mermaid."

The broadcast of November 20, 1948 entitled "The Golden Fleece" was the same script later dramatized as "Jason and the Golden Fleece." The June 18, 1949 broadcast of "The Three Terrible Heads" was a rewritten version of "The Bushy Bride." The broadcast of September 11, 1954 entitled "The Song of Roland" was probably the same script as "Childe Roland." Strangely, the broadcast of September 1, 1951 was entitled "Childe Roland to the Dark Tower Came." "The Enchanted Frog" was possibly a rewritten version of "The Stuttering Girl." "The Donkey, The Table and the Stick" was dramatized numerous times, however, the broadcast of October 10, 1953 was entitled slightly differently, "The Table, the Donkey and the Stick."

THE ADVENTURES OF HELEN AND MARY

Written and directed by Yolanda Langworthy. 59 programs were broadcast consecutive Saturday mornings from June 29, 1929 through August 9, 1930. Nila Mack became writer and director beginning with the broadcast of August 16, 1930.

60. "Sinbad the Sailor" (8/16/30)
61. "Gulnare of the Sea" (8/23/30)
62. *No title known* (8/30/30)
63. *No title known* (9/6/30)
64. "Aladdin and His Wonderful Lamp" [part one] (9/13/30)
65. "Aladdin and His Wonderful Lamp" [part two] (9/20/30)

66. "Prince Agib" (9/27/30)
67. "Prince Codadad" (10/4/30)
68. *No title known* (10/11/30)
69. *No title known* (10/18/30)
70. *No title known* (10/25/30)
71. "Palace of Tears" (11/15/30)
72. "Portrait of a Sick Girl" (12/20/30)
73. *No title known* (12/27/30)
74. *No title known* (1/3/31)
75. *No title known* (1/17/31)
76. "The Magic Carpet of Baghdad" (1/24/31)
77. *No title known* (1/31/31)
78. *No title known* (2/7/31)
79. *No title known* (2/14/31)
80. "Prince Darling" (2/21/31)
81. "Puss in Boots" (2/28/31)
82. "The Leprechaun" (3/7/31)
83. "The Goose Girl" (3/14/31)
84. "The Youth Who Learned to Shiver and Shake" (3/21/31)
85. "Graciosa and Percinary" (3/28/31)
86. "Bluebeard" (4/11/31)
87. "Rapunzel" (4/18/31)
88. "Babes in the Wood" (4/25/31)
89. "One Eye, Two Eyes, Three Eyes" (5/2/31)
90. "Dick Whittington and His Cat" (5/9/31)
91. "The Six Swans" (5/16/31)
92. "The Frog Prince" (5/23/31)
93. *No title known* (6/6/31)
94. "Hop O' My Thumb" (6/13/31)
95. *No title known* (6/20/31)
96. "Goldilocks and the Three Bears" (6/27/31)
97. "The Yellow Dwarf" (7/4/31)
98. "The Youth Who Learned to Shiver and Shake" (7/25/31)
99. "Thumbalina" (8/1/31)
100. "Beauty and the Beast" (8/8/31)
101. "Snow Drop and the Seven Dwarfs" (8/15/31)
102. "Cinderella" (8/22/31)
103. "Sleeping Beauty" (8/29/31)
104. "Snow White and Rose Red" (9/5/31)
105. *No title known* (9/12/31)
106. "The Bronze Ring" (9/19/31)
107. "Why the Sea is Salt" (9/26/31)
108. "The Princess and the Pea" (10/3/31)
109. *No title known* (10/10/31)
110. "The Magic Carpet of Baghdad" (10/24/31)
111. "Fairer Than a Fairy" (10/31/31)
112. "Goody Two Shoes" (11/7/31)
113. "The Princess on the Glass Mountain" (11/14/31)
114. "Ali Baba and the Forty Thieves" (11/21/31)
115. "Little Red Riding Hood" (11/28/31)
116. "The Flower Queen's Daughter" (12/5/31)

117. "Hansel and Gretel" (12/12/31)
118. "Portrait of a Sick Girl" (12/19/31)
119. "The Little Tin Soldier" (12/26/31)
120. "The Fisherman and His Wife" (1/2/32)
121. "One Eye, Two Eyes, Three Eyes" (1/9/32)
122. *No title known* (1/16/32)
123. "The Ferryman and the Mermaid" (1/23/32)
124. "The Elves and the Shoemaker" (1/30/32)
125. "The Six Swans" (2/6/32)
126. "Faithful John" (2/13/32)
127. "Cinderella" (2/20/32)
128. *No title known* (2/27/32)
129. "The Palace of Tears" (3/5/32)
130. "The Blue Light" (3/12/32)
131. "The Leprechaun" (3/19/32)
132. "Rumpelstiltskin" / "Babes in the Wood" (3/26/32)
133. "Donkey Skin" (4/2/32)
134. "Bluebeard" (4/9/32)
135. "The Winged Princess of Bronze Mountain" (4/16/32)
136. "King Thrushbeard" (4/23/32)
137. "Jack and the Beanstalk" (5/7/32)
138. "The Twelve Dancing Princesses" (5/14/32)
139. "Goldilocks and the Three Bears" (5/21/32)
140. "Jorinda and Joringel" (5/28/32)
141. "Hop O' My Thumb" (6/4/32)
142. "Beauty and the Beast" (6/11/32)
143. "Snow Drop and the Seven Dwarfs" (6/18/32)
144. "The Three Golden Hairs" (6/25/32)
145. "Brother and Sister" (7/2/32)
146. "The Enchanted Frog" (7/9/32)
147. "Drakestail" (7/16/32)
148. "The Three Feathers" (7/23/32)
149. "Hansel and Gretel" (7/30/32)
150. "Princess Goldenhair and the Wonderful Flower" [part one] (8/6/32)
151. "Princess Goldenhair and the Wonderful Flower" [part two] (8/13/32)
152. "Goldilocks and Prince Charming" (8/20/32)
153. "Snow White and Rose Red" (8/27/32)
154. "The Tinderbox" (9/3/32)
155. *No title known* (9/10/32)
156. "Fur Ball" (9/17/32)
157. "The Youth Who Learned to Shiver and Shake" (9/24/32)
158. "The Bremen Town Musicians" / "East of the Sun, West of the Moon" (10/1/32)
159. "Graciosa and Percinary" (10/8/32)
160. "The Little Mermaid" (10/15/32)
161. "Dick Whittington and His Cat" (10/22/32)
162. "Fairer Than a Fairy" (10/29/32)
163. "The Bushy Bride" (11/5/32)
164. "Puss in Boots" (11/12/32)
165. "Junior Meet the Artist" (11/19/32)
166. "The Flying Trunk" (11/26/32)
167. "Aladdin and His Wonderful Lamp" [part one] (12/3/32)

168. "Aladdin and His Wonderful Lamp" [part two] (12/10/32)
169. "Beauty and the Beast" (12/17/32)
170. "Portrait of a Sick Girl" (12/24/32)
171. "The Princess on the Glass Mountain" (12/31/32)
172. *No title known* (1/7/33)
173. "The White Cat" (1/14/33)
174. "Goody Two Shoes" (1/21/33)
175. "The Fisherman and His Wife" (1/28/33)
176. "The Enchanted Canary" (2/4/33)
177. "One Eye, Two Eyes, Three Eyes" (2/11/33)
178. "Cinderella" (2/18/33)
179. "Faithful John" (2/25/33)
180. *No title known* (3/11/33)
181. "Childe Roland" (3/18/33)
182. "Rumpelstiltskin" (3/25/33)
183. "The Blue Light" (4/1/33)
184. "The Juniper Tree" (4/8/33)
185. "Sleeping Beauty" (4/15/33)
186. "The Bronze Ring" (4/22/33)
187. "The Water of Life" (4/29/33)
188. "Hansel and Gretel" (5/6/33)
189. "Princess Moonbeam" (5/13/33)
190. "The Twelve Months" (5/20/33)
191. "Rapunzel" (5/27/33)
192. "The Goose Girl" (6/3/33)
193. "Snow Drop and the Seven Dwarfs" (6/10/33)
194. "The Yellow Dwarf" (6/17/33)
195. "The Donkey, the Table and the Stick" (6/24/33)
196. "Little Red Riding Hood" (7/1/33)
197. "The Emperor's New Clothes" (7/8/33)
198. "The Twelve Dancing Princesses" (7/15/33)
199. "The Wishing Ring" (7/22/33)
200. "Goldilocks and Prince Charming" (7/29/33)
201. "Rosanella" (8/5/33)
202. "The Ferryman and the Mermaid" (8/12/33)
203. "The Rusted Knight" (8/19/33)
204. "Snow White and Rose Red" (8/26/33)
205. "The Enchanted Frog" (9/2/33)
206. "The Six Swans" (9/9/33)
207. "The Queen Who Couldn't Make Spice Nuts" (9/16/33)
208. "The Riddle" (9/23/33)
209. "The Blue Bird" [part one] (10/14/33)
210. "The Blue Bird" [part two] (10/28/33)
211. "The Blue Bird" [part three] (11/4/33)
212. "The Elves and the Shoemaker" (11/18/33)
213. "Thanksgiving Playlet" (11/25/33)
214. "The Little Mermaid" (12/2/33)
215. "The Crystal Coffin" (12/9/33)
216. "Thumbelina" (12/16/33)
217. "The House of the World" (12/23/33)
218. "Dick Whittington and His Cat" (12/30/33)

219. "The Little Soldier" (1/6/34)
220. *No title known* (1/13/34)
221. "Jorinda and Joringel" (1/20/34)
222. "Ali Baba and the Forty Thieves" (1/27/34)
223. "The Invisible Kingdom" (2/3/34)
224. "Brother and Sister" (2/10/34)
225. "Prince Darling" (2/17/34)
226. "The King of the Golden Mountain" (2/24/34)
227. "The Three Feathers" (3/3/34)
228. "Melilot" (3/10/34)
229. No title known (3/17/34)

TITLE CHANGED TO "LET'S PRETEND"

1. "Cinderella" (3/24/34)
2. "Heavenly Music" (3/31/34)
3. "Beauty and the Beast" (4/7/34)
4. "The Golden Bud" (4/14/34)
5. "Rumpelstiltskin" (4/21/34)
6. "Gigi and The Magic Ring" (4/28/34)
7. "Sleeping Beauty" (5/5/34)
8. "Jack and the Beanstalk" (5/12/34)
9. "East of the Sun, West of the Moon" (5/19/34)
10. "The Flying Trunk" (5/26/34)
11. "Hansel and Gretel" (6/2/34)
12. "The Three Snake Leaves" (6/9/34)
13. "One Eye, Two Eyes, Three Eyes" (6/16/34)
14. "Puss in Boots" (6/23/34)
15. "The Chinese Nightingale" [part one] (6/30/34)
16. "The Chinese Nightingale" [part two] (7/7/34)
17. "Fur Ball" (7/14/34)
18. "Bluebeard" (7/21/34)
19. "The Maiden Without Hands" (7/28/34)
20. "The White Cat" (8/4/34)
21. "The Snow Queen" [part one] (8/11/34)
22. "The Snow Queen" [part two] (8/18/34)
23. "King Thrushbeard" (8/25/34)
24. "Princess Goldenhair and the Wonderful Flower" [part one] (9/1/34)
25. "Princess Goldenhair and the Wonderful Flower" [part two] (9/8/34)
26. "Princess Moonbeam" (9/15/34)
27. "The King of the Golden River" [part one] (9/22/34)
28. "The King of the Golden River" [part two] (9/29/34)
29. "The Fisherman and His Wife" (10/13/34)
30. "The Giant Who Had No Heart" (10/20/34)
31. "Babes in the Woods" (10/27/34)
32. "The Twelve Months" (11/3/34)
33. "The Princess on the Glass Mountain" (11/10/34)
34. "Snow Drop and the Seven Dwarfs" (11/17/34)
35. *No title known* (11/24/34)
36. "The Queen Who Couldn't Make Spice Nuts" (12/1/34)
37. "Aladdin and His Wonderful Lamp" [part one] (12/8/34)
38. "Aladdin and His Wonderful Lamp" [part two] (12/15/34)

39. "House of the World" (12/22/34)
40. "The Emperor's New Clothes" (12/29/34)
41. "Snow White and Rose Red" (1/5/35)
42. "The Winged Princess of Bronze Mountain" (1/12/35)
43. "Cinderella" (1/19/35)
44. "How Six Traveled Thru the World" (1/26/35)
45. "The Little Mermaid" (2/2/35)
46. "Hop O' My Thumb" (2/9/35)
47. "Donkey Skin" (2/16/35)
48. "Childe Roland" (2/23/35)
49. "Why the Sea is Salt" (3/2/35)
50. "The Yellow Dwarf" (3/9/35)
51. "The Tinder Box" (3/16/35)
52. "Beauty and the Beast" (3/23/35)
53. "The Bushy Bride" (3/20/35)
54. "The Juniper Tree" (4/6/35)
55. "Jack and the Beanstalk" (4/13/35)
56. "The Rusted Knight" (4/20/35)
57. "The Silver Knight" (4/27/35)
58. "Hansel and Gretel" (5/4/35)
59. *No title known* (5/11/35)
60. "House in the Wood" (5/18/35)
61. "The Wishing Ring" (5/25/35)
62. "The Castle of Hatred" (6/1/35)
63. "Sleeping Beauty" (6/8/35)
64. "Faithful John" (6/15/35)
65. "The Golden Blackbird" (6/22/35)
66. "One Eye, Two Eyes, Three Eyes" (6/29/35)
67. "Dick Whittington and His Cat" (7/6/35)
68. "Rapunzel" (7/13/35)
69. "The Brave Little Tailor" (8/3/35)
70. "The Twelve Dancing Princesses" (8/10/35)
71. "The Blue Bird" [part one] (8/17/35)
72. "The Blue Bird" [part two] (8/24/35)
73. "The Blue Bird" [part three] (8/31/35)
74. "Rumpelstiltskin" (9/7/35)
75. "The Enchanted Canary" (9/14/35)
76. "The Frog Prince" (9/21/35)
77. "The Goose Girl" (9/28/35)
78. "The Riddle" (10/5/35)
79. "East of the Sun, West of the Moon" (10/12/35)
80. "Brother and Sister" (10/19/35)
81. "The Nuremburg Stove" (10/26/35)
82. "Ali Baba and the Forty Thieves" (11/2/35)
83. "The White Cat" (11/9/35)
84. "Heart of Ice" [part one] (11/16/35)
85. "Heart of Ice" [part two] (11/23/35)
86. "Gigi and The Magic Ring" (11/30/35)
87. *No title known* (12/7/35)
88. "Cinderella" (12/14/35)
89. "House of the World" (12/21/35)

90. "The Queen Who Couldn't Make Spice Nuts" (12/28/35)
91. "Princess Goldenhair and the Wonderful Flower" [part one] (1/4/36)
92. "Princess Goldenhair and the Wonderful Flower" [part two] (1/11/36)
93. "Snow White and Rose Red" (1/18/36)
94. "Bluebeard" (1/25/36)
95. "The Fisherman and His Wife" (2/1/36)
96. "Snow Drop and the Seven Dwarfs" (2/8/36)
97. "Three Golden Hairs" (2/15/36)
98. "The Snow Queen" [part one] (2/29/36)
99. "The Snow Queen" [part two] (3/7/36)
100. "Puss in Boots" (3/14/36)
101. "The Blue Light" (3/21/36)
102. "Jorinda and Joringel" (3/28/36)
103. "The Emperor's New Clothes" (4/4/36)
104. "Heavenly Music" (4/11/36)
105. "The Water of Life" (4/18/36)
106. "The Twelve Months" (5/2/36)
107. "The Bremen Town Musicians" / "King Thrushbeard" (5/9/36)
108. "Aladdin and His Wonderful Lamp" [part one] (5/16/36)
109. "Aladdin and His Wonderful Lamp" [part two] (5/23/36)
110. "The Flower Queen's Daughter" (5/30/36)
111. "The Crystal Coffin" (6/6/36)
112. "The Flying Trunk" (6/13/36)
113. "The Tinder Box" (6/20/36)
114. "Rosanella" (6/27/36)
115. "Douban the Physician" (7/11/36)
116. "How Six Traveled Thru the World" (7/18/36)
117. "The Giant Who Had No Heart" (7/25/36)
118. "The Chinese Nightingale" [part one] (8/1/36)
119. "The Chinese Nightingale" [part two] (8/8/36)
120. "The Invisible Kingdom" (8/15/36)
121. "Beauty and the Beast" (8/22/36)
122. "The King of the Golden River" [part one] (8/29/36)
123. "The King of the Golden River" [part two] (9/5/36)
124. "The Enchanted Frog" (9/12/36)
125. "Babes in the Woods" (9/19/36)
126. "The Yellow Dwarf" (9/26/36)
127. "The Donkey, the Table and the Stick" (10/3/36)
128. "Melilot" (10/10/36)
129. "The Princess on the Glass Mountain" (10/17/36)
130. "Thumbelina" (10/24/36)
131. "Fairer Than a Fairy" (10/31/36)
132. "The Nuremburg Stove" (11/7/36)
133. "The Queen Who Couldn't Make Spice Nuts" (11/14/36)
134. "Sleeping Beauty" (11/21/36)
135. "Faithful John" (11/28/36)
136. "One Eye, Two Eyes, Three Eyes" (12/5/36)
137. "Princess Moonbeam" (12/12/36)
138. "The House of the World" (12/19/36)
139. "Hansel and Gretel" (12/26/36)
140. "King of the Golden Mountain" (1/2/37)

141. "House in the Wood" (1/9/37)
142. "The Juniper Tree" (1/16/37)
143. "The Three Feathers" (1/23/37)
144. "The Bronze Ring" (1/30/37)
145. "The Maiden Without Hands" (2/6/37)
146. "The Brave Little Tailor" (2/13/37)
147. "Rapunzel" (2/20/37)
148. "The White Cat" (2/27/37)
149. "The Six Swans" (3/6/37)
150. *No title known* (3/13/37)
151. "The Twelve Dancing Princesses" (3/20/37)
152. "The Rusted Knight" (3/27/37)
153. "The Golden Blackbird" (4/3/37)
154. "The Goose Girl" (4/10/37)
155. "Jack and the Beanstalk" (4/17/37)
156. "Princess Goldenhair and the Wonderful Flower" [part one] (4/24/37)
157. "Princess Goldenhair and the Wonderful Flower" [part two] (5/1/37)
158. "Why the Sea is Salt" (5/8/37)
159. "The Little Black Pot" (5/15/37)
160. "Cinderella" (5/22/37)
161. "Rumpelstiltskin" (5/29/37)
162. "The Castle of Hatred" (6/5/37)
163. "Fur Ball" (6/12/37)
164. "East of the Sun, West of the Moon" (6/19/37)
165. "Goldilocks and Prince Charming" (6/26/37)
166. "Brother and Sister" (7/3/37)
167. "The Blue Light" (7/10/37)
168. "The Bushy Bride" (7/24/37)
169. "The Enchanted Canary" / "Hop O' My Thumb" (8/14/37)
170. "Aladdin and His Wonderful Lamp" [part one] (8/21/37)
171. "Aladdin and His Wonderful Lamp" [part two] (8/28/37)
172. "Snow Drop and the Seven Dwarfs" (9/4/37)
173. "The Three Golden Hairs" (9/11/37)
174. "The Fisherman and His Wife" (9/18/37)
175. "Jorinda and Joringel" (9/25/37)
176. "Ali Baba and the Forty Thieves" (10/2/37)
177. "The Emperor's New Clothes" (10/9/37)
178. "Beauty and the Beast" (10/16/37)
179. *No title known* (10/23/37)
180. "Fairer Than a Fairy" (10/30/37)
181. *No title known* (11/6/37)
182. "The Giant Who Had No Heart" (11/13/37)
183. "Princess Moonbeam" (11/20/37)
184. "Sleeping Beauty" (11/27/37)
185. "The Water of Life" (12/4/37)
186. "The Bremen Town Musicians" (12/11/37)
187. "Snow White and Rose Red" (12/18/37)
188. "The House of the World" (12/25/37)
189. "The Nuremburg Stove" (1/1/38)
190. "The Tinder Box" (1/8/38)
191. "Gigi and The Magic Ring" (1/15/38)

192. "King Thrushbeard" (1/20/38)
193. "The Enchanted Frog" (1/25/38)
194. "The Invisible Kingdom" (1/27/38)
195. "The Twelve Months" (2/1/38)
196. "Dick Whittington and His Cat" (2/3/38)
197. "Gigi and the Magic Ring" (2/8/38)
198. "Hansel and Gretel" (2/10/38)
199. "Faithful John" (2/15/38)
200. "The Queen Who Couldn't Make Spice Nuts" (2/17/38)
201. "Snow Drop and the Seven Dwarfs" (2/22/38)
202. "The Riddle" (2/24/38)
203. "How Six Traveled Thru the World" (3/1/38)
204. "Rapunzel" (3/3/38)
205. "The Yellow Dwarf" (3/8/38)
206. "Beauty and the Beast" (3/10/38)
207. *No title known* (3/15/38)
208. "The Leprechaun" (3/17/38)
209. "The Snow Queen" [part one] (3/22/38)
210. "The Snow Queen" [part two] (3/24/38)
211. "The Donkey, the Table and the Stick" (3/29/38)
212. "Thumbelina" (3/31/38)
213. "Rosanella" (4/5/38)
214. "The Six Swans" (4/7/38)
215. "Childe Roland" (4/12/38)
216. "Heavenly Music" (4/14/38)
217. "The Flying Trunk" (4/19/38)
218. "Bluebeard" (4/21/38)
219. "The White Cat" (4/26/38)
220. "Jack and the Beanstalk" (4/28/38)
221. "East of the Sun, West of the Moon" (5/3/38)
222. "Melilot" (5/5/38)
223. "The Rusted Knight" (5/10/38)
224. "The Goose Girl" (5/12/38)
225. "The Little Mermaid" (5/17/38)
226. "Cinderella" (5/19/38)
227. "Rumpelstiltskin" (5/24/38)
228. "The Twelve Dancing Princesses" (5/26/38)
229. "The Maiden Without Hands" / "The Wishing Ring" (5/31/38)
230. "The Maiden Without Hands" / "The Wishing Ring" (6/2/38)
231. "The Winged Princess of Bronze Mountain" (6/7/38)
232. "The Crystal Coffin" (6/9/38)
233. "The Chinese Nightingale" [part one] (6/14/38)
234. "The Chinese Nightingale" [part two] (6/16/38)
235. "Donkey Skin" (6/21/38)
236. "Prince Darling" (6/23/38)
237. "The Juniper Tree" (6/28/38)
238. "The Emperor's New Clothes" (6/30/38)
239. "Goldilocks and Prince Charming" (7/5/38)
240. "The Golden Blackbird" (7/7/38)
241. "Snow Drop and the Seven Dwarfs" (7/12/38)
242. "Why the Sea is Salt" (7/14/38)

243. "Princess Goldenhair and the Wonderful Flower" [part one] (7/19/38)
244. "Princess Goldenhair and the Wonderful Flower" [part two] (7/21/38)
245. "King of the Golden Mountain" (7/26/38)
246. "The Flower Queen's Daughter" (7/28/38)
247. "Brother and Sister" (8/2/38)
248. "The Brave Little Tailor" (8/4/38)
249. "The Blue Light" (8/9/38)
250. "The Bushy Bride" (8/11/38)
251. "The Castle of Hatred" (8/16/38)
252. "The Enchanted Canary" (8/18/38)
253. "Heart of Ice" [part one] (8/23/38)
254. "Heart of Ice" [part two] (8/25/38)
255. *No title known* (8/30/38)
256. "Snow White and Rose Red" (9/1/38)
257. "The Three Feathers" (9/6/38)
258. "Babes in the Woods" (9/8/38)
259. "Aladdin and His Wonderful Lamp" [part one] (9/13/38)
260. "Aladdin and His Wonderful Lamp" [part two] (9/15/38)
261. "Three Golden Hairs" (9/22/38)
262. *No title known* (9/27/38)
263. "Ali Baba and the Forty Thieves" (9/29/38)
264. "Fur Ball" (10/4/38)
265. "The Fisherman and His Wife" (10/6/38)
266. "Drakestail" (10/10/38)
267. "The Giant Who Had No Heart" (10/13/38)
268. "Jorinda and Joringel" (10/17/38)
269. "The Magic Horse" (10/20/38)
270. "Hop O' My Thumb" (10/24/38)
271. "The Bronze Ring" (10/27/38)
272. "Fairer Than a Fairy" (10/31/38)
273. "Sleeping Beauty" (11/3/38)
274. "The Frog Prince" (11/7/38)
275. "Douban, the Physician" (11/10/38)
276. "The Enchanted Toystore of Fairyland" [part one] (11/14/38)
277. "The Enchanted Toystore of Fairyland" [part two] (11/17/38)
278. "One Eye, Two Eyes, Three Eyes" (11/21/38)
279. "Princess Moonbeam" (11/24/38)
280. "The Water of Life" (11/28/38)
281. "The Magic Carpet of Baghdad" (12/1/38)
282. *No title known* (12/5/38)
283. "House in the Wood" / "The Snake Leaves" (12/8/38)
284. *No title known* (12/12/38)
285. "Dog of Flanders" (12/15/38)
286. "The Nuremburg Stove" (12/19/38)
287. "The House of the World" (12/22/38)
288. "Cinderella" (12/26/38)
289. "The Elves and the Shoemaker" (12/29/38)
290. "Palace of Tears" (1/5/39)
291. "The Tinder Box" (1/9/39)
292. "Hansel and Gretel" (1/12/39)
293. "Gigi and The Magic Ring" (1/16/39)

294. "The Enchanted Frog" (1/19/39)
295. *No title known* (1/23/39)
296. "King Thrushbeard" (1/26/39)
297. "The Twelve Months" (1/30/39)
298. "Gigi and the Magic Ring" (2/2/39)
299. "Dick Whittington and His Cat" (2/6/39)
300. "The Invisible Kingdom" (2/9/39)
301. "The Queen Who Couldn't Make Spice Nuts" (2/13/39)
302. "The Riddle" (2/16/39)
303. "How Six Traveled Thru the World" (2/20/39)
304. "Faithful John" (2/23/39)
305. "Rapunzel" (2/27/39)
306. "The Bremen Town Musicians" (3/2/39)
307. "Thumbalina" (3/6/39)
308. "Beauty and the Beast" (3/9/39)
309. "The White Cat" (3/13/39)
310. "The Leprechaun" (3/16/39)
311. "The Snow Queen" [part one] (3/20/39)
312. "The Snow Queen" [part two] (3/23/39)
313. "Rumpelstiltskin" (3/27/39)
314. "Snow Drop and the Seven Dwarfs" (3/30/39)
315. "The Donkey, the Table and the Stick" (4/3/39)
316. "Heavenly Music" (4/6/39)
317. "Rosanella" (4/10/39)
318. *No title known* (4/13/39)
319. "Jack and the Beanstalk" (4/22/39)
320. "Childe Roland" (4/29/39)
321. "The Flying Trunk" (5/6/39)
322. "The Castle of Hatred" (5/13/39)
323. "East of the Sun, West of the Moon" (5/20/39)
324. "The Yellow Dwarf" (5/27/39)
325. "Melilot" (6/10/39)
326. "The Rusted Knight" (6/17/39)
327. "The Fisherman and His Wife" (6/24/39)
328. "The Goose Girl" (7/1/39)
329. "The Golden Touch" (7/8/39)
330. "The Emperor's New Clothes" (7/15/39)
331. "The Juniper Tree" (7/22/39)
332. "Puss in Boots" (7/29/39)
333. "The Twelve Dancing Princesses" (8/5/39)
334. "The Maiden Without Hands" (8/12/39)
335. "Prince Darling" (8/19/39)
336. "Bluebeard" (8/26/39)
337. "Cinderella" (9/2/39)
338. "Brother and Sister" (9/9/39)
339. "Snow Drop and the Seven Dwarfs" (9/16/39)
340. "The Little Mermaid" (9/23/39)
341. "The Brave Little Tailor" (9/30/39)
342. "The Flower Queen's Daughter" (10/7/39)
343. "Ali Baba and the Forty Thieves" (10/14/39)
344. "Snow White and Rose Red" (10/21/39)

345. "Fairer Than a Fairy" (10/28/39)
346. "The Three Feathers" (11/4/39)
347. "The Winged Princess of Bronze Mountain" (11/18/39)
348. "The Crystal Coffin" (11/25/39)
349. "Sleeping Beauty" (12/2/39)
350. "Why the Sea is Salt" (12/9/39)
351. "The Nuremburg Stove" (12/16/39)
352. "The House of the World" (12/23/39)
353. "The Twelve Months" (12/30/39)
354. "Hansel and Gretel" / "One Eye, Two Eyes, Three Eyes" (1/6/40)
355. "The Blue Light" (1/13/40)
356. "Three Golden Hairs" (1/20/40)
357. "Rapunzel" (1/27/40)
358. "The Flying Trunk" (2/3/40)
359. "Drakestail" (2/10/40)
360. "The Chinese Nightingale" (2/17/40)
361. "Goldilocks and Prince Charming" (2/24/40)
362. "The Bushy Bride" (3/2/40)
363. "Dick Whittington and His Cat" (3/9/40)
364. "The Three Feathers" (3/16/40)
365. "Heavenly Music" (3/23/40)
366. "The Princess and the Pea" (3/30/40)
367. "The Enchanted Canary" (4/6/40)
368. "Donkey Skin" (4/13/40)
369. "The Queen Who Couldn't Make Spice Nuts" (4/20/40)
370. "The Castle of Hatred" (4/27/40)
371. "Thumbelina" (5/4/40)
372. "The Invisible Kingdom" (5/11/40)
373. "Hop O' My Thumb" (5/18/40)
374. "The Enchanted Frog" (5/25/40)
375. "East of the Sun, West of the Moon" (6/1/40)
376. "The Bremen Town Musicians" (6/8/40)
377. "Jorinda and Joringel" (6/15/40)
378. "Rumpelstiltskin" (6/22/40)
379. "The House in the Wood" (6/29/40)
380. "Jack and the Beanstalk" (7/6/40)
381. "The Water of Life" (7/13/40)
382. "The Tinder Box" (7/20/40)
383. "Beauty and the Beast" (7/27/40)
384. "The Wishing Ring" (8/3/40)
385. "The Giant Who Had No Heart" (8/10/40)
386. "The Frog Prince" (8/17/40)
387. "Snow Drop and the Seven Dwarfs" (8/24/40)
388. "The White Cat" (8/31/40)
389. "Gigi and the Magic Ring" (9/7/40)
390. "The Donkey, the Table and the Stick" (9/14/40)
391. "The Bronze Ring" (9/21/40)
392. "Cinderella" (9/28/40)
393. "King Thrushbeard" (10/5/40)
394. "The Riddle" (10/12/40)
395. "The Six Swans" (10/19/40)

396. "Puss in Boots" (10/26/40)
397. "The Goose Girl" (11/2/40)
398. "Princess Moonbeam" (11/9/40)
399. "The Brave Little Tailor" (11/16/40)
400. "Childe Roland" (11/23/40)
401. "The Twelve Dancing Princesses" (11/30/40)
402. "The Elves and the Shoemaker" (12/7/40)
403. "The Emperor's New Clothes" (12/14/40)
404. "The House of the World" (12/21/40)
405. "Snow White and Rose Red" (12/28/40)
406. "How Six Traveled Thru the World" (1/4/41)
407. "The Yellow Dwarf" (1/11/41)
408. "The Flying Trunk" (1/18/41)
409. *No title known* (1/25/41)
410. "Sleeping Beauty" (2/1/41)
411. "The Three Feathers" (2/8/41)
412. "Rosanella" (2/15/41)
413. "The Fisherman and His Wife" (2/22/41)
414. "Melilot" (3/1/41)
415. "Prince Darling" (3/8/41)
416. "The Leprechaun" (3/15/41)
417. "The Little Mermaid" (3/22/41)
418. "Why the Sea is Salt" (3/29/41)
419. "The Golden Blackbird" (4/5/41)
420. "Heavenly Music" (4/12/41)
421. "The Juniper Tree" (4/19/41)
422. "Beauty and the Beast" (4/26/41)
423. "Brother and Sister" (5/3/41)
424. "Three Golden Hairs" (5/10/41)
425. "Gigi and The Magic Ring" (5/17/41)
426. "The Chinese Nightingale" (5/24/41)
427. "The Flower Queen's Daughter" (5/31/41)
428. "Ali Baba and the Forty Thieves" (6/7/41)
429. *No title known* (6/14/41)
430. "Fur Ball" (6/21/41)
431. "The Little Black Pot" (6/28/41)
432. "Drakestail" (7/5/41)
433. "The Golden Touch" (7/12/41)
434. "The Invisible Kingdom" (7/19/41)
435. "King of the Golden Mountain" (7/26/41)
436. "Hansel and Gretel" (8/2/41)
437. "Puss in Boots" (8/9/41)
438. "The Enchanted Canary" (8/16/41)
439. "Rumpelstiltskin" (8/23/41)
440. *No title known* (8/30/41)
441. "One Eye, Two Eyes, Three Eyes" (9/6/41)
442. "The Castle of Hatred" / "Faithful John" (9/13/41)
443. "The Tinder Box" (9/20/41)
444. "Goldilocks and Prince Charming" (9/27/41)
445. "Jack and the Beanstalk" (10/4/41)
446. "The Winged Princess of Bronze Mountain" (10/11/41)

447. "The Bremen Town Musicians" (10/18/41)
448. "Rapunzel" (10/25/41)
449. "Donkey Skin" (11/8/41)
450. "The Queen Who Couldn't Make Spice Nuts" (11/15/41)
451. "Princess Moonbeam" (11/22/41)
452. "The Bushy Bride" (11/29/41)
453. "Dick Whittington and His Cat" (12/6/41)
454. "Jorinda and Joringel" (12/13/41)
455. "The House of the World" (12/20/41)
456. "The Nuremburg Stove" (12/27/41)
457. "The Goose Girl" (1/3/42)
458. "Hop O' My Thumb" (1/10/42)
459. "Snow Drop and the Seven Dwarfs" (1/17/42)
460. "The Little Lame Prince" (1/24/42)
461. "The House in the Wood" (1/31/42)
462. "Cinderella" (2/7/42)
463. "The Brave Little Tailor" (2/14/42)
464. "King Thrushbeard" (2/28/42)
465. "Snow White and Rose Red" (3/7/42)
466. "The Leprechaun" (3/14/42)
467. "The Giant Who Had No Heart (3/21/42)
468. "The Three Feathers" (3/28/42)
469. "The Emperor's New Clothes" (4/4/42)
470. "Childe Roland" (4/11/42)
471. "The Twelve Dancing Princesses" (4/18/42)
472. "The Twelve Months" (4/25/42)
473. "The Rusted Knight" (5/2/42)
474. "Gigi and the Magic Ring" (5/9/42)
475. "The Bronze Ring" (5/16/42)
476. "East of the Sun, West of the Moon" (5/23/42)
477. "The Flying Trunk" (5/30/42)
478. "The Riddle" (6/6/42)
479. "The Donkey, the Table and the Stick" (6/13/42)
480. "Rosanella" (6/20/42)
481. "Beauty and the Beast" (6/27/42)
482. "The Three Snake Leaves" (7/4/42)
483. "Thumbelina" (7/11/42)
484. "The Wishing Ring" (7/18/42)
485. "How Six Traveled Thru the World" (7/25/42)
486. "Sleeping Beauty" (8/1/42)
487. "Prince Darling" (8/8/42)
488. "Three Golden Hairs" (8/15/42)
489. "Why the Sea is Salt" (8/22/42)
490. "The Little Mermaid" (8/29/42)
491. "The Elves and the Shoemaker" (9/5/42)
492. "The Water of Life" (9/12/42)
493. "Gigi and The Magic Ring" (9/19/42)
494. "The Flower Queen's Daughter" (9/26/42)
495. "The Crystal Coffin" (10/3/42)
496. "The Chinese Nightingale" (10/10/42)
497. "The Blue Light" (10/17/42)

498. "Brother and Sister" (10/24/42)
499. "The Fisherman and His Wife" (11/7/42)
500. "The Juniper Tree" (11/14/42)
501. "Rumpelstiltskin" (11/21/42)
502. "Ali Baba and the Forty Thieves" (11/28/42)
503. "Fur Ball" (12/5/42)
504. "Princess Moonbeam" (12/12/42)
505. "Gigi and The Magic Ring" (12/19/42)
506. "The House of the World" (12/26/42)
507. "One Eye, Two Eyes, Three Eyes" (1/2/43)
508. "The Queen Who Couldn't Make Spice Nuts" (1/9/43)
509. "The Twelve Months" (1/16/43)
510. "The Golden Touch" (1/23/43)
511. "The Little Lame Prince" (1/30/43)
512. "Drakestail" (2/6/43)
513. "The Six Swans" (2/20/43)
514. "The Castle of Hatred" (2/27/43)
515. "The Enchanted Frog" (3/6/43)
516. "The Invisible Kingdom" (3/13/43)
517. "Princess Moonbeam" (3/20/43)
518. "Rapunzel" (3/27/43)
519. "Dick Whittington and His Cat" (4/3/43)
520. "The Enchanted Canary" (4/10/43)
521. "Jack and the Beanstalk" (4/17/43)
522. "The Rusted Knight" (4/24/43)
523. "Faithful John" (5/1/43)
524. "Hansel and Gretel" (5/8/43)
525. "Puss in Boots" (5/15/43)
526. "Jorinda and Joringel" (5/22/43)
527. "Goldilocks and Prince Charming" (5/29/43)
528. "The Nuremburg Stove" (6/5/43)
529. "The White Cat" (6/12/43)
530. "The Golden Blackbird" (6/19/43)
531. "The Bushy Bride" (6/26/43)
532. "Snowdrop and the Seven Dwarfs" (7/3/43)
533. "Hop O' My Thumb" (7/10/43)
534. "King Thrushbeard" (7/17/43)
535. "Snow White and Rose Red" (7/24/43)
536. "The Brave Little Tailor" (7/31/43)
537. "The Maiden Without Hands" (8/7/43)
538. "Babes in the Wood" (8/14/43)
539. "The Twelve Dancing Princesses" (8/21/43)
540. "Bluebeard" (8/28/43)
541. "The Flying Trunk" (9/4/43)
542. "Melilot" (9/11/43)
543. "The Winged Princess of Bronze Mountain" (9/18/43)
544. "Cinderella" (9/25/43)
545. "Childe Roland" (10/2/43)
546. "The Goose Girl" (10/9/43)
547. "The Three Feathers" (10/16/43)
548. "The Emperor's New Clothes" (10/23/43)

549. "Fairer Than a Fairy" (10/30/43)
550. "The Princess and the Pea" (11/6/43)
551. "The House in the Woods" (11/13/43)
552. "Princess Moonbeam" (11/20/43)
553. "Sleeping Beauty" (11/27/43)
554. "The Bremen Town Musicians" (12/4/43)
555. "The Bronze Ring" (12/11/43)
556. "The Night Before Christmas" (12/18/43)
557. "The House of the World" (12/25/43)
558. "The Twelve Months" (1/1/44)
559. "The Three Golden Hairs" (1/8/44)
560. "Beauty and the Beast" (1/15/44)
561. "The Little Lame Prince" (1/22/44)
562. "The Fisherman and His Wife" (1/29/44)
563. "The Little Mermaid" (2/5/44)
564. "The Golden Touch" (2/12/44)
565. "East of the Sun, West of the Moon" (2/19/44)
566. "Rumpelstiltskin" (2/26/44)
567. "The Frog Prince" (3/4/44)
568. "The Leprechaun" (3/11/44)
569. "How Six Traveled Thru the World" (3/18/44)
570. "Babes in the Woods" (3/25/44)
571. "Gigi and the Magic Ring" (4/1/44)
572. "The Rusted Knight" (4/8/44)
573. "Ali Baba and the Forty Thieves" (4/15/44)
574. "The Donkey, the Table and the Stick" (4/22/44)
575. "The Giant Who Had No Heart" (4/29/44)
576. "Why the Sea is Salt" (5/6/44)
577. "Hansel and Gretel" (5/13/44)
578. "One Eye, Two Eyes, Three Eyes" (5/20/44)
579. "Dick Whittington and His Cat" (5/27/44)
580. "Thumbelina" (6/3/44)
581. "Jack and the Beanstalk" (6/10/44)
582. "Jorinda and Joringel" (6/17/44)
583. "The Six Swans" (6/24/44)
584. "The Enchanted Frog" (7/1/44)
585. "Rapunzel" (7/8/44)
586. "Gigi and The Magic Ring" (7/15/44)
587. "The Chinese Nightingale" (7/22/44)
588. "Snow White and Rose Red" (7/29/44)
589. "The Queen Who Couldn't Make Spice Nuts" (8/5/44)
590. "The Enchanted Stag" (8/12/44)
591. "The Elves and the Shoemaker" (8/19/44)
592. "The Water of Life" (8/26/44)
593. "The Invisible Kingdom" (9/2/44)
594. "Aladdin and His Wonderful Lamp" (9/9/44)
595. "Hop O' My Thumb" (9/16/44)
596. "Cinderella" (9/23/44)
597. "The Castle of Hatred" (9/30/44)
598. "The Youth Who Learned to Shiver and Shake" (10/7/44)
599. "The Brave Little Tailor" (10/14/44)

600. "The Juniper Tree" (10/21/44)
601. "Goldilocks and Prince Charming" (10/28/44)
602. "King Thrushbeard" (11/4/44)
603. "Snowdrop and the Seven Dwarfs" (11/11/44)
604. "Faithful John" (11/18/44)
605. "The Twelve Dancing Princesses" (11/25/44)
606. "The Yellow Dwarf" (12/2/44)
607. "The Nurembourg Stove" (12/9/44)
608. "The Night Before Christmas" (12/16/44)
609. "The House of the World" (12/23/44)
610. "Drakestail" / "The Wishing Ring" (12/30/44)
611. "Bluebeard" (1/6/45)
612. "The Flying Trunk" (1/13/45)
613. "Prince Darling" (1/20/45)
614. "The Little Lame Prince" (1/27/45)
615. "The Three Feathers" (2/3/45)
616. "Childe Roland" (2/10/45)
617. "The Goose Girl" (2/17/45)
618. "The Crystal Coffin" (2/24/45)
619. "Princess Moonbeam" (3/3/45)
620. "The Princess and the Pea" (3/10/45)
621. "The Leprechaun" (3/17/45)
622. "The Enchanted Canary" (3/24/45)
623. "Heavenly Music" (3/31/45)
624. "Sleeping Beauty" (4/7/45)
625. "The Emperor's New Clothes" (4/21/45)
626. "The Riddle" (4/28/45)
627. "The Flower Queen's Daughter" (5/5/45)
628. "The House in the Woods" (5/12/45)
629. "Puss in Boots" (5/19/45)
630. "Beauty and the Beast" (5/26/45)
631. "Rosanella" (6/2/45)
632. "Hansel and Gretel" (6/9/45)
633. "The Golden Touch" (6/16/45)
634. "The Fisherman and His Wife" (6/23/45)
635. "The Bronze Ring" (6/30/45)
636. "The Little Mermaid" (7/7/45)
637. "Rumpelstiltskin" (7/14/45)
638. "The White Cat" (7/21/45)
639. "One Eye, Two Eyes, Three Eyes" (7/28/45)
640. "East of the Sun, West of the Moon" (8/4/45)
641. *No title known* (8/11/45)
642. "The Elves and the Shoemaker" (8/18/45)
643. "Three Golden Hairs" (8/25/45)
644. "Gigi and the Magic Ring" (9/1/45)
645. "Ali Baba and the Forty Thieves" (9/8/45)
646. "How Six Traveled Thru the World" (9/15/45)
647. "The Rusted Knight" (9/22/45)
648. "Cinderella" (9/29/45)
649. "Dick Whittington and His Cat" (10/6/45)
650. "Babes in the Wood" (10/13/45)

651. "Why the Sea is Salt" (10/20/45)
652. "The Giant Who Had No Heart" (10/27/45)
653. "The Enchanted Frog" (11/3/45)
654. "The Queen Who Couldn't Make Spice Nuts" (11/10/45)
655. "The Six Swans" (11/17/45)
656. "Jack and the Beanstalk" (11/24/45)
657. "Thumbelina" (12/1/45)
658. "The Nuremburg Stove" (12/8/45)
659. "The Twelve Months" (12/15/45)
660. "The Night Before Christmas" (12/22/45)
661. "The House of the World" (12/29/45)
662. "Bluebeard" (1/5/46)
663. "The Brave Little Tailor" (1/12/46)
664. "Brother and Sister" (1/19/46)
665. "The Little Lame Prince" (1/26/46)
666. "Donkey Skin" (2/2/46)
667. "Gigi and The Magic Ring" (2/9/46)
668. "Rapunzel" (2/16/46)
669. "The Chinese Nightingale" (2/23/46)
670. "Melilot" (3/2/46)
671. "Snow Drop and the Seven Dwarfs" (3/9/46)
672. "Old Pipes and the Dryad" (3/16/46)
673. "The Youth Who Learned to Shiver and Shake" (3/23/46)
674. "The Donkey, the Table and the Stick" (3/30/46)
675. "Aladdin and His Wonderful Lamp" (4/6/46)
676. "The Twelve Dancing Princesses" (4/13/46)
677. "Heavenly Music" (4/20/46)
678. "Hop O' My Thumb" (4/27/46)
679. "Jorinda and Joringel" (5/4/46)
680. "The Three Snake Leaves" (5/11/46)
681. "The Frog Prince" (5/18/46)
682. "The Water of Life" (5/25/46)
683. "The Castle of Hatred" (6/1/46)
684. "The Juniper Tree" (6/8/46)
685. "The Bronze Mountain" (6/15/46)
686. "Drakestail" (6/22/46)
687. "The Invisible Kingdom" (6/29/46)
688. "Snow White and Rose Red" (7/6/46)
689. "King Thrushbeard" (7/13/46)
690. "The Bremen Town Musicians" (7/20/46)
691. "The Yellow Dwarf" (7/27/46)
692. "The Goose Girl" (8/3/46)
693. "Faithful John" (8/10/46)
694. "The Elves and the Shoemaker" (8/17/46)
695. "Goldilocks and Prince Charming" (8/24/46)
696. "Prince Darling" (8/31/46)
697. "The Flying Trunk" (9/7/46)
698. "Childe Roland" (9/14/46)
699. "Beauty and the Beast" (9/21/46)
700. "The Crystal Coffin" (9/28/46)
701. "The Three Feathers" (10/5/46)

702. "The Riddle" (10/12/46)
703. "Cinderella" (10/19/46)
704. "Jack and the Beanstalk" (10/26/46)
705. "Puss in Boots" (11/2/46)
706. "The Emperor's New Clothes" (11/9/46)
707. "The Princess and the Pea" (11/16/46)
708. "Princess Moonbeam" (11/23/46)
709. "The Fisherman and His Wife" (11/30/46)
710. "The House in the Woods" (12/7/46)
711. "The Golden Touch" (12/14/46)
712. "The Night Before Christmas" (12/21/46)
713. "The House of the World" (12/28/46)
714. "One Eye, Two Eyes, Three Eyes" (1/4/47)
715. "The Flower Queen's Daughter" (1/11/47)
716. "Hansel and Gretel" (1/18/47)
717. "The Little Lame Prince" (1/25/47)
718. "Rosanella" (2/1/47)
719. "The Three Golden Hairs" (2/8/47)
720. "The Golden Blackbird" (2/15/47)
721. "The Giant Who Had No Heart" (2/22/47)
722. "East of the Sun, West of the Moon" (3/1/47)
723. "The Queen Who Couldn't Make Spice Nuts" (3/8/47)
724. "The Leprechaun" (3/15/47)
725. "The White Cat" (3/22/47)
726. "Why the Sea is Salt" (3/29/47)
727. "Heavenly Music" (4/5/47)
728. "Gigi and the Magic Ring" (4/12/47)
729. "Ali Baba and the Forty Thieves" (4/19/47)
730. "The Bronze Mountain" (4/26/47)
731. "How Six Traveled Thru the World" (5/3/47)
732. "The Little Mermaid" (5/10/47)
733. "Babes in the Wood" (5/17/47)
734. "Dick Whittington and His Cat" (5/31/47)
735. "The Six Swans" (6/7/47)
736. "The Rusted Knight" (6/14/47)
737. "Bluebeard" (6/21/47)
738. "Thumbelina" (6/28/47)
739. "Brother and Sister" (7/5/47)
740. "The Brave Little Tailor" (7/12/47)
741. "Rapunzel" (7/19/47)
742. "The Chinese Nightingale" (7/26/47)
743. "Gigi and The Magic Ring" (8/2/47)
744. "Snow Drop and the Seven Dwarfs" (8/9/47)
745. "The Youth Who Learned to Shiver and Shake" (8/16/47)
746. "Melilot" (8/23/47)
747. "Aladdin and His Wonderful Lamp" (8/30/47)
748. "The Twelve Months" (9/6/47)
749. "The Donkey, the Table and the Stick" (9/13/47)
750. "The Enchanted Frog" (9/20/47)
751. "Cinderella" (9/27/47)
752. "Hop O' My Thumb" (10/4/47)

753. "The Maiden Without Hands" (10/11/47)
754. "Drakestail" (10/18/47)
755. "Fairer Than a Fairy" (10/25/47)
756. "Faithful John" (11/1/47)
757. "The Tinder Box" (11/8/47)
758. "The Twelve Dancing Princesses" (11/15/47)
759. "Rumpelstiltskin" (11/22/47)
760. "Donkey Skin" (11/29/47)
761. "The Nuremburg Stove" (12/6/47)
762. "Snow White and Rose Red" (12/13/47)
763. "The Night Before Christmas" (12/20/47)
764. "The House of the World" (12/27/47)
765. "One Eye, Two Eyes, Three Eyes" (1/3/48)
766. "Beauty and the Beast" (1/10/48)
767. "The Little Lame Prince" (1/17/48)
768. "The Bremen Town Musicians" (1/24/48)
769. "The Three Feathers" (1/31/48)
770. "The Yellow Dwarf" (2/7/48)
771. "King Thrushbeard" (2/14/48)
772. "The Bronze Ring" (2/21/48)
773. "Childe Roland" (2/28/48)
774. "The Crystal Coffin" (3/6/48)
775. "The Elves and the Shoemaker" (3/13/48)
776. "Jorinda and Joringel" (3/20/48)
777. "Heavenly Music" (3/27/48)
778. "Alice in Wonderland" (4/3/48)
779. "Alice Through the Looking Glass" (4/10/48)
780. "Goldilocks and Prince Charming" (4/17/48)
781. "The Castle of Hatred" (4/24/48)
782. "The Emperor's New Clothes" (5/1/48)
783. "The Goose Girl" (5/8/48)
784. "The Fisherman and His Wife" (5/15/48)
785. "Jack and the Beanstalk" (5/22/48)
786. "Sleeping Beauty" (5/29/48)
787. "The Juniper Tree" (6/5/48)
788. "The Invisible Kingdom" (6/12/48)
789. "Puss in Boots" (6/19/48)
790. "The Riddle" (6/26/48)
791. "The Flying Trunk" (7/3/48)
792. "House in the Wood" (7/10/48)
793. "The Golden Touch" (7/17/48)
794. "Rosanella" (7/24/48)
795. "East of the Sun, West of the Moon" (7/31/48)
796. "Princess Moonbeam" (8/7/48)
797. "The Water of Life" (8/14/48)
798. "Prince Darling" (8/21/48)
799. "Why the Sea is Salt" (8/28/48)
800. "The Three Snake Leaves" (9/4/48)
801. "The Giant Without a Heart" (9/11/48)
802. "Gigi and The Magic Ring" (9/18/48)
803. "The 500 Hats of Bartholomew Cubbins" (9/25/48)

804. "Ali Baba and the Forty Thieves" (10/2/48)
805. "The Princess and the Pea" (10/9/48)
806. "Bluebeard" (10/16/48)
807. "The Queen Who Couldn't Make Spice Nuts" (10/23/48)
808. "Fairer Than A Fairy" (10/30/48)
809. "The White Cat" (11/6/48)
810. "Cinderella" (11/13/48)
811. "The Golden Fleece" (11/20/48)
812. "Hansel and Gretel" (11/27/48)
813. "The Brave Little Tailor" (12/4/48)
814. "The Flower Queen's Daughter" (12/11/48)
815. "Snowdrop and the Seven Dwarfs" (12/18/48)
816. "The Night Before Christmas" (12/25/48)
817. "The House of the World" (1/1/49)
818. "Drakestail" (1/8/49)
819. "Dick Whittington and His Cat" (1/15/49)
820. "Donkey Skin" (1/22/49)
821. "The Little Lame Prince" (1/29/49)
822. "Gigi and The Magic Ring" (2/5/49)
823. "The Enchanted Stag" (2/12/49)
824. "The Youth Who Learned to Shiver and Shake" (2/19/49)
825. "Thumbelina" (2/26/49)
826. "Aladdin and His Wonderful Lamp" (3/5/49)
827. "The Leprechaun" (3/12/49)
828. "The Six Swans" (3/19/49)
829. "How Six Traveled Thru the World" (3/26/49)
830. "The Snow Queen" (4/2/49)
831. "The Enchanted Frog" (4/9/49)
832. "Heavenly Music" (4/16/49)
833. "Hop O' My Thumb" (4/23/49)
834. "The Little Mermaid" (4/30/49)
835. "The Donkey, the Table and the Stick" (5/7/49)
836. "The Twelve Dancing Princesses" (5/14/49)
837. "Rumpelstiltskin" (5/21/49)
838. "The Three Golden Hairs" (5/28/49)
839. "Snow White and Rose Red" (6/4/49)
840. "The Enchanted Canary" (6/11/49)
841. "The Three Terrible Heads" (6/18/49)
842. "One Eye, Two Eyes, Three Eyes" (6/25/49)
843. "Melilot" (7/2/49)
844. "The Tinder Box" (7/9/49)
845. "The Elves and the Shoemaker" (7/16/49)
846. "The Chinese Nightingale" (7/23/49)
847. "The Maiden Without Hands" (7/30/49)
848. "Rapunzel" (8/6/49)
849. "The Three Feathers" (8/13/49)
850. "The Rusted Knight" (8/20/49)
851. "Alice in Wonderland" (8/27/49)
852. "Alice Through the Looking Glass" (9/3/49)
853. "Beauty and the Beast" / "Sleeping Beauty" (9/10/49)
854. "Cinderella" (9/17/49)

855. "Faithful John" (9/24/49)
856. "The Emperor's New Clothes" (10/1/49)
857. "The Goose Girl" (10/8/49)
858. "The Fisherman and His Wife" (10/15/49)
859. "The Flying Trunk" (10/22/49)
860. "The Nuremburg Stove" (10/29/49)
861. "Goldilocks and the Three Bears" (11/5/49)
862. "King Thrushbeard" (11/12/49)
863. "East of the Sun and West of the Moon" (11/19/49)
864. "Jorinda and Joringel" (11/26/49)
865. "The Bremen Town Musicians" (12/3/49)
866. "The Three Spinners" (12/10/49)
867. "The Brave Little Tailor" (12/17/49)
868. "The Night Before Christmas" (12/24/49)
869. "The House of the World" (12/31/49)
870. "Ali Baba and the Forty Thieves" (1/7/50)
871. *No title known* (1/14/50)
872. *No title known* (1/21/50)
873. "The Little Lame Prince" (1/28/50)
874. *No title known* (2/4/50)
875. *No title known* (2/11/50)
876. "The Yellow Dwarf" (2/18/50)
877. "The Golden Touch" (2/25/50)
878. "Why the Sea is Salt" (3/4/50)
879. *No title known* (3/11/50)
880. "The Leprechaun" (3/18/50)
881. "Little Red Riding Hood" (3/25/50)
882. *No title known* (4/1/50)
883. "Heavenly Music" (4/8/50)
884. "Bluebeard" (4/15/50)
885. "The Queen Who Couldn't Make Spice Nuts" (4/22/50)
886. "The Castle of Hatred" (4/29/50)
887. *No title known* (5/6/50)
888. *No title known* (5/13/50)
889. *No title known* (5/20/50)
890. *No title known* (5/27/50)
891. *No title known* (6/3/50)
892. "The Riddle" (6/10/50)
893. *No title known* (6/17/50)
894. *No title known* (6/24/50)
895. *No title known* (7/1/50)
896. *No title known* (7/8/50)
897. *No title known* (7/15/50)
898. *No title known* (7/22/50)
899. *No title known* (7/29/50)
900. *No title known* (8/5/50)
901. *No title known* (8/12/50)
902. *No title known* (8/19/50)
903. *No title known* (8/26/50)
904. "Water of Life" (9/2/50)
905. "Alice in Wonderland" [part one] (9/9/50)

906. "Alice in Wonderland" [part two] (9/16/50)
907. "Alice Through the Looking Glass" [part one] (9/23/50)
908. "Alice Through the Looking Glass" [part two] (9/30/50)
909. *No title known* (10/7/50)
910. *No title known* (10/14/50)
911. *No title known* (10/21/50)
912. "Fairer Than a Fairy" (10/28/50)
913. *No title known* (11/4/50)
914. *No title known* (11/11/50)
915. *No title known* (11/18/50)
916. *No title known* (11/25/50)
917. "The Twelve Months" (12/2/50)
918. *No title known* (12/9/50)
919. *No title known* (12/16/50)
920. "The Night Before Christmas" (12/23/50)
921. "The House of the World" (12/30/50)
922. "The Enchanted Frog" (1/6/51)
923. "Aladdin and His Wonderful Lamp" (1/13/51)
924. "One Eye, Two Eyes, Three Eyes" (1/20/51)
925. "The Little Lame Prince" (1/27/51)
926. "The Emperor and the Nightingale" (2/3/51)
927. "The Donkey, the Table and the Stick" (2/10/51)
928. "Rapunzel" (2/17/51)
929. "Hop O' My Thumb" (2/24/51)
930. "The Twelve Dancing Princesses" (3/3/51)
931. "The Fisherman and His Wife" (3/10/51)
932. "The Leprechaun" (3/17/51)
933. "The Castle of Harmony" (3/24/51)
934. "East of the Sun, West of the Moon" (3/31/51)
935. "The Three Golden Hairs" (4/7/51)
936. "The Rusted Knight" (4/14/51)
937. "Faithful John" (4/21/51)
938. "The Princess and the Pea" (4/28/51)
939. "Snow White and Rose Red" (5/5/51)
940. "The Little Mermaid" (5/12/51)
941. "The Bremen Town Musicians" (5/19/51)
942. "Snow Drop and the Seven Dwarfs" (5/26/51)
943. "King Thrushbeard" (6/2/51)
944. "The Goose Girl" (6/9/51)
945. "The Brave Little Tailor" (6/16/51)
946. "The King of the Golden River" (6/23/51)
947. "Donkey Skin" (6/30/51)
948. "Princess Moonbeam" (7/7/51)
949. "The Emperor's New Clothes" (7/14/51)
950. "Ali Baba and the Forty Thieves" (7/21/51)
951. "Beauty and the Beast" (7/28/51)
952. "The Three Terrible Heads" (8/4/51)
953. "The Golden Touch" (8/11/51)
954. "The Flying Trunk" (8/18/51)
955. "Little Red Riding Hood" (8/25/51)
956. "Childe Roland to the Dark Tower Came" (9/1/51)

957. "The Queen Who Couldn't Make Spice Nuts" (9/8/51)
958. "Prince Darling" (9/15/51)
959. "Cinderella" (9/22/51)
960. "The Light Princess" (9/29/51)
961. "The Enchanted Canary" (10/6/51)
962. "The Crystal Coffin" (10/13/51)
963. "The Castle of Hatred" (10/20/51)
964. "Fairer Than a Fairy" (10/27/51)
965. "The Three Feathers" (11/3/51)
966. "The Tinder Box" (11/10/51)
967. "Hansel and Gretel" (11/17/51)
968. "Alice in Wonderland" (11/24/51)
969. "Alice Through the Looking Glass" (12/1/51)
970. "Jorinda and Joringel" (12/8/51)
971. "Drakestail" (12/15/51)
972. "The Night Before Christmas" (12/22/51)
973. "The House of the World" (12/29/51)
974. "The Shrine of Tears" (1/5/52)
975. "The Youth Who Learned to Shiver and Shake" (1/12/52)
976. "The Little Lame Prince" (1/19/52)
977. "Sleeping Beauty" (1/26/52)
978. "The Elves and the Shoemaker" (2/2/52)
979. "The Maiden Without Hands" (2/9/52)
980. *No title known* (2/16/52)
981. *No title known* (2/23/52)
982. "Dick Whittington and His Cat" (3/1/52)
983. *No title known* (3/8/52)
984. *No title known* (3/15/52)
985. *No title known* (3/22/52)
986. *No title known* (3/29/52)
987. *No title known* (4/5/52)
988. *No title known* (4/12/52)
989. "The Emperor and the Nightingale" (4/19/52)
990. *No title known* (4/26/52)
991. "Goldilocks and the Three Bears" (5/3/52)
992. "Half-Chicks" (5/10/52)
993. *No title known* (5/17/52)
994. *No title known* (5/24/52)
995. *No title known* (5/31/52)
996. *No title known* (6/7/52)
997. "The Enchanted Stag" (6/14/52)
998. "The White Cat" (6/21/52)
999. "The Invisible Kingdom" (6/28/52)
1000. *No title known* (7/5/52)
1001. *No title known* (7/12/52)
1002. *No title known* (7/19/52)
1003. *No title known* (7/26/52)
1004. *No title known* (8/2/52)
1005. *No title known* (8/9/52)
1006. "The White Cat" (8/16/52)
1007. *No title known* (8/23/52)

1008. *No title known* (8/30/52)
1009. *No title known* (9/6/52)
1010. *No title known* (9/13/52)
1011. *No title known* (9/20/52)
1012. "The Magic Doctor" (9/27/52)
1013. *No title known* (10/4/52)
1014. *No title known* (10/11/52)
1015. "The Water of Life" (10/18/52)
1016. "The Bronze Ring" (10/25/52)
1017. "Fairer Than a Fairy" (11/1/52)
1018. *No title known* (11/8/52)
1019. "The Juniper Tree" (11/15/52)
1020. *No title known* (11/22/52)
1021. "One Eye, Two Eyes, Three Eyes" (11/29/52)
1022. *No title known* (12/6/52)
1023. "Drakestail" (12/13/52)
1024. "The Night Before Christmas" (12/20/52)
1025. "The Husband Who Was to Mind the House" (12/27/52)
1026. "The Twelve Months" (1/3/53)
1027. "The Story of Robin Hood" (1/9/53)
1028. "Three Golden Hairs" (1/10/53)
1029. *No title known* (1/17/53)
1030. "The Little Lame Prince" (1/24/53)
1031. "The Brave Little Tailor" (1/31/53)
1032. "The Twelve Dancing Princesses" (2/7/53)
1033. "Beauty and the Beast" (2/14/53)
1034. "The Bremen Town Musicians" (2/21/53)
1035. *No title known* (2/28/53)
1036. *No title known* (3/7/53)
1037. *No title known* (3/14/53)
1038. "Babes in the Woods" (3/21/53)
1039. *No title known* (3/28/53)
1040. "Thumbelina" (4/4/53)
1041. "Ali Baba and the Forty Thieves" (4/11/53)
1042. "The Enchanted Canary" (4/18/53)
1043. "The Light Princess" (4/25/53)
1044. "Hansel and Gretel" (5/2/53)
1045. "The Little Mermaid" (5/9/53)
1046. *No title known* (5/23/53)
1047. *No title known* (5/30/53)
1048. "Jorinda and Joringel" (6/6/53)
1049. "King Thrushbeard" (6/13/53)
1050. "Princess Moonbeam" (6/20/53)
1051. "Snow White and Rose Red" (6/27/53)
1052. "Why the Sea is Salt" (7/4/53)
1053. "Cinderella" (7/11/53)
1054. "The Emperor's New Clothes" (7/18/53)
1055. "Dick Whittington and His Cat" (7/25/53)
1056. "Donkey Skin" (8/1/53)
1057. "Jack and the Beanstalk" (8/8/53)
1058. "Jason and the Golden Fleece" (8/15/53)

1059. "House in the Wood" (8/22/53)
1060. "The Song of Hiawatha" (8/29/53)
1061. *No title known* (9/5/53)
1062. "Aladdin and His Wonderful Lamp" (9/12/53)
1063. "Rosanella" (9/19/53)
1064. "The Frog Prince" (9/26/53)
1065. "King Arthur and How He Won the Sword" (10/3/53)
1066. "The Table, the Donkey and the Stick" (10/10/53)
1067. "Sleeping Beauty" (10/17/53)
1068. "Sinbad the Sailor" (11/7/53)
1069. "Ceres and Proserpina" (11/28/53)
1070. "Puss in Boots" (12/5/53)
1071. "The Snow Queen" (12/12/53)
1072. "The Night Before Christmas" (12/19/53)
1073. "The House of the World" (12/26/53)
1074. "The Twelve Months" (1/2/54)
1075. "The Story of Robin Hood" (1/9/54)
1076. "The Emperor's Nightingale" (1/16/54)
1077. "The Little Lame Prince" (1/23/54)
1078. "Gigi and The Magic Ring" (1/30/54)
1079. "The Six Swans" (2/6/54)
1080. "The Bremen Town Musicians" (2/13/54)
1081. "The Elves and the Shoemaker" (2/20/54)
1082. "The Princess on the Glass Mountain" (2/27/54)
1083. "The Nuremburg Stove" (3/6/54)
1084. "Charlotte's Web" [part one] (3/13/54)
1085. "Charlotte's Web" [part two] (3/20/54)
1086. "The Husband Who Was to Mind the House" (3/27/54)
1087. *No title known* (4/3/54)
1088. "The Magic Cuckoo" (4/10/54)
1089. "Thumbelina" (4/17/54)
1090. "The Miraculous Pitcher" (4/24/54)
1091. "The Twelve Dancing Princesses" (5/1/54)
1092. "The Fisherman and His Wife" (5/8/54)
1093. "The Princess and the Pea" (5/15/54)
1094. "The Giant Who Had No Heart in His Body" (5/22/54)
1095. "How Six Traveled Thru the World" (5/29/54)
1096. "Beauty and the Beast" (6/5/54)
1097. "The Tinder Box" (6/12/54)
1098. "Ondine" (6/19/54)
1099. "King Thrushbeard" (6/26/54)
1100. "The Song of Hiawatha" (7/3/54)
1101. "Why the Sea is Salt" (7/10/54)
1102. "The Light Princess" (7/17/54)
1103. "King of the Golden River" (7/24/54)
1104. "Hans, Who Made the Princess Laugh" (7/31/54)
1105. "The Little Mermaid" (8/7/54)
1106. "Drakestail" (8/14/54)
1107. *No title known* (8/21/54)
1108. "Hop O' My Thumb" (8/28/54)
1109. "Ali Baba and the Forty Thieves" (9/4/54)

1110. "The Song of Roland" (9/11/54)
1111. "Rapunzel" (9/18/54)
1112. "Dick Whittington and His Cat" (9/25/54)
1113. "King Arthur and How He Won His Sword" (10/2/54)
1114. "Hansel and Gretel" (10/9/54)
1115. "Jorinda and Joringel" (10/23/54)

Selected sources of information:

Jay Hickerson's *Ultimate History of Network Radio Programming*, Preston Print II, December 2001.
John Dunning's *On the Air: The Encyclopedia of Old-Time Radio*, Oxford University Press, 1998.

Special thanks to Terry Salomonson who assisted with the ratings chart featured.
Acknowledgements: Kermyt Anderson, Bob Taylor and Arlene Osborne.
Nila Mack Papers at the Performing Arts Library, New York Public Library.
The *Let's Pretend* script collection at Emerson College located in Boston, Mass.

Selected Reading

John Dunning, *On The Air: The Encyclopedia of Old-Time Radio*. Oxford University Press, 1998

Frank Buxton and Bill Owen, *The Big Broadcast: An Encyclopedia of Radio's Golden Age, 1920-1950*. Scarecrow Press, Inc., 1997

J. Fred MacDonald, *Don't Touch That Dial! Radio Programming in American Life from 1920 to 1960*. Nelson-Hall, 1979

Robert L. Mott, *Radio Live! Television Live! Those Golden Days When Horses Were Coconuts*. McFarland & Co., 2000

Robert L. Mott, *Radio Sound Effects: Who Did It, and How, In the Era of Live Broadcasting*. McFarland & Co., Inc. 1993

Ron Lackmann, *An Encyclopedia of American Radio*. Facts On File, Inc., 2000

Leonard Maltin, *The Great American Broadcast: A Celebration of Radio's Golden Age*. Dutton, 1997

Marilyn Lawrence Boemer, *The Children's Hour: Radio Programs for Children 1926-1956*. Scarecrow Press, Inc., 1989

Thomas A. DeLong, *Radio Stars: An Illustrated Biographical Dictionary, 1920-1960*. McFarland & Co, Inc., 1996

Index

Printed in the United States
21966LVS00004B/55-153